• Bartholomew •

GLASGOW
Streetfinder
COLOUR ATLAS

Contents

0141
4451472

Bartholomew
An Imprint of HarperCollins*Publishers*

Bartholomew
An Imprint of HarperCollins*Publishers*
77-85 Fulham Palace Road, Hammersmith, London W6 8JB

Copyright © Bartholomew 1997

Printed in Great Britain

ISBN 0 7028 3632 X   CDNR   KI9076

Key to map symbols

M73	Motorway
	Motorway proposed/under contruction
26	Motorway junction
A77	Primary route
A89	'A' class road
B757	'B' class road
	Pedestrianised area
→	One way street
	Administration boundary
	Postal boundary
Ⓟ	Car park
	Railway/bus/coach station
	Underground railway & station
Cinema	Places of interest, leisure and entertainment
ℹ	Tourist information centre
Hospital	Hospital
	Park, wood, sports ground, cemetery
57	Page continuation numbers
42	National Grid reference system

Scale   4 inches to 1 mile

0	¼	½	¾	1 mile
0	500	1000	1500	metres

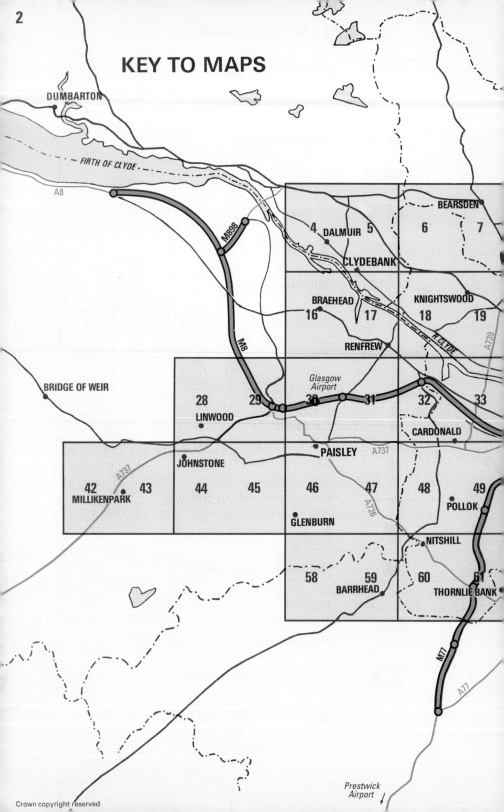

2

KEY TO MAPS

DUMBARTON

FIRTH OF CLYDE

A8

M898

M8

BRIDGE OF WEIR

BEARSDEN

4 DALMUIR   5   6   7

CLYDEBANK

BRAEHEAD   KNIGHTSWOOD

16   17   18   19

RENFREW

R.CLYDE   A739

Glasgow
Airport

28   29   30   31   32   33

LINWOOD   CARDONALD

PAISLEY   A737

JOHNSTONE

42   43   44   45   46   47   48   49
MILLIKENPARK   A737   A726   POLLOK

GLENBURN

NITSHILL

58   59   60   61
BARRHEAD   THORNLIE BANK

M77

A77

Prestwick
Airport

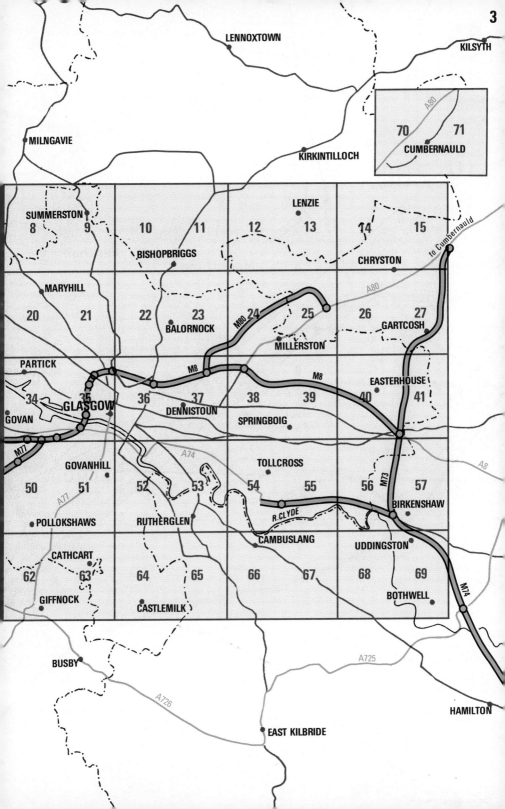

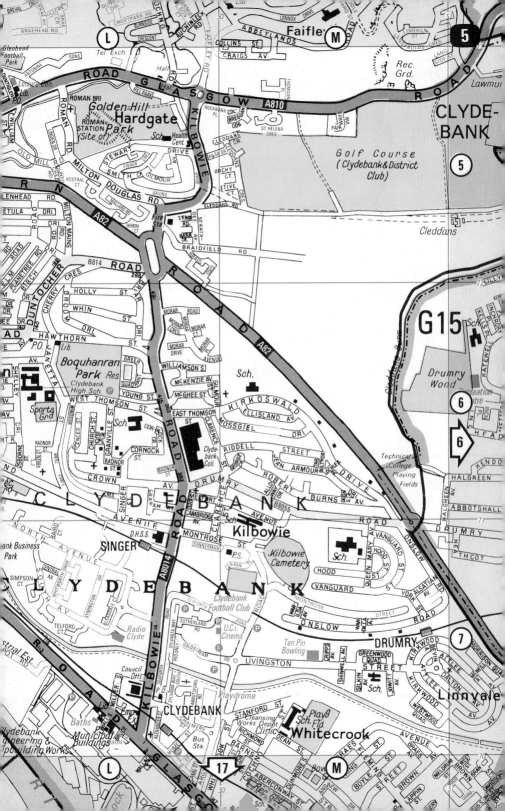

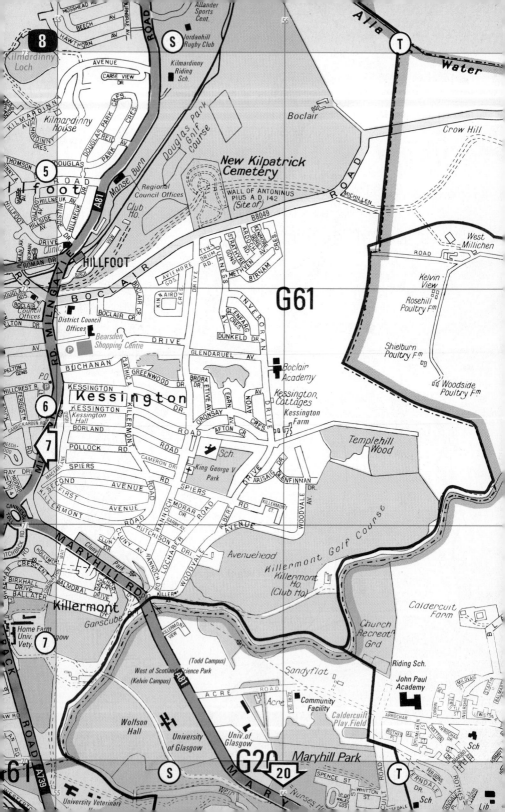

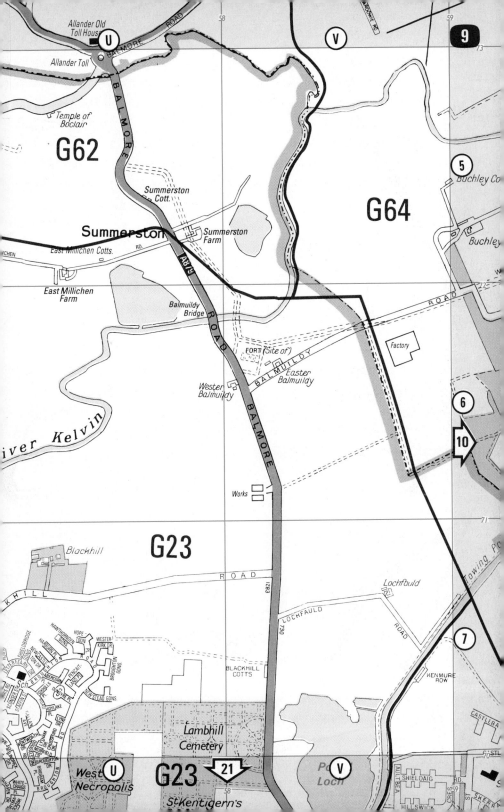

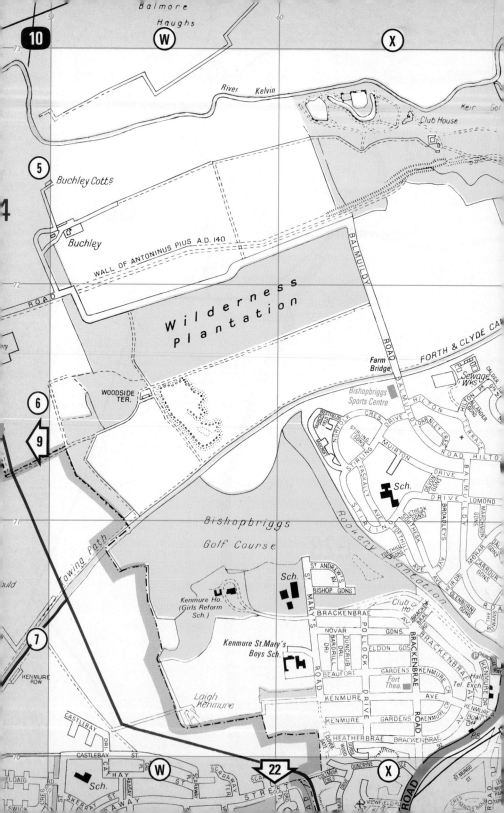

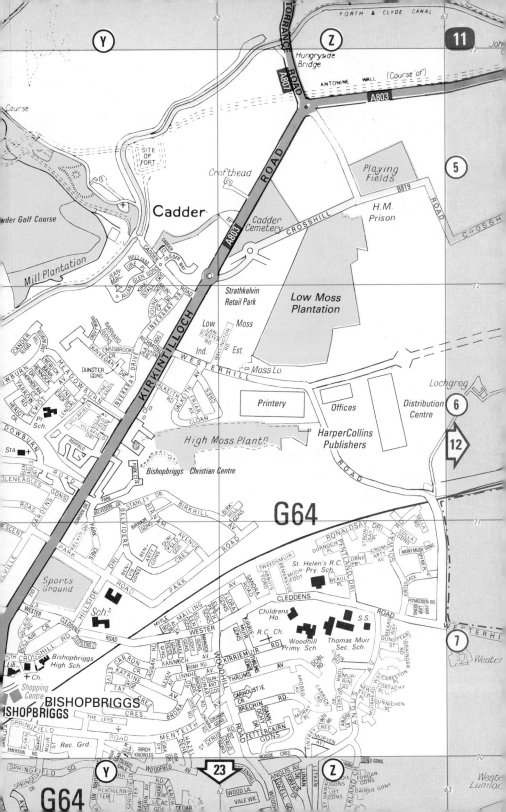

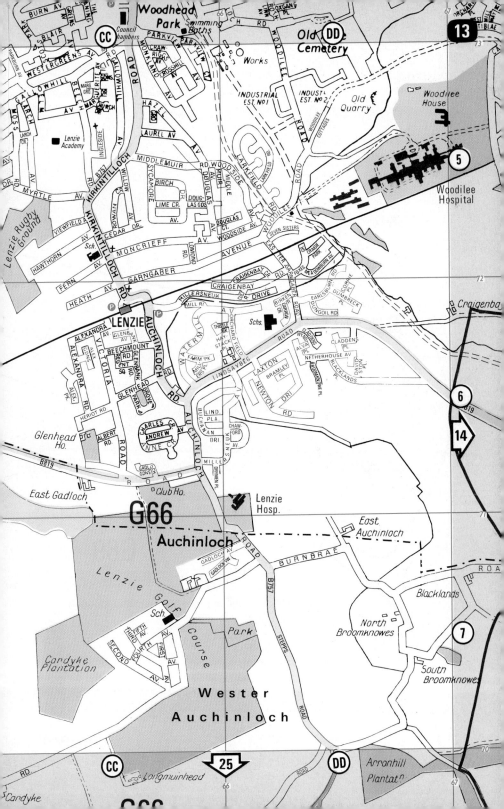

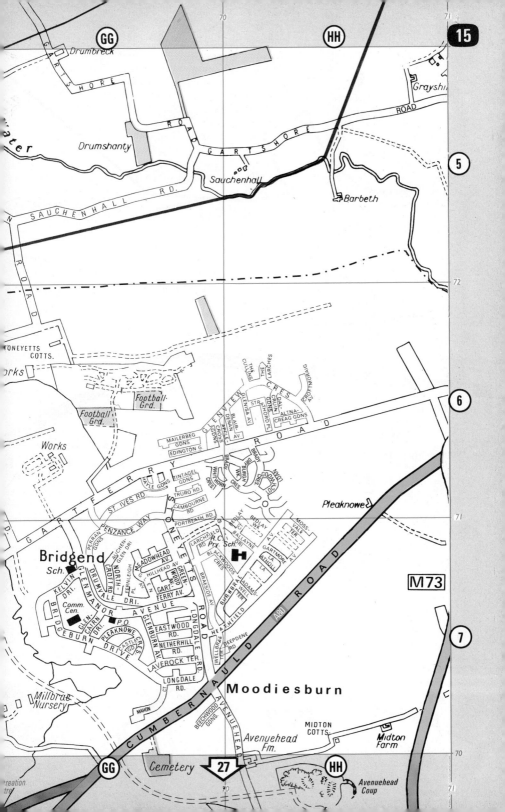

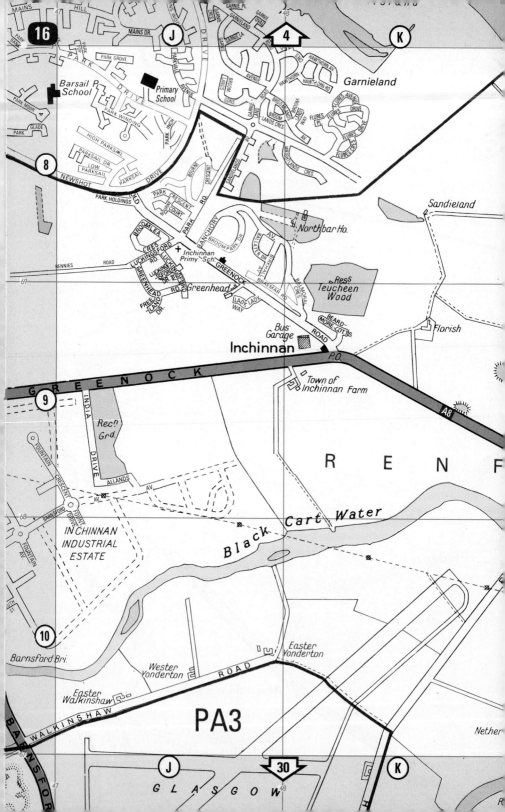

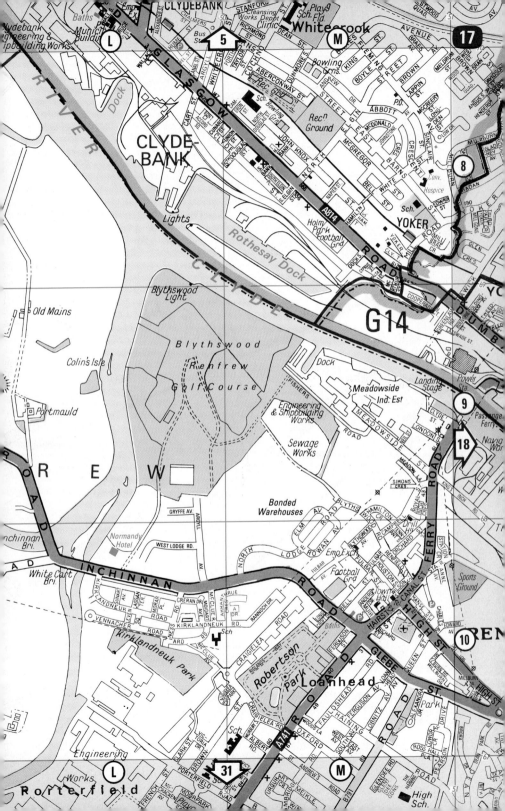

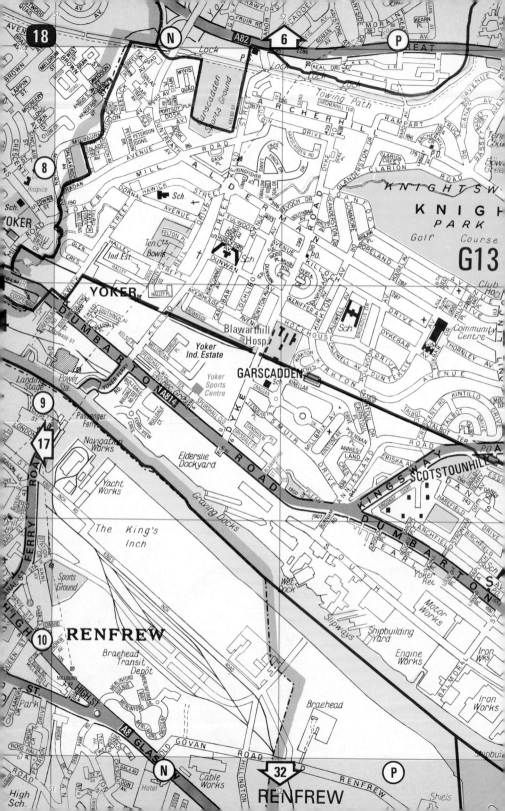

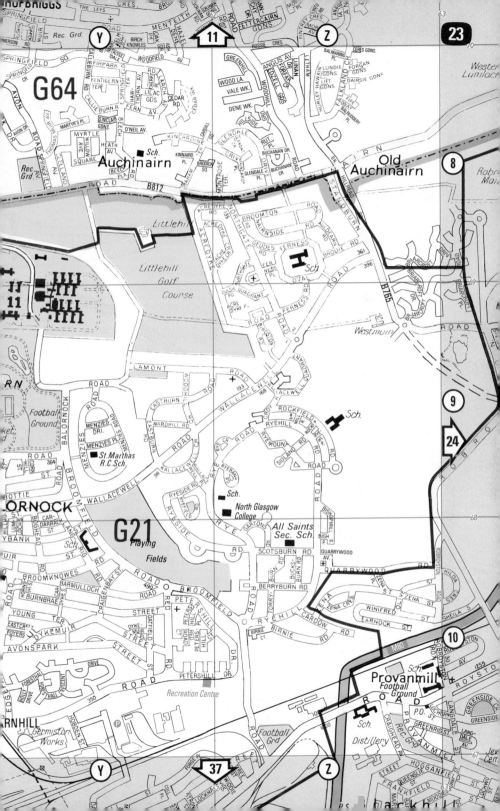

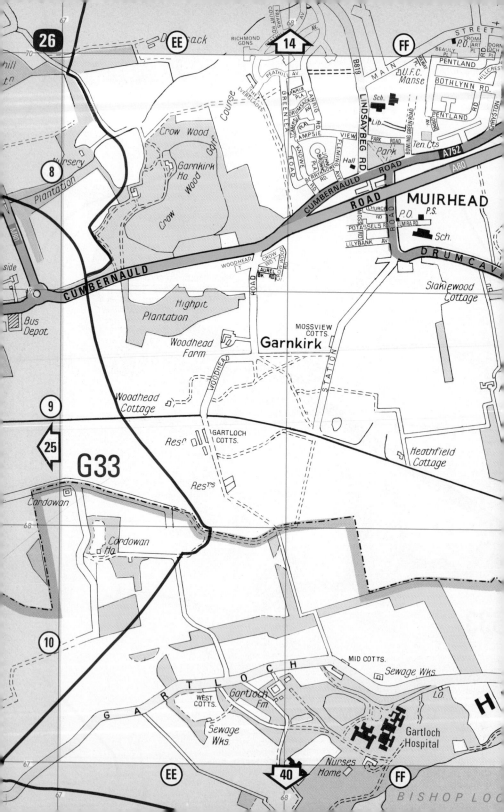

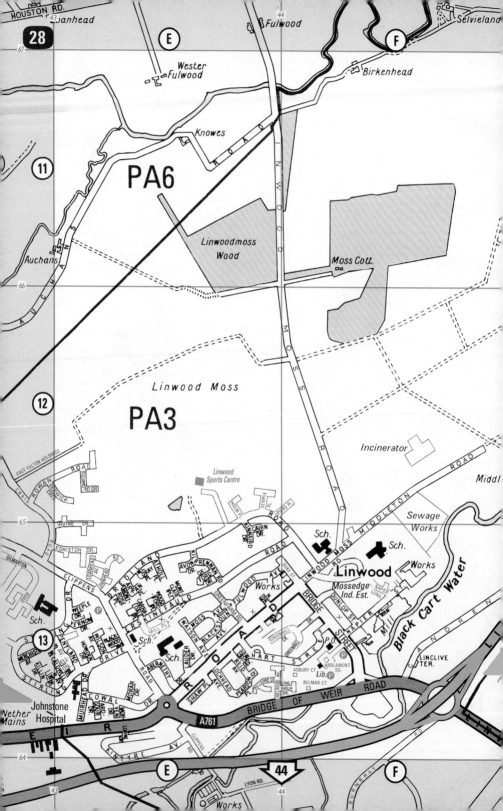

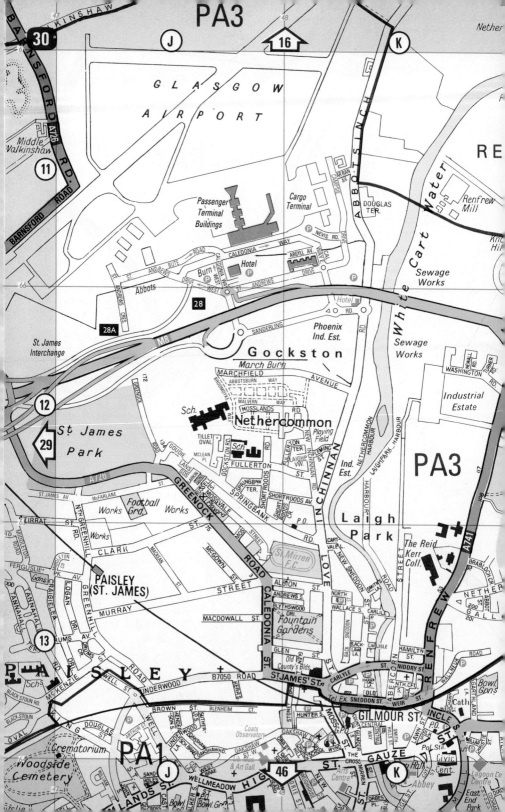

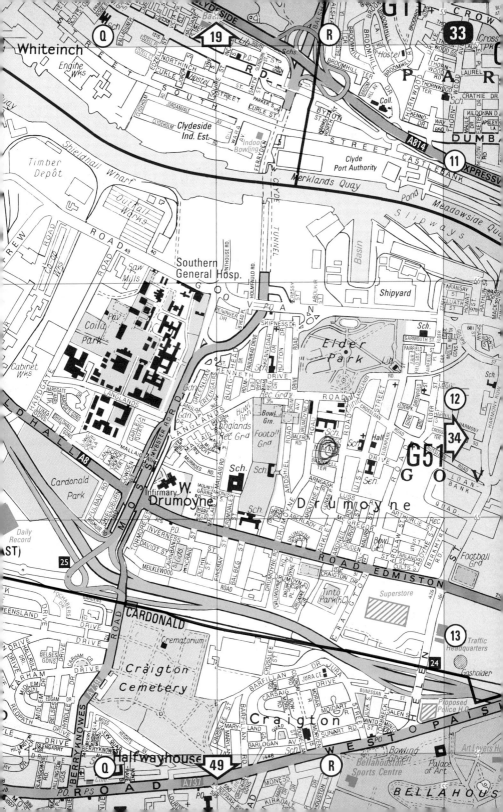

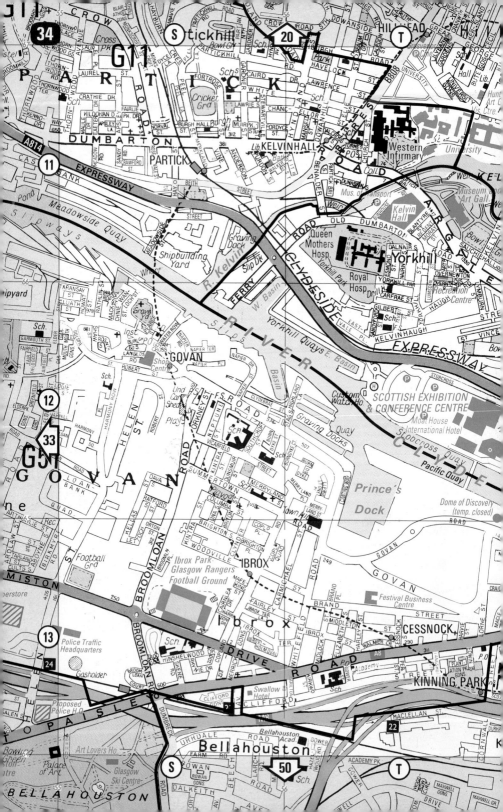

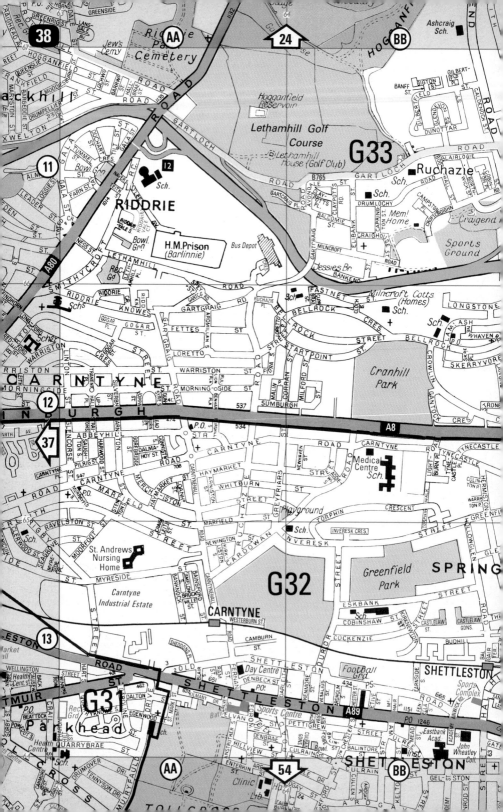

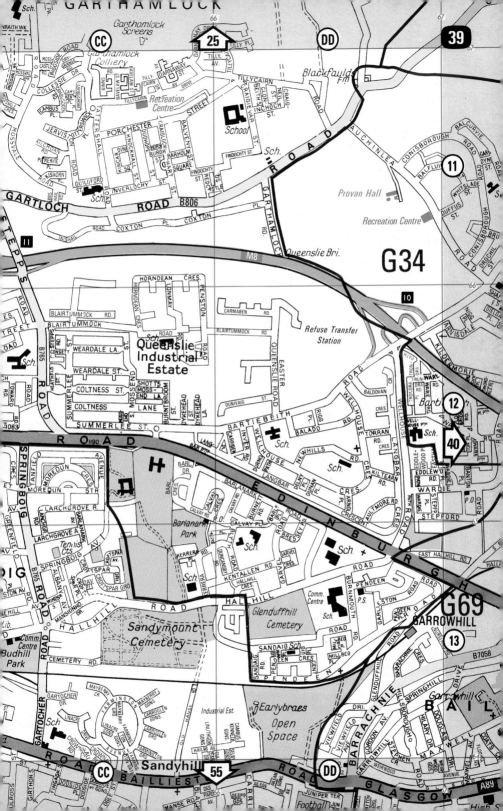

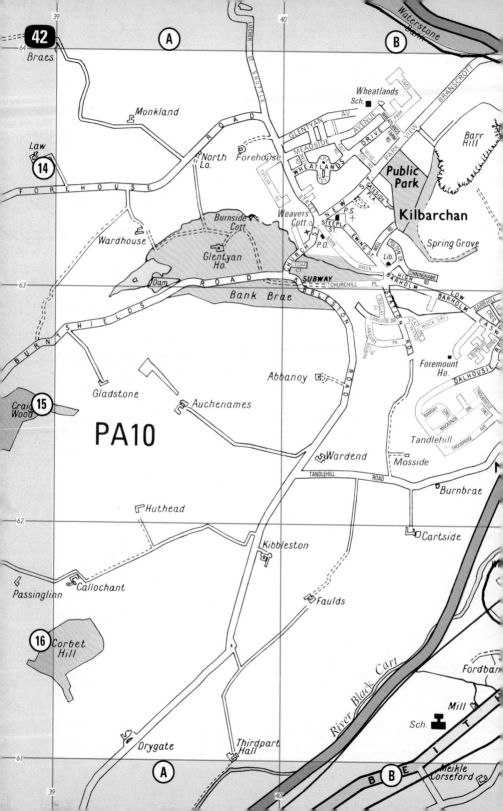

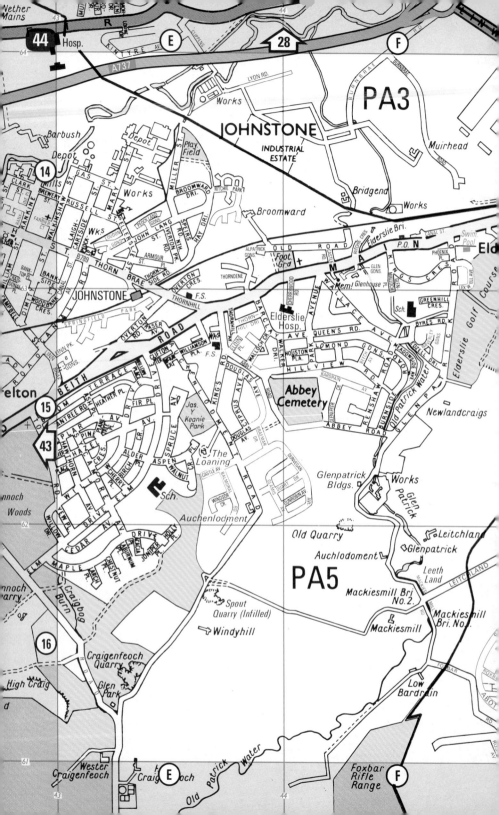

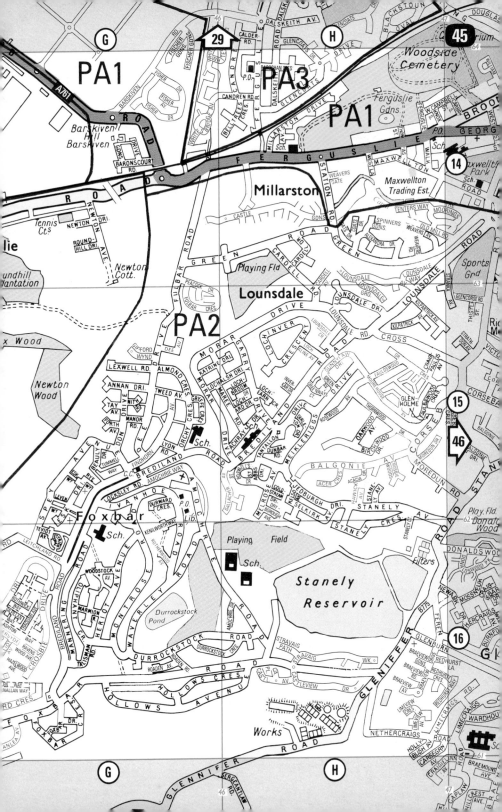

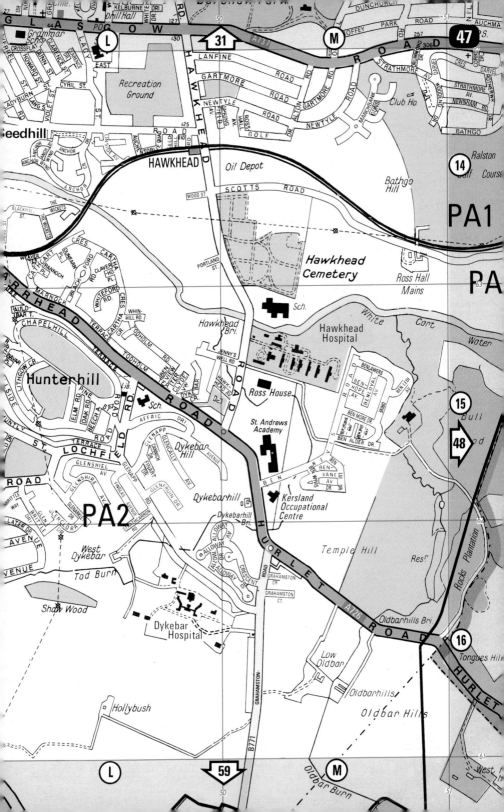

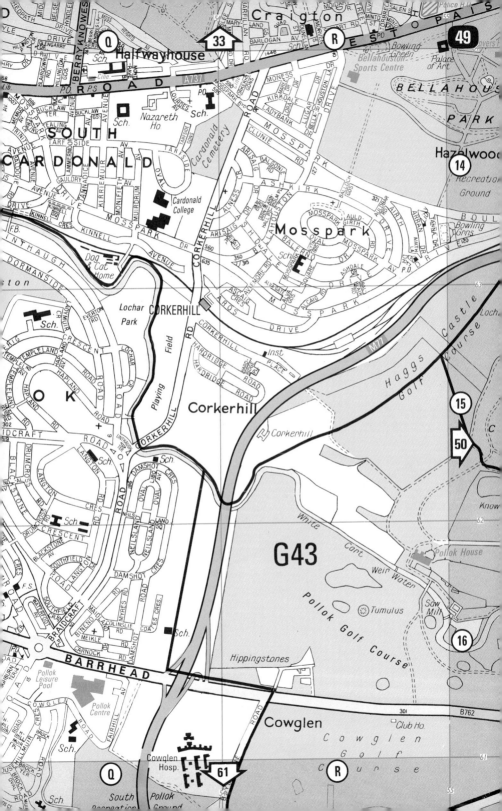

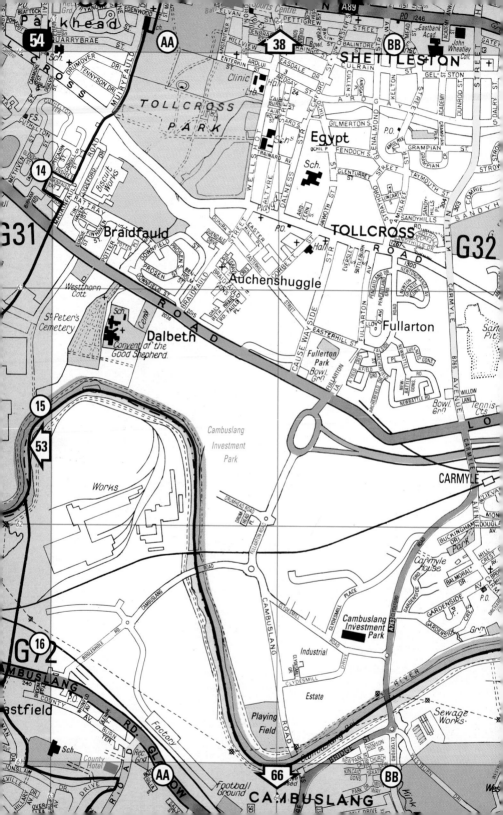

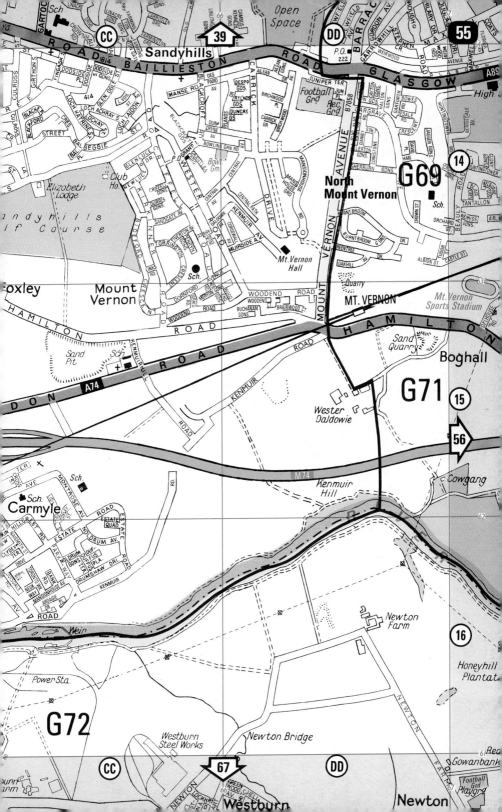

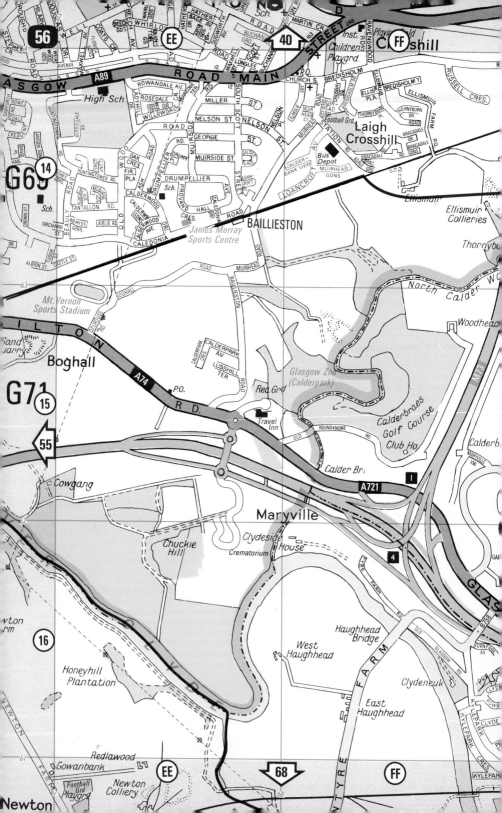

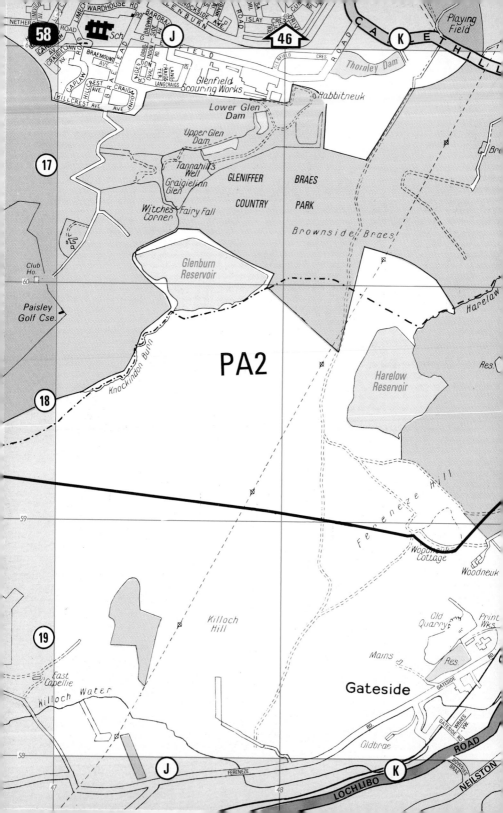

58

J

46

K

Playing Field

NETHER... WARDHOUSE RD.
LIMECR... KILMACOLM ... ISLAY CRES.
ROAD ... GLENBURN

CAKETHILL

Sch

Thornley Dam

Glenfield Scouring Works

FITZ FIELD CRES.

Rabbitneuk

BRAEMOUNT AVE.
CAPLAW ... BRAEHEAD
WEST AVE.
HILLCREST AVE.
CRAIGA...
LANGCRAIGS

Lower Glen Dam

Upper Glen Dam

17

Tannahills Well
Craigielinn Glen

GLENIFFER   BRAES

Witches Corner   Fairy Fall

COUNTRY   PARK

Brownside Braes

Club Ho.

60

Glenburn Reservoir

Harelaw

Paisley Golf Cse.

Knockindon Burn

PA2

Harelow Reservoir

Res

18

Fereneze Hill

59

Woodneuk Cottage

Woodneuk

19

Killoch Hill

Old Quarry

Print Wks

Mains

Res

East Capellie

Gateside

Killoch Water

GATESIDE RD.

Oldbrae

GATESIDE RD.
BRAES VW.

58

J

FERENEZE

K

LOCHLIBO   ROAD

NEILSTON

DOWNIE...

47

48

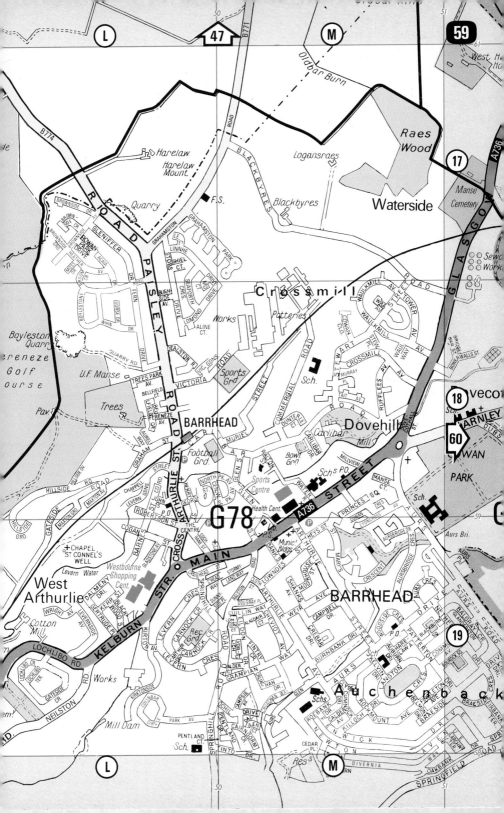

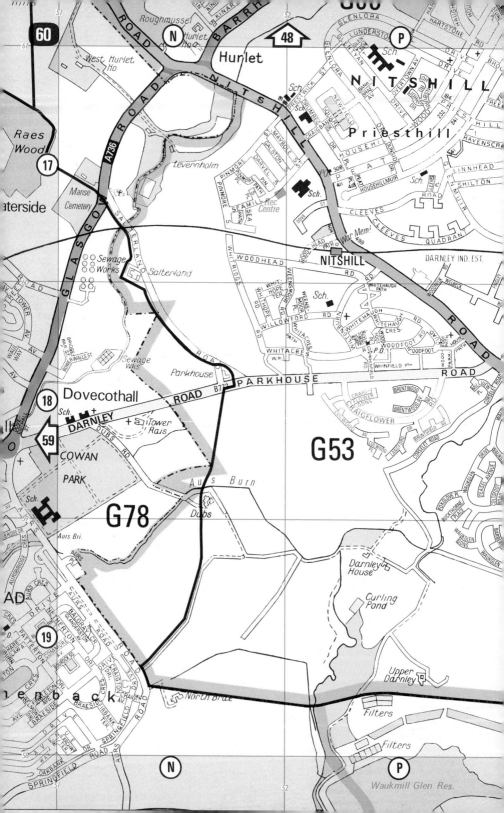

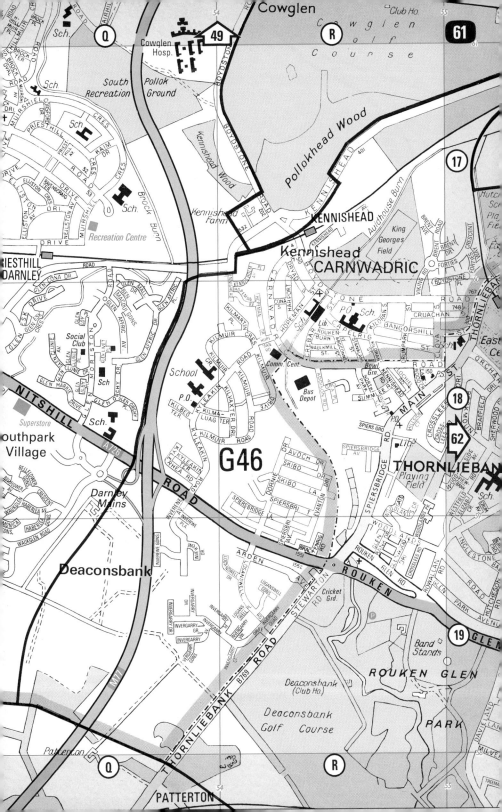

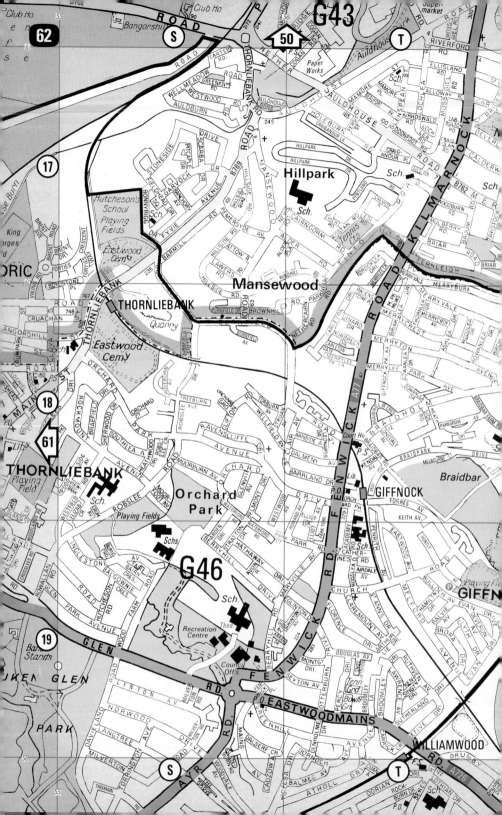

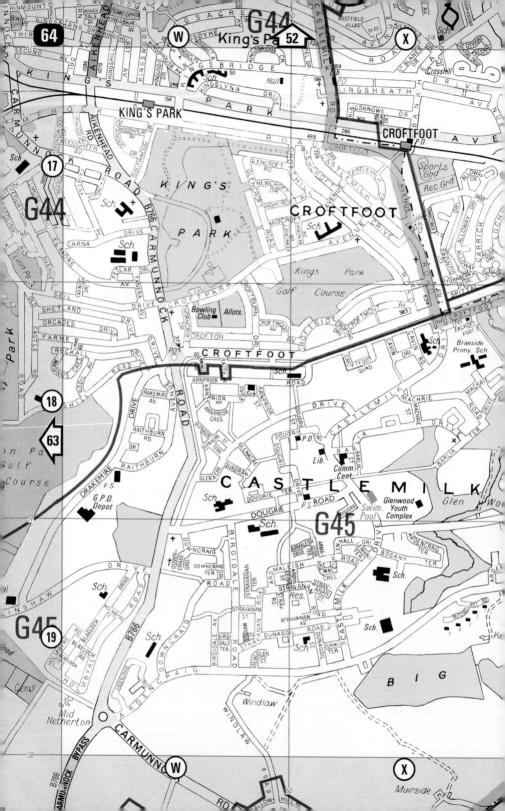

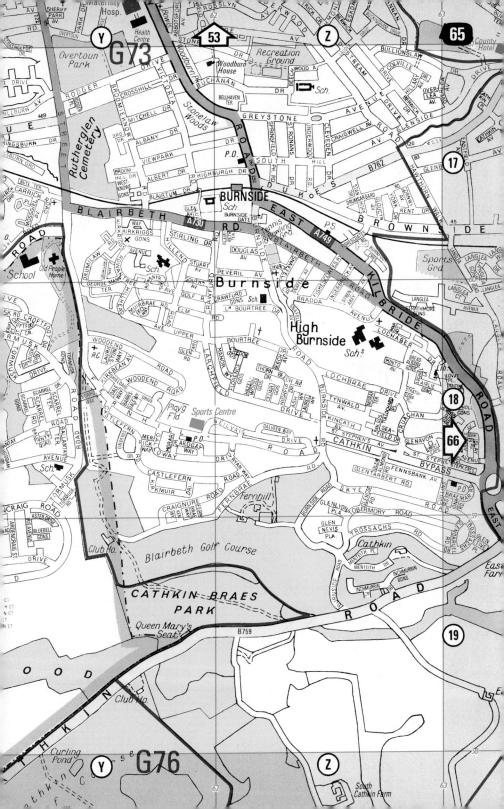

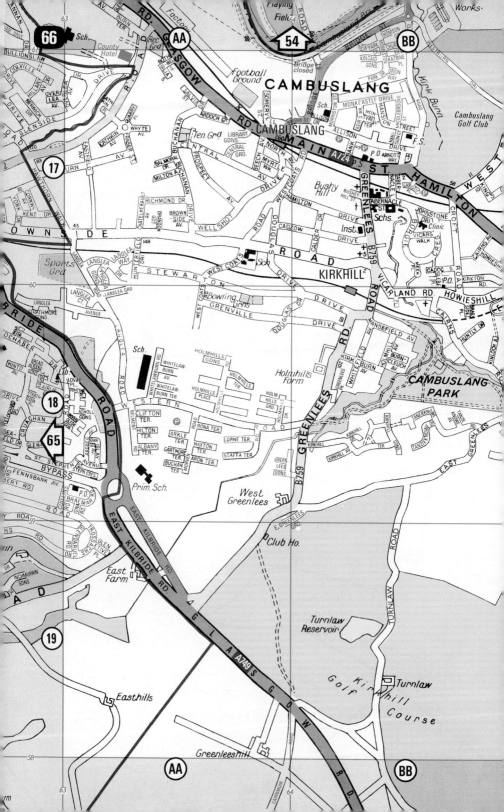

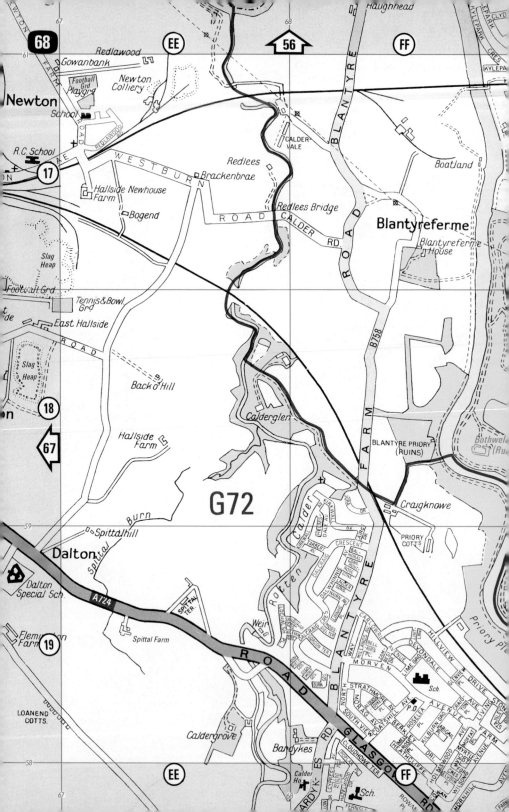

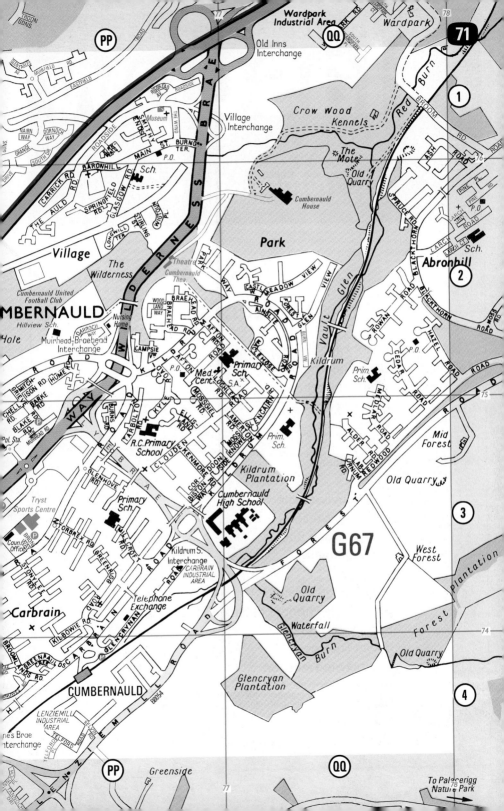

Glasgow

Information

Contents

The City of Glasgow began life as a makeshift hamlet of huts huddled round a 6thC church, built by St. Mungo on the banks of a little salmon river - the Clyde. It was called Gleschow, meaning 'beloved green place' in Celtic. The cathedral was founded in 1136; the university, the second oldest in Scotland, was established in the 15thC; and in 1454 the flourishing medieval city wedged between the cathedral and the river was made a Royal burgh. The city's commercial prosperity dates from the 17thC when the lucrative tobacco, sugar and cotton trade with the New World flourished. The River Clyde, Glasgow's gateway to the Americas, was dredged, deepened and widened in the 18thC to make it navigable to the city's heart.

By the 19thC, Glasgow was the greatest shipbuilding centre in the world. From the 1820s onwards, it grew in leaps and bounds westwards along a steep ridge of land running parallel with the river. The hillside became encased in an undulating grid of streets and squares. Gradually the individualism, expressed in one-off set pieces characteristic of the 18thC and early 19thC, gave way to a remarkable coherent series of terraced squares and crescents of epic proportions - making Glasgow one of the finest of Victorian cities. But the price paid for such rapid industrialisation, the tremendous social problems manifest in the squalor of some of the worst of 19thC slums, was high. Today the city is still the commercial and industrial capital of the West of Scotland. The most notorious of the slums have been cleared but the new buildings lack that sparkling clenchfisted Glaswegian character of the 19thC. Ironically, this character was partially destroyed when the slums were cleared for it wasn't the architecture that had failed, only the bureaucrats, who designated such areas as working class ghettos.

Districts
Little remains of medieval Glasgow, which stood on the wedge of land squeezed between the cathedral and the River Clyde. Its business centre was The Cross, a space formed by the junction of several streets - the tall, square Tolbooth Steeple, 1626, in the middle. Opposite is Trongate, an arch astride a footpath, complete with tower and steeple salvaged from 17thC St. Mary's Church - destroyed by fire in 1793. The centre of 20thC Glasgow is George Square, a tree-lined piazza planned in 1781 and pinned down by more than a dozen statues including an 80 foot high Doric column built in 1837 to carry a statue of Sir Walter Scott. Buildings of interest: the monumental neo-Baroque City Chambers 1883-88 which takes up the east side and the Merchants' House 1874, on the west. To the south of the square, in a huddle of narrow streets, is the old Merchant City. Of interest here is the elegant Trades House, 85 Glassford Street, built by Robert Adam in 1794. An elegant Ionic portico stands on a rusticated ground storey flanked by domed towers. Hutcheson's Hospital, 158 Ingram Street, is an handsome Italianate building designed by David Hamilton in 1805. Nearby is Stirling's Library, originally an 18thC private residence, it became the Royal Exchange in 1827 when the Corinthian portico was added. To the north west is Kelvingrove, Victorian Glasgow at its best. Built around a steep saddle of land, landscaped by Paxton in 1850 and lined along its edge with handsome terraces.

Last but not least are the banks of the River Clyde. From Clyde Walkway on the north bank you can see: the Suspension Bridge of 1871 with its pylons in the form of triumphal arches; 17thC Merchants' Steeple; the Gothic Revival St. Andrew's R.C. Cathedral of 1816; the church, built 1739, in nearby St. Andrew's Square is a typical copy of London's St. Martin-in-the-Fields.

City of Glasgow Local Information Guide

Useful Information

Area of City 79 sq. miles (approx)

Population (Glasgow City)
1995 618,000

Early Closing Days
Tuesday with alternative of Saturday.
Most of the shops in the central area
operate six-day trading.

Electricity
240 volts A.C.

Emergency Services
Police, Fire and Ambulance. Dial 999
on any telephone.

Licensing Hours
Public Houses
City Centre
Daily except Sundays 11 a.m.-12 p.m.
Sundays 12.30a.m.-12p.m.

Restaurants, Hotels and Public Houses
with catering facilities; same as above
but can be extended for drinks with
meals.

Information Bureau

Tourist Information Centres:
35 St. Vincent Place, Glasgow.
0141 204 4400

Town Hall, Abbey Close, Paisley.
0141 889 0711

Glasgow Airport (Abbotsinch), Paisley.
0141 848 4440

Pier Head, Gourock
(Summer only)
01475 639467

Help & Advice

British Broadcasting Corporation
Queen Margaret Drive, G12 8DG
0141 339 8844

British Council
6 Belmont Crescent, G12 8ES.
0141 339 8651

**British Telecom Scotland
Glasgow Area**
Westergate Chambers,
11 Hope Street,
Glasgow, G2 6AB.
All Enquiries 0141 220 1234
FREEFONE 0800 309 409

Chamber of Commerce
30 George Square, G2 1EQ.
0141 204 2121

Citizens Advice Bureau
87 Bath Street, Glasgow, G2 2EE
0141 331 2345/6/7/8

119 Main Street,
Bridgeton, Glasgow, G40 1QD
0141 554 0336

27 Dougrie Drive, Castlemilk, Glasgow,
G45 9AD
0141 634 0338/9

139 Main Street (Town Hall),
Rutherglen, G73 2JJ
0141 647 5100

216 Main Street, Barrhead, G78 1SN
0141 881 2032

1145 Maryhill Road, Glasgow, G20 9AZ
0141 945 5900

4 Shandwick Square, Easterhouse,
Glasgow, G34 9DS
0141 771 2328

Drumchapel, 49 Dunkenny Square,
G15 8NE
0141 944 2612

1361-1363 Gallowgate
Parkhead
G31 4DN
0141 554 004

Consumer Advice Centre
9 Queen Street,
Glasgow, GL1 3ED
0141 204 0262

Customs and Excise
21 India Street, G2 4PZ 01412213828

H.M. Immigration Office
Public Enquiry Office
Dumbarton Court,
Admin Block D, Argyll Avenue,
Abbotsinch, Paisley
0141 887 2225

Housing Aid and Advice
Shelter, 53 St. Vincent Crescent,
Glasgow, G3 8NQ 0141 221 8895

Legal Aid and Advice
Castlemilk Advice and Law Centre
27 Dougrie Drive, Glasgow, G45 9AD
0141 6340338

Law Centre
32 Dougrie Drive, G45 9AD
0141 634 0313

Lost Property
There is a railway switchboard number
that will put you through to Lost
Property (whichever station).
0141 335 3276

Buses - Office of bus company
Trains - Station of arrival.
Elsewhere in City - Strathclyde Police.
Lost Property Department,
173 Pitt Street, G2 4JS
0141 532 2000

**Registrar of Births, Deaths and
Marriages**
1 Martha Street, G1 1JJ
0141 287 7652

Marriages only:
22 Park Circus, G3 6BE
0141 287 8350
Hours: Monday 9.15 a.m. - 5.00p.m.
Tuesday to Friday 9.15 a.m. - 4.00 p.m.

Births must be registered within twenty
one days, deaths within eights days
and marriages within three days. The
Registrar should be consulted at least
one month before intended date of
marriage.

Children First
31 Burleigh Street, Govan, G51 3LA
0141 445 4541

**RNID - Royal National Institute for
the Deaf**
9 Clairmont Gardens, Glasgow, G3 7LW
0141 332 0343

Samaritans
210 West George Street, Glasgow,
G2 2PQ
0141 248 4488

**Scottish Society for the Mentally
Handicapped**
6th Floor
7 Buchanan Street
Glasgow, G1 3HL
0141 248 4541

Scottish Television
Cowcaddens, G2 3PR
0141 300 3000

**Society for the Prevention of Cruelty
to Animals**
125 Kinnell Avenue, Cardonald G52 3RY
0141 882 3338

Newspapers

Morning Daily
Daily Record
40 Anderston Quay, G3 8DA.
0141 248 7000

The Herald
195 Albion Street, G1 1QP
0141 552 6255

Scottish Daily Express
Park House, Park Circus Place,
G3 6AF
0141 332 9600

The Scotsman
Regent Court, 76 West Regent Street
G2 2QZ
0141 332 6177

Evening Daily
Evening Times
195 Albion Street, G1 1QP
0141 552 6255

Weekly
Scottish Sunday Express
Park House, Park Circus Place, G3 6AF
0141 332 9600

Sunday Mail
40 Anderston Quay, G3 8DA
0141 248 7000

Sunday Post
144 Port Dundas Road, G4 0HZ
0141 332 9933

Parking

Car Parking in the central area of Glasgow is controlled. Parking meters are used extensively and signs indicating restrictions are displayed at kerbsides and on entry to the central area. Traffic Wardens are on duty.

British Rail Car Parks
(Open 24 hours)
Central Station
Queen Street Station

Multi-Storey Car Parks
(Open 24 hours)
Anderston Cross: Cambridge Street: George Street: Mitchell Street: Port Dundas Road: Waterloo Street.

(Limited Opening)
Charing Cross: Cowcaddens Road: St. Enoch Centre: Sauchiehall Street Centre

Surface Car Parks
Cathedral Street (Concert Hall): Dunlop Street: High Street: Ingram Street: King Street: McAlpine Street: Oswald Street: Shuttle Street:

Post Offices

Head Post Office
47 St. Vincent Street, Glasgow G2 5QX
0141 204 3689
Open Monday to Friday 8.30a.m. - 5.45p.m.
Saturdays 9 a.m. - 7.00 p.m.

Branch Offices
228 Hope Street, Glasgow G2 3PN
0141 332 4598

87-91 Bothwell Street, Glasgow G2 7AA

Taxis

Glasgow has over 1400 traditional London type taxis, all licensed by the Glasgow District Council and all fitted with meters sealed and approved by the Council. A fare card stating the current tariff is displayed in a prominent position within each taxi. At the time of publishing a three mile journey costs approximately £5. The total price of each journey is shown on the meter. Fares are normally reviewed annually by the council. Each taxi can carry a maximum of five passengers.

The major taxi companies in the city offer City tours at fixed prices, listing the places of interest to be visited, leaflets are available at all major hotel reception areas. Tours vary from 2 to 3 hours and in price between £20 and £28. A tour "Glasgow by Night" is also available.

Any passenger wishing to travel to a destination outside the Glasgow District Boundary should ascertain from the driver the fare to be charged or the method of calculating the fare PRIOR to making the journey.

Complaints
Any complaints regarding the conduct of a taxi driver should be addressed to the Taxi Enforcement Officer, City Building Department, 73 Hawthorn Street, Glasgow G22 6HY.
0141 287 3326

Local Government

East Dunbartonshire
PO Box 4, Tom Johnston House, Civic Way, Kirkintilloch, G66 4TJ
0141 776 9000

East Renfrewshire
Council Offices, Eastwood Park, Rouken Glen Road, Giffnock G46 6UG
0141 621 3000

Glasgow City
City Chambers, George Square, Glasgow G2 1DU
0141 287 2000

North Lanarkshire
Civic Centre, Motherwell, ML1 1TW
01698 302222

Renfrewshire
South Buildings, Cotton Street, Paisley, PA1 1BU
0141 842 5000

South Lanarkshire
Council Offices, Almada Street, Hamilton ML3 0AA
01698 454444

West Dunbartonshire
Council Offices
Garshake Road
Dumbarton
G82 3PU
01389 737000

Glasgow Cathedral is a perfect example of pre-Reformation Gothic architecture. Begun in 1238, it has a magnificent choir and handsome nave with shallow projecting transepts. On a windy hill to the east is the Necropolis, a cemetery with a spiky skyline of Victoriana consisting of pillars, temples and obelisks, dominated by an 1825 Doric column carrying the statue of John Knox. Other churches of interest: Landsdowne Church built by J. Honeyman in 1863; St. George's Tron Church by William Stark 1807; Caledonian Road Church, a temple and tower atop a storey-high base, designed by Alexander Thomson in 1857; a similar design is to be found at the United Presbyterian Church, St. Vincent Street, 1858, but on a more highly articulated ground storey; Queen's Cross Church 1897 is an amalgam of Art Nouveau and Gothic Revival by the brilliant Charles Rennie Mackintosh.

Churches within the central area of Glasgow are:

Church of Scotland
Glasgow Cathedral
Castle Street
Renfield St. Stephen's Church
262 Bath Street
St. George's Tron Church
165 Buchanan Street
St. Columba Church (Gaelic)
300 St. Vincent Street

Baptist
Adelaide Place Church
209 Bath Street

Congregational
Hillhead Centre
1 University Avenue

Episcopal Church in Scotland
Cathedral Church of St. Mary
300 Great Western Road

First Church of Christ Scientist
1 La Bell Place, Clifton Street
(off Sauchiehall Street)

Free Church of Scotland
265 St. Vincent Street

German Speaking Congregation
Services held at 7 Hughenden Terrace

Greek Orthodox Cathedral
St. Luke's, 27 Dundonald Road

Jewish Orthodox Synagogue
Garnethill, 29 Garnet Street

Methodist
Woodlands Church
229 Woodlands Road

Roman Catholic
St. Andrew's Cathedral
190 Clyde Street
St. Aloysius' Church
25 Rose Street

Unitarian Church
72 Berkeley Street

United Free
Wynd Church
427 Crown Street

Interesting Buildings

Victorian Glasgow was extremely eclectic architecturally. Good examples of the Greek Revival style are Royal College of Physicians 1845, by W.H. Playfair and the Custom House 1840, by G.L. Taylor. The Queen's Room 1857, by Charles Wilson, is a handsome temple used now as a Christian Science church. The Gothic style is seen at its most exotic in the Stock Exchange 1877, by J. Burnet. The new Victorian materials and techniques with glass, wrought and cast iron were also ably demonstrated in the buildings of the time. Typical are: Gardener's Stores 1856, by J. Baird; the Buck's Head, Argyle Street, an amalgam of glass and cast iron; and the Egyptian Halls of 1873, in Union Street, which has a masonry framework. Both are by Alexander Thomson. The Templeton Carpet Factory 1889, Glasgow Green, by William Leiper, is a Venetian Gothic building complete with battlemented parapet.

Glasgow University

The great genius of Scottish architecture is Charles Rennie Mackintosh whose major buildings are in Glasgow. In the Scotland Street School 1904-6, he punctuated a 3-storey central block with flanking staircase towers in projecting glazed bays. His most famous building - Glasgow School of Art 1897-9 - is a magnificent Art Nouveau building of taut stone and glass; the handsome library, with its gabled facade, was added later in 1907-9.

Stirling's Library

78

Galleries & museums

Scotland's largest tourist attraction, The Burrell Collection, is situated in Pollok Country Park, Haggs Road and has more than 8,000 objects, housed in an award winning gallery. The Museum and Art Gallery, Kelvingrove Park, Argyle Street, a palatial sandstone building with glazed central court, has one of the best municipal collections in Britain; superb Flemish, Dutch and French paintings, drawings, prints, also ceramics, silver, costumes and armour, as well as a natural history section. The recently refurbished McLellan Galleries in Sauchiehall Street provide an important venue for touring and temporary art exhibitions. Provand's Lordship c1471, in Castle Street, is Glasgow's oldest house and now a museum of 17th-18thC furniture and household articles. Pollok House, Pollok Country Park, a handsome house designed by William Adam in 1752, has paintings by William Blake and a notable collection of Spanish paintings, including works by El Greco. The Museum of Transport, housed in Kelvin Hall, Bunhouse Road, has a magnificent collection of trams, cars, ships models, bicycles, horse-drawn carriages and 7 steam locos. The People's Palace, The Green built 1898 with a huge glazed Winter Garden, has a lively illustrated history of the city. But the oldest museum in Glasgow is the Hunterian Museum, University of Glasgow, University Avenue, opened in 1807, it has a fascinating collection of manuscripts, early painted books, as well as some fine archaeological and geological exhibits. 400-year old Haggs Castle, St. Andrew's Drive, is now a children's museum with practical demonstrations and exhibits showing how everyday life has changed over the centuries.

Streets & shopping

The Oxford Street of Glasgow is Sauchiehall (meaning 'willow meadow') Street. This together with Buchanan Street, Argyle Street, Princes Square and St. Enoch Centre form the main shopping area. Here you will find the department stores, boutiques and

Old Sheriff Court

general shops. All three streets are partly pedestrianised, but the most exhilarating is undoubtedly Buchanan Street. Of particular interest is the spatially elegant Argyll Arcade 1828, the Venetian Gothic-style Stock Exchange 1877, the picturesque Dutch gabled Buchanan Street Bank building 1896 and the Glasgow Royal Concert Hall (opened 1990). In Glasgow Green is The Barras, the city's famous street market, formed by the junction of London Road and Kent Street. The Market is open weekends. Some parts of the city have early closing on Tuesdays.

Museum & Art Gallery Kelvingrove

Entertainment

As Scotland's commercial and industrial capital, Glasgow offers a good choice of leisure activities. The city now has many theatres where productions ranging from serious drama to pantomime, pop and musicals are performed. The Theatre Royal, Hope Street is Scotland's only opera house and has been completely restored to its full Victorian splendour. The Royal Scottish National Orchestra gives concerts at the Glasgow Royal Concert Hall every Saturday night in winter and is the venue for the proms in June. Cinemas are still thriving in Glasgow, as are the many public houses, some of which provide meals and live entertainment. In the city centre and Byres Road, West End, there is a fair number of restaurants where traditional home cooking, as well as international cuisines, can be sampled. More night life can be found at the city's discos and dance halls.

Outdoors, apart from the many parks and nature trails, there is Calderpark Zoological Gardens, situated 6 miles from the centre between Mount Vernon and Uddingston. Here you may see white rhinos, black panthers and iguanas among many species. Departing from Stobcross Quay, you can also cruise down the Clyde in 'P.S. Waverley' - the last sea-going paddle-steamer in the world.

Cinemas

ABC Cinema, 380 Clarkston Road
0141 637 2641
ABC Cinema
326 Sauchiehall Street 0141 332 9513
Admin Dept 0141 332 1592
Glasgow Film Theatre
12 Rose Street (Box Office)
0141 332 6535
Grosvenor Cinema
Ashton Lane
0141 339 4298
Kelburne Cinema
(Manager), Glasgow Road, Paisley
PA1 3BD. 0141 889 3612
Odeon Film Centre
56 Renfield Street 0141 332 8701

Virgin Centre
The Forge Shopping Centre
1221 Gallowgate,
G31 4EB
0141 556 4282

Halls

City Halls, Candleriggs
Couper Institute
86 Clarkston Road, G44
Glasgow Royal Concert Hall
2 Sauchiehall Street, G2 3NY
Langside Hall, 5 Langside Avenue
Partick Burgh Hall, 9 Burgh Hall Street,
Pollokshaws Hall
2025 Pollokshaws Road,
Woodside Hall, Glenfarg Street
More information about the above
G.C.C. halls and others contact,
Performing Arts and Venues, Exchange
House, 229 George Street, G1 1QU
0141 287 5008

Theatres

Arches Theatre
30 Midland Street G1 4PR
0141 221 9736
Citizens' Theatre
119 Gorbals Street G5 9DS
0141 429 0022
King's Theatre
297 Bath Street 0141 227 5511
Mitchell Theatre and Moir Hall
Granville Street G3 0141 227 5511
New Athenaeum Theatre
100 Renfrew Street G2 3DB
0141 332 5057
Old Athenaeum Theatre
179 Buchanan Street G1 2JZ
0141 332 2333
Pavilion Theatre
121 Renfield Street G2 3AX
0141 332 1846
Theatre Royal
282 Hope Street G2 3QA
0141 332 9000
Tramway
25 Albert Drive G41 2PE
0141 552 4267
Tron Theatre
63 Trongate, Glasgow G1 5HB
0141 552 4267

The Ticket Centre
Candleriggs, G1 1NQ
Glasgow's Central Box Office for Arches Theatre, Centre for Contemporary Arts, Citizens'
Theatre, City Hall at Candleriggs, King's Theatre, Mitchell Theatre, Tron Theatre, Scottish
Exhibition Centre and Glasgow Royal Concert Hall.
Telephone lines open Mon.- Sat. 9a.m. - 9.00 p.m. Sun. 12.00 - 5 p.m.
0141 227 5511
Counter Service: Mon.- Sat. 9.00 a.m.-6.00 p.m.
Sun. 12.00 - 5.pm

Weather

The City of Glasgow is on the same latitude as the City of Moscow, but because of its close
proximity to the warm Atlantic Shores, and the prevailing westerly winds, it enjoys a more
moderate climate. Summers are generally cool and winters mostly mild, this gives Glasgow
fairly consistent summer and winter temperatures. Despite considerable cloud the City is
sheltered by hills to the south-west and north and the average rainfall for Glasgow is usually
less than 40 inches per year. The following table shows the approximate average figures for
sunshine, rainfall and temperatures to be expected in Glasgow throughout the year.

Weather Forecasts
For the Glasgow Area including Loch Lomond and the Clyde Coast:
Weatherline 0891 232 791 (Recording)
The Glasgow Weather Centre (Meteorological Office), St. Vincent Street, G2 5QD
0141 248 3451

Month	Hours of Sunshine	Inches of Rainfall	Temperature °C		
			Ave. Max.	Ave. Min.	High/Low
January	36	3.8	5.5	0.8	-18
February	62	2.8	6.3	0.8	-15
March	94	2.4	8.8	2.2	21
April	147	2.4	11.9	3.9	22
May	185	2.7	15.1	6.2	26
June	181	2.4	17.9	9.3	30
July	159	2.9	18.6	10.8	29
August	143	3.5	18.5	10.6	31
September	106	4.1	16.3	9.1	-4
October	76	4.1	13.0	6.8	-8
November	47	3.7	8.7	3.3	-11
December	30	4.2	6.5	1.9	-12

Sport & Recreation

For both spectator and participant, football is Glasgow's favourite sport. Both Celtic and Rangers, Scotland's most famous rival teams, have their grounds within the City. Glasgow houses Scotland's national football stadium at Hampden Park.

Badminton
Scottish Badminton Union's Cockburn Centre, 40 Bogmoor Place, G51 4TQ. 0141 445 1218

Bowling Greens
There are greens in all the main Parks. Information about clubs from the Scottish Bowling Association: 50 Wellington Street, G2 6EF. 0141 221 8999

Cricket Grounds
Huntershill Crowhill Road, Bishopbriggs.
Poloc Dawholm, 2060 Pollokshaws Road, G43.
West of Scotland Peel Street, G11.

Football Grounds
Broadwood (Clyde F.C.) Cumbernauld
Celtic Park (Celtic F.C.) 95 Kerrydale Street, G40
Firhill Park (Partick ThistleF.C.) Firhill Road, G20
Hampden Park (Queen's Park F.C.) Somerville Drive, G42
Ibrox Stadium (Rangers F.C.) Edmiston Drive, G51
Kilbowie Park (Clydebank F.C.) Argyll Road, Clydebank
St. Mirren Park (St. Mirren F.C.) Love Street, Paisley

Golf Courses
Glasgow District Council
9 holes
Alexandra Park, Cumbernauld Road, G31
Cambuslang, Westburn Drive, Cambuslang.
King's Park, Carmunnock Road, Croftfoot, G44
Knightswood, Lincoln Avenue, G13

Ruchill, Brassey Street, G20

18 holes
Barshaw, Glasgow Road, Paisley.
Douglaston, Strathblane Road, Milngavie. (Five miles from Glasgow).
Elderslie, Main Road, Johnstone.
Lethamhill, Cumbernauld Road, G33
Littlehill, Auchinairn Road, G64.
Linn Park, Simshill Road,G4
Pollok, Barrhead Road, Pollokshaws, G43

Putting Greens
There are putting greens in some of the main parks.

Pitch & Putt
Courses at Bellahouston Park, Queen's Park, and several others.

Rugby Grounds
Auldhouse (Hutchesons'/Aloysians) Thornliebank
Cartha Queens Park Haggs Road, G41
Garscube Estate Switchback Road, Maryhill, Glasgow, G61
Hughenden (Hillhead High School) Hughenden Road, G12.
New Anniesland (Glasgow Acad.) Helensburgh Drive, G13.
Old Anniesland (Glasgow High School F.P. & Kelvinside Academicals) Crow Road, G11.

Sports Centres
Barrhead, Main Street, Barrhead G78 1SW 0141 881 1900

Bellahouston 31 Bellahouston Drive, G52 1HH. 0141 427 5454
Burnhill 60 Toryglen Road, Rutherglen, G73 1NE. 0141 643 0327
Crownpoint Crownpoint Road, Bridgeton, G40. 0141 554 8274
Linwood, Brediland Road, Linwood PA3 3RA. 01505 329 461
Springburn Key Street, Springburn, G21 1JY. 0141 557 5878
Tryst, Tryst Walk, Cumbernauld G67 1EW. 01236 728138

Swimming Pools
Drumchapel, 199 Drumry Road East, G15 8NS. 0141 944 5812
Easterhouse, Bogbain Road, G34 9LA. 0141 771 7978
Elderslie, 3 Stoddard Square, Elderslie. PA5 9AS 01505 328133
Govan, 1 Harhill Street, G51. 0141 445 1899
Lagoon Leisure Centre, Mill St., Paisley PA1 1LZ. 0141 889 4000
North Woodside, Braid Square, G4 9YB. 0141 332 8102
Pollok Leisure Pool, Cowglen Road, G53. 0141 881 3313
Renfrew, Inchinnan Road, Renfrew PA4 8ND. 0141 886 2088
Scotstown Leisure Centre 72 Danes Drive, Scotstown, G14. 0141 959 4000
Temple, 354 Netherton Road, G13. 0141 954 6537
Tollcross Park Leisure Centre Wellshot Road, Tollcross G32 8TF 0141 763 1222

Tennis
There are courts in some of the main parks. Information about clubs from theSecretary of the West of Scotland Lawn Tennis Association: Mr J Stevenson 01505 812336.

Strathclyde
Further Education

Anniesland College
Hatfield Drive, Glasgow, G12 OYE
0141 357 3969

Ayr College
Dam Park, Ayr, KA8 OEU
01292 265184

Bell College of Technology
Almada Street, Hamilton, Lanarkshire,
ML3 OJB
01698 283100

Cambuslang College
Hamilton Road, Cambuslang, Glasgow,
G72 7BS
0141 641 6600

**Cardonald College of Further
Education**
690 Mosspark Drive, Glasgow, G52 3AY
0141 883 6151

Central College of Commerce
300 Cathedral Street, G1 2TA
0141 552 3941

Clydebank College
Kilbowie Road, Clydebank,
Dunbartonshire, G81 2AA
0141 952 7771

Coatbridge College
Kildonan Street, Coatbridge,
Lanarkshire, ML5 3LS
01236 422316

Cumbernauld College
Town Centre, Cumbernauld, Glasgow,
G67 1HU
01236 731811

Glasgow Caledonian University
Cowcaddens Road, Glasgow G4 0BA
0141 331 3000

**Glasgow College of Building and
Printing**
60 North Hanover Street, Glasgow,
G1 2BP
0141 332 9969

**Glasgow College of Food
Technology**
230 Cathedral Street, Glasgow, G1 2TG
0141 552 3751

Glasgow College of Nautical Studies
21 Thistle Street, Glasgow, G5 9XB
0141 429 3201

James Watt College
Finnart Street, Greenock, Renfrewshire,
PA16 8HF
01475 724433

John Wheatley College
1346-1364 Shettleston Road, Glasgow,
G32 9AT
0141 778 2426

Kilmarnock College
Holehouse Road, Kilmarnock, Ayrshire,
KA3 7AT
01563 23501

Langside College
50 Prospecthill Road, Glasgow, G42 9LB
0141 649 4991

Motherwell College
Dalzell Drive, Motherwell, Lanarkshire,
ML4 2DD
01698 232323

North Glasgow College
110 Flemington Street, Glasgow,
G21 4BX
0141 558 9001

Reid Kerr Gollege, The
Renfrew Road, Paisley, Renfrewshire,
PA13 4DR
0141 889 4225

Stow College
43 Shamrock Street, Glasgow, G4 9LD
0141 332 1786

University of Glasgow
University Avenue, Glasgow
0141 339 8855

University of Paisley
High St, Paisley
0141 848 3000

University of Strathclyde
George Street, Glasgow, G1 1XQ
0141 552 4400

Parks & Gardens

There are over 70 public parks within the city. The most famous is Glasgow Green. Abutting the north bank of the River Clyde, it was acquired in 1662. Of interest are the Winter Gardens attached to the People's Palace. Kelvingrove Park is an 85-acre park laid out by Sir Joseph Paxton in 1852. On the south side of the city is the 148-acre Queen's Park, Victoria Road, established 1857-94. Also of interest: Rouken Glen, Thornliebank, with a spectacular waterfall, walled garden, nature trail and boating facilities; Victoria Park, Victoria Park Drive, with its famous Fossil Grove flower gardens and yachting pond. In Great Western Road are the Botanic Gardens. Founded in 1817, the gardens' 42 acres are crammed with natural attractions, including the celebrated Kibble Palace glasshouse with its fabulous tree ferns, exotic plants and white marble Victorian statues.

Alexandra
671 Alexandra Parade, G31.

Barshaw
Glasgow Road, Paisley.

Bellahouston
Paisley Road West, G52.

Botanic Gardens
730 Great Western Road, G12.

Hogganfield Loch
Cumbernauld Road, G33.

Kelvingrove
Sauchiehall Street, G3.

King's
325 Carmunnock Road, G44.

Linn
Clarkston Road at Netherlee Road, G44.

Pollok Country Park
Pollokshaws Road, G43

Queen's
Victoria Road, G42.

Rouken Glen
Rouken Glen Road, G46.

Springburn
Broomfield Road, G21.

Tollcross
461 Tollcross Road, G32.

Victoria
Victoria Park Drive North, G14.

Kibble Palace

Public Transport

The City of Glasgow has one of the most advanced, fully integrated public transport systems in the whole of Europe. The Strathclyde Transport network consists of: the local railway network, the local bus services and the fully modernised Glasgow Underground, with links to Glasgow Airport and the Steamer and Car Ferry Services.
For information contact:
Strathclyde Transport Travel Centre
St. Enoch Square G1 4BW
0141 226 4826
Open Monday to Saturday 9.30 a.m. - 5.30 p.m.
Phone enquiries Monday to Saturday 9.00 a.m. - 9.00 p.m.
Sunday 9 a.m. - 7.30 p.m.
For City services, ferry services, local train services. Free timetables are available.

Bus Services and Tours
Long Distance Coach Service
0990 505050
Scottish Citylink Coaches Ltd and National Express provide express services to London and most parts of Scotland including Campbeltown, Tarbert, Ardrishaig, Inverary, Oban, Fort William, Skye, Stirling, Perth, Dundee, Arbroath, Montrose, Aberdeen, Aviemore, Inverness and Edinburgh.

Local Bus Services
A comprehensive network of local bus services is provided by a variety of operators within the City of Glasgow and also direct to the following destinations:
Airdrie, Ardrossan, Ayr, Balfron, Barrhead, Bearsden, Beith, Bellshill, Bishopbriggs, Bishopton, Blantyre, Bo'ness, Caldercruix, Cambuslang, Campsie Glen, Carluke, Clydebank, Coatbridge, Cumbernauld, Denny, Drymen, Dunfermline, Duntocher, Eaglesham, East Kilbride, Erskine, Falkirk, Glenrothes, Grangemouth, Hamilton, Irvine, Johnstone, Kilbarchan, Kilbirnie, Killearn, Kilmarnock, Kilsyth, Kirkintilloch, Kirkcaldy, Lanark, Largs, Larkhall, Lennoxtown, Lochwinnoch, Motherwell, Milngavie, Newton Mearns, Old Kilpatrick, Paisley, Prestwick, Renfrew, Saltcoats, Shotts, Stirling, Strathblane, Strathaven,

Uddingston, Wishaw.
These services depart from City Centre bus stops or from Buchanan Bus Station.
0141 332 7133

Coach Hire and Day, Half Day and Extended Tours
Scottish City Link Coaches Ltd
0990 505050
Private hire and seasonal tours
Freephone 0800 080001

Haldane's of Cathcart
12, Delvin Road, G44 3AA
Private hire and tours
0141 637 2234

Strathclyde Buses Ltd.
197 Victoria Road, G42 7AD
0141 636 3190
Private hire and seasonal tours
Freephone 0800 0800 01

Railway Services
Passenger enquiries: 0345 484 950
Sleeper reservations: 0345 5500 33

ScotRail trains serve over 170 stations in Glasgow and Strathclyde (see map). ScotRail services operate to most destinations in Scotland.
East Coast Ltd., West Coast Ltd. and Cross Country Trains Ltd. operate services to England.

Glasgow Queen Street Station
for services to Cumbernauld, Edinburgh, Falkirk, Stirling, Perth, Dundee, Arbroath, Montrose, Aberdeen, Pitlochry, Aviemore, Inverness, Durnbarton, Balloch, Helensburgh, Oban, Fort William, Mallaig, Coatbridge, Airdrie.

Glasgow Central Station
for services to Gourock (ferry connection to Dunoon), Greenock, Wemyss Bay (ferry connection to Rothesay), Paisley, Johnstone, Largs, Ardrossan (ferry connection to Brodick), Irvine, Ayr, Girvan, Stranraer, East Kilbride, Kilmarnock, Dumfries, Motherwell, Hamilton, Lanark, Carlisle, Shotts, Edinburgh, Berwick, Newcastle.
London and destinations on West and East Coast Main Lines.

Strathclyde Transport

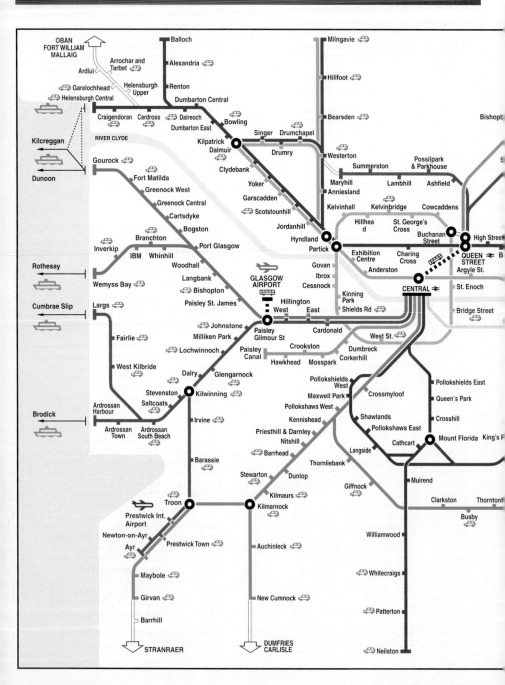

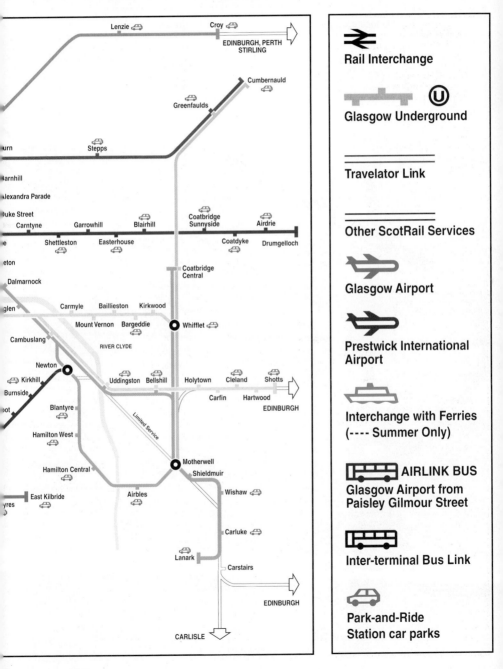

Glasgow Airport

Glasgow Airport is located eight miles west of Glasgow alongside the M8 motorway at Junction 28. It is linked by a bus service to Buchanan Street Bus Station, which runs every 10 minutes from 8.00 a.m.-5.00p.m. Monday to Saturday and less frequently at off peak times. There is a frequent coach service linking the Airport with all major bus and rail terminals in the City. Gilmour Street railway station in Paisley is 2 miles away and is linked by a frequent local bus service or by taxi.
Car parking is available with a graduated scale of charges. The Airport telephone number is 0141 887 1111

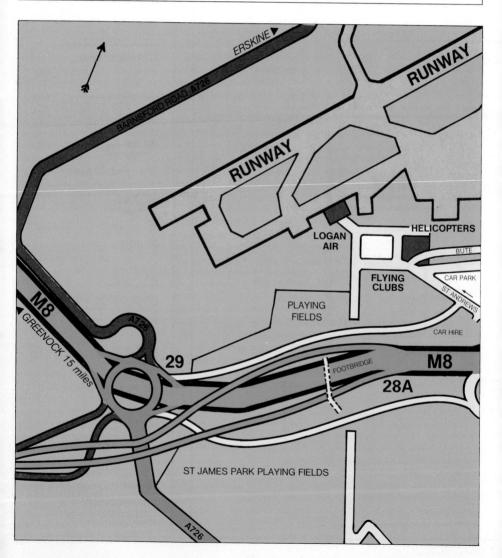

Airlines

Aer Lingus Flights to: Dublin
Reservations 0141 248 4121
Air Canada Flights to: Calgary, Toronto, Calgary.
Reservations 0345 181313
Air U.K. Flights to: Amsterdam, London Gatwick, London Stansted.
Reservations 0345 666777
British Airways Flights to: Boston, New York, Paris, London Heathrow, Manchester, Birmingham, and Inter Scottish Routes.
Reservations 0345 222111
British Airways Express Flights to: Barra, Belfast, Donegal, Islay, Inverness, Kirkwall, Londonderry, Sumburgh, Tiree.

British Midland Flights to: London Heathrow, Jersey, Copenhagen, East Midlands.
Reservations 0345 554554
Business Air Flights to: Aberdeen, Manchester.
Reservations 01500 340146
Easy Jet Flights to: London Luton.
Reservatons 01582 445566
Icelandair Flights to: Reykjavik.
Reservations 0171 388 5599
Manx Airlines Flights to: Isle of Man
Reservations 0141 221 0162
Sabena Flights to: Brussels
Reservations 0345 125245

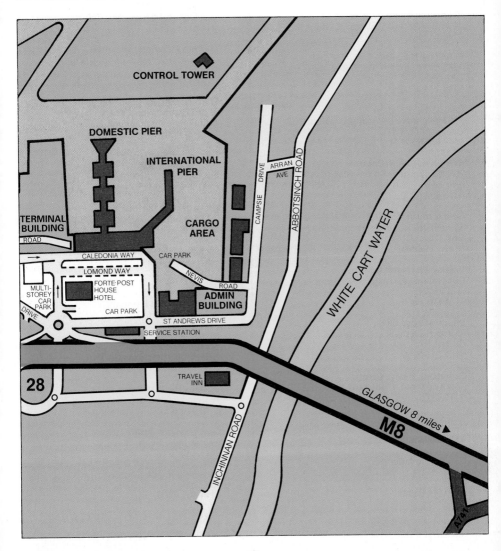

Hospitals

Greater Glasgow Health Board
(Administration)
112 Ingram Street, Glasgow, G1 1ET
0141 201 4444

Acorn Street Psychiatric Day Hospital
23 Acorn Street, Bridgeton, Glasgow,
G40 4AA
0141 556 4789

Baillieston Health Centre
20 Muirside Road, Glasgow, G69 7AD
0141 531 8000

Belvidere Hospital
1362-1452 London Road, Glasgow,
G31 4PG
0141 211 8500

Blawarthill Hospital
129 Holehouse Drive, Knightswood,
Glasgow, G13 3TG
0141 954 9547

Bridgeton Health Centre
201 Abercromby Street, Glasgow,
G40 2AD
0141 531 6500

Canniesburn Hospital
Switchback Road, Bearsden, Glasgow,
G61 1QL
0141 211 5600

Castlemilk Health Centre
Dougrie Drive, Castlemilk, Glasgow,
G45 9AW
0141 531 8500

Charing Cross Clinic
8 Woodside Crescent, Glasgow,
G3 7UL
0141 211 8100

Clydebank Health Centre
Kilbowie Road, Clydebank, G81 2TQ
0141 531 6400

Cowglen Hospital
Boydstone Road, Glasgow, G53 6XJ
0141 632 9106

Douglas Inch Centre
2 Woodside Terrace, Glasgow,
G3 7UY
0141 211 8000

Drumchapel Hospital
129 Drumchapel Road, Glasgow,
G15 6PX
0141 211 6000

Easterhouse Health Centre
9 Auchinlea Road, Glasgow, G34 9QU
0141 531 8100

Gartloch Hospital
Gartloch Road,Glasgow, G69 8EJ
0141 771 0771

Gartnavel General Hospital
1053 Great Western Road, Glasgow,
G12 0YN
0141 211 3000

Gartnavel Royal Hospital
1055 Great Western Road, Glasgow,
G12 0XH
0141 211 3600

Glasgow Dental Hospital and School
378 Sauchiehall Street, Glasgow,
G2 3JZ
0141 211 9600

Glasgow Eye Infirmary
3 Sandyford Place, Glasgow, 63 7NB
0141 211 6767

Glasgow Homeopathic Hospital
1000 Great Western Road, Glasgow,
G12 0AA
0141 211 1600

Glasgow Royal Infirmary
84 Castle Street, Glasgow, G4 0NA
0141 211 4000

Glasgow Royal Maternity Hospital
Rottenrow, Glasgow, G4 0NA
0141 211 3400

Gorbals Health Centre
45 Pine Place, Glasgow, G5 0BQ
0141 429 6291

Govan Health Centre
5 Drumoyne Road, Glasgow G51 4BJ
0141 440 1212

Govanhill Health Centre
233 Calder Street, Glasgow, G42 7DR
0141 531 8300

Knightswood Hospital
125 Knightswood Road, Glasgow,
G13 2XG
0141 211 6900

Lennox Castle Hospital
Lennoxtown, Glasgow, G65 7LB
01360 329200

Lenzie Hospital
Auchinloch Road, Kirkintilloch,
Glasgow, G66 5DF
0141 776 1208

Leverndale Hospital
510 Crookston Road, Glasgow,
G53 7TU
0141 211 6400

Lightburn Hospital
966 Carntyne Road, Glasgow, G32 6ND
0141 774 5102

Maryhill Health Centre
41 Shawpark Street, Glasgow, G20 9DR
0141 531 8700

Mearnskirk Hospital
Newton Mearns, Glasgow, G77 5RZ
0141 201 6000

Parkhead Health Centre
101 Salamanca Street, Glasgow,
G31 5NA
0141 531 9000

Parkhead Hospital
81 Salamanca Street, Glasgow,
G31 5ES
0141 554 7951

Pollock Health Centre
21 Cowglen Road, Glasgow, G53 6EQ
0141 880 8899

Possilpark Health Centre
85 Denmark Street, Glasgow, G22 5EG
0141 531 6120

Queen Mother's Hospital
Yorkhill, Glasgow, 63 8SH
0141 201 0550

Royal Hospital for Sick Children
Yorkhill, Glasgow, G3 8SJ
0141 201 0000

Ruchill Hospital
Bilsland Drive, Glasgow, G20 9NB
0141 946 7120

Rutherglen Health Centre
130 Stonelaw Road, Rutherglen,
Glasgow, G73 2PQ
0141 531 6000

Rutherglen Maternity Hospital
120 Stonelaw Road, Rutherglen,
Glasgow, G73 2PG 0141 201 6060

Shettleston Health Centre
420 Old Shettleston Road, Glasgow,
G32 7JZ
0141 531 6200

Southern General Hospital
1345 Govan Road, Glasgow, G51 4TF
0141 201 1100

Springburn Health Centre
200 Springburn Way, Glasgow, G21 1TR
0141 558 0101

Stobhill General Hospital
133 Balornock Road, Glasgow, G21 3UW
0141 201 3907

Thornliebank Health Centre
20 Kennishead Road, Glasgow, G46 8NY
0141 531 6900

Townhead Health Centre
16 Alexandra Parade, Glasgow, G31 2ES
0141 531 8900

Victoria Geriatric Unit
100 Mansionhouse Road, Glasgow,
G41 3DX
0141 201 6167

Victoria Infirmary
Langside Road, Glasgow, G42 9TY
0141 201 6000

Western Infirmary
Dumbarton Road, Glasgow, G11 6NT
0141 211 2000

Woodilee Hospital
Lenzie, Glasgow, G66 3UG
0141 777 8000

Woodside Health Centre
Barr Street, Glasgow, G20 7LR
0141 531 9200

Renfrew District

A selection of leisure, recreational and cultural attractions in Renfrew District:

Barrhead Sports' Centre
The Centre contains swimming pools, sports halls, activity rooms and saunasuite. Bar and restaurant facilities add to the wide range of sporting and leisure activities available.

Barshaw Park, Glasgow Road, Paisley
The park is extensive with formal and informal areas. It adjoins the public golf course and incorporates a boating pond, playgrounds, model "ride-on" railway and a nature corner.

Castle Semple Country Park, Lochwinnoch
Castle Semple Loch is a popular feature for sailing and fishing. Canoes, rowing boats and sailing boards for hire. Fishing permits available. 01505 842882

Coats Observatory
The Observatory has traditionally recorded astronomical and meteorological information since 1882. Now installed with a satellite picture receiver, it is one of the best equipped Observatories in the country. Monday, Tuesday, Thursday 2-8 p.m., Wednesday, Friday, Saturday 10 a.m. - 5 p.m. 0141 889 3151

Erskine Bridge (Toll)
The bridge is an impressive high level structure opened by HRH Princess Anne in 1971 and provides a direct link from Renfrew District to Loch Lomond and the Trossachs. The bridge replaced the Erskine Ferry and affords extensive views up and down river to pedestrian users.

Finlaystone Estate
Off the A8 at Langbank. The Estate is now a garden centre with woodland walks. The house has connections with John Knox and Robert Burns and is open April to August on Sundays from 2.30 - 4.30 p.m. At other times groups by appointment. Estate open all year round. 0147 554 285

Formakin Estate, By Bishopton
A group of buildings and landscaped grounds designed in the Arts and Crafts style at the turn of the century. The estate has a visitor centre, tea room and offers walks, trails, picnic areas and play areas. Open 7 days 11a.m. - 6 p.m. 01505 863400

Gleniffer Braes Country Park, Glenfield Road, Paisley
1,000 breathtaking acres including Glen Park nature trail, picnic and children's play areas. Open dawn till dusk, the park affords extensive walks and spectacular views from this elevated moorland area, and contains an area reserved for model aero flying. 0141 884 3794

Houston Village
Houston was developed in the 18th century as an estate village. The traditional smiddy building, village pubs and terraced houses combine to create a quiet, sleepy atmosphere which has successfully survived the development of extensive modern housing on its periphery.

Inchinnan Bridges
Early 19th century stone bridges over the White Cart and Black Cart rivers close to St. Conval's stone, and the site of the Inchinnan Church which houses the graves of the Knights Templar, whose order was introduced to Scotland in 1153 by King David I.

Johnstone Castle
The remnants of a 1700 building formerly a much larger structure but demolished in the 1950's. The castle has significant historical links with the Cochrane and Houston families, major landowners who were instrumental in the development of the Burgh of Johnstone.

Kilbarchan Village
A good example of an 18th Century weaving village with many original buildings still fronting the narrow streets. A focal point is the steeple building in the square, originally a school and meal market and now used as public meeting rooms. A cycle route/footpath system links it to Glasgow and the Clyde Coast.

Lagoon Leisure Centre, Paisley
Ultra-modern complex housing superb ice rink and extensive "fun" pool featuring artificial wave machine and water slides. Also has cafe/bar facilities. Unique within the area, the complex is easily reached by public transport and has ample parking. Monday - Friday 10 a.m. - 10 p.m., Saturday and Sunday 10 a.m. - 5.00 p.m. 0141 889 4000

Laigh Kirk, Paisley
Originally built in 1738, the Laigh Kirk has been converted to an Arts Centre, with a theatre, workshop, bistro and bar open daily 10 a.m. - 11 p.m. For further information 0141 887 1010

Linwood Sports Centre
A wide range of indoor and outdoor sporting activities include football and rugby pitches, games hall, squash courts, BMX track, fitness trail, tennis courts and conditioning suite.

Lochwinnoch Village
An attractive rural village close to the Castle Semple Water Park, Muirshiel Country Park and the R.S.P.B. nature reserve, Lochwinnoch contains a small local museum with displays reflecting agricultural, social and industrial aspects of village life. Museum open Monday, Wednesday and Friday 10 a.m. - 1 p.m., 2 - 5 p.m. and 6 - 8 p.m. Tuesday and Saturday 10 a.m. - 1 p.m. and 2- 5 p.m. Open most days throughout the year, visitors should telephone 01505 842615

Muirshiel Country Park
Four miles north of Lochwinnoch, the park features trails of varying length radiating from the Information Centre. Open daily 9a.m.-4.30 p.m. (Winter), 9a.m. - 7.30 p.m. (Summer). 01505 842803

Paisley Abbey
Birthplace of the Stewart Dynasty, the Abbey dates, in part, to the 12th century and features regimental flags, relics, the Barochan Cross and beautiful stained glass windows.
Monday - Saturday 10 a.m. - 12.30 p.m., 1.30- 3.30 p.m. 0141 889 3630

Paisley Arts Centre
Converted 18th century church. Performing arts, works by local artists and participatory events and includes bar and bistro. Box office open 7 days 10 a.m. - 8 p.m. Further information 0141 887 1007

Paisley Museum and Art Gallery, High Street, Paisley
In addition to the world famous collection of Paisley shawls, the Museum traces the history of the Paisley pattern, the development of weaving techniques and houses collections of local and natural history, ceramics and paintings. Monday - Saturday 10 a.m - 5 p.m. 0141 8893151

Paisley Town Hall
A Renaissance style building by the River Cart in the heart of Paisley, it features a slim clock tower and houses a Tourist Information Centre. It accommodates many exhibitions during the year and it is also available for conferences and functions. Monday - Saturday 9 a.m. - 5 p.m. 0141 887 1007

Paisley Town Trail
An easy to follow route taking in the town's historic and architecturally significant buildings. Visitors can spend an hour or two walking round the trail and referring to a printed guide and wall plaques on the main buildings.

Renfrew Town Hall
The Town Hall has a "fairy-tale" style to its 105 feet high spire and was the administrative centre of the Royal Burgh of Renfrew. Originally the principal town in the area, Renfrew was strategically placed on the River Clyde, and a passenger ferry continues to operate daily.

Robert Tannahill, Weaver Poet
The works of Tannahill rank with those of Burns. Born in 1774 he took his own life in 1810 and is buried in a nearby graveyard. Visitors can visit his early home, site of his death, and his grave, and read his works in Paisley Library.

Royal Society for Protection of Birds, Lochwinnoch
An interesting visitor centre with observation tower, hides, displays and gift shop. Thursday, Friday, Saturday and Sunday 10a.m. - 5 p.m. Shop open 7 days. 01505 842663

Sma' Shot Cottages, Paisley
Fully restored and furnished artisan's house of the Victorian era; exhibition roomdisplaying photographs plus artefacts of local interest. 18th Century weaver's loomshop with combined living quarters. Open Wednesday & Saturday May - September 1-5 p.m. Group visits arranged by appointment. Tel: 0141 812 2513 or 0141 889 0530

The Clyde Estuary
Visitors travelling along the rural route to the Old Greenock Road above Langbank village at the western end of the District are able to take advantage of extensive views of the upper and lower Clyde Estuary, the Gareloch and the mountains beyond.

Thomas Coats Memorial Church
Open Monday - Friday 9 a.m. - 12 noon. Visitors should check in advance. Another gift from the Coats family to Paisley, the church was built in 1894 and constructed of red sandstone, is one of the finest Baptist Churches in the country. Tel: 0141 889 9980

Wallace Monument, Elderslie
The monument was erected in 1912 and marks the birthplace of the Scottish Patriot, Sir William Wallace. It stands adjacent to the reconstructed foundation plan of the adjacent Wallace Buildings which dated from the 17th Century.

Weaver's Cottage, Kilbarchan
This cottage, built in 1723, houses the last of the village's 800 looms and demonstrations are still given. It contains displays of weaving and domestic utensils, with Cottage garden and refreshments. Open Monday, Tuesday, Thursday, Friday 2 - 5 p.m., Saturday 10 a.m.- 1 p.m. and 2 - 5 p.m.

INDEX TO STREETS

General Abbreviations

Arc.	Arcade	Dr.	Drive	Mans.	Mansions	Sta.	Station
Av.	Avenue	E.	East	Ms.	Mews	Ter.	Terrace
Bk.	Bank	Est.	Estate	N.	North	Trd.	Trading
Bldgs.	Buildings	Ex.	Exchange	Par.	Parade	Twr.	Tower
Boul.	Boulevard	Fm.	Farm	Pas.	Passage	Vill.	Villa
Bri.	Bridge	Gdns.	Gardens	Pk.	Park	Vills.	Villas
Cen.	Centre,Central	Gra.	Grange	Pl.	Place	Vw.	View
Cft.	Croft	Grn.	Green	Quad.	Quadrant	W.	West
Circ.	Circus	Gro.	Grove	Rd.	Road	Wd.	Wood
Clo.	Close	Ho.	House	Ri.	Rise	Wds.	Woods
Cor.	Corner	Ind.	Industrial	S.	South	Wf.	Wharf
Cotts.	Cottages	La.	Lane	Sch.	School	Wk.	Walk
Cres.	Crescent	Ln.	Loan	Sq.	Square		
Ct.	Court	Lo.	Lodge	St.	Street,Saint		

Postal Town Abbreviations

Clyde.	Clydebank	Ersk.	Erskine	Pais.	Paisley
Coat.	Coatbridge	John.	Johnstone	Renf.	Renfrew

District Abbreviations

Abbots.	Abbotsinch	Clark.	Clarkston	Kirk.	Kirkintilloch
Bail.	Baillieston	Cumb.	Cumbernauld	Linw.	Linwood
Barr.	Barrhead	Cumb.V.	Cumbernauld Village	Mill.Pk.	Milliken Park
Bears.	Bearsden	Dunt.	Duntocher	Mood.	Moodiesburn
Bishop.	Bishopbriggs	Elder.	Elderslie	Muir.	Muirhead
Blan.	Blantyre	Gart.	Gartcosh	Old Kil.	Old Kilpatrick
Both.	Bothwell	Giff.	Giffnock	Ruther.	Rutherglen
Camb.	Cambuslang	Inch.	Inchinnan	Thorn.	Thornliebank
Chry.	Chryston	Kilb.	Kilbarchan	Udd.	Uddingston

NOTES

This index contains some street names in standard text which are followed by another street named in italics. In these cases the street in standard text does not actually appear on the map due to insufficient space but can be located close to the street named in italics.

For streets outwith the Glasgow post town area, the appropriate post town abbreviation is used. Thus the post town for Abbey Close is Paisley and it will be found on page 46 in square K14.

Name	Page	Grid
Airlour Rd. G43	63	U17
Airth Dr. G52	49	R14
Airth La. G52	49	R14
Airth Pl. G52	49	R14
Airthrey Av. G14	19	R10
Airthrey La. G14	19	Q10
Airthrey Av.		
Aitken St. G31	37	Z12
Aitkenhead Av., Coat. ML5	57	HH14
Aitkenhead Rd. (Udd.) G71	57	HH16
Alasdair Ct. (Barr.) G78	59	M19
Albany Av. G32	39	CC13
Albany Cotts. G13	19	R9
Crow Rd.		
Albany Dr. (Ruther.) G73	65	Y17
Albany Pl. (Both.) G71	69	HH19
Marguerite Gdns.		
Albany Quad. G32	39	CC13
Mansionhouse Dr.		
Albany St. G40	53	Y14
Albany Ter. (Camb.) G72	66	AA18
Albany Way, Pais. PA3	30	K12
Abbotsburn Way		
Albert Av. G42	51	U15
Albert Bri. G1	36	W13
Albert Bri. G5	36	W13
Albert Ct. G41	51	U14
Albert Dr.		
Albert Cross G41	51	U14
Albert Dr. G41	50	T15
Albert Dr. (Bears.) G61	8	S7
Albert Dr. (Ruther.) G73	65	Y17
Albert Rd. G42	51	V15
Albert Rd. (Lenzie) G66	13	CC6
Albert Rd., Clyde. G81	5	L6
Albert Rd., Renf. PA4	17	M10
Alberta Ter. G12	20	T10
Saltoun St.		
Albion Gate, Pais. PA3	30	J13
Mossvale St.		
Albion St. G1	36	W12
Albion St. (Bail.) G69	55	DD14
Albion St., Pais. PA3	30	J13
Alcaig Rd. G52	49	R15
Alder Av. (Kirk.) G66	12	BB5
Alder Ct. (Barr.) G78	59	M19
Alder Pl. G43	62	T17
Alder Pl., John. PA5	44	E15
Alder Rd. G43	62	T17
Alder Rd. (Cumb.) G67	71	QQ3
Alder Rd., Clyde. G81	4	K5
Alderman Pl. G13	19	Q9
Alderman Rd. G13	18	N8
Aldersdyke Pl. (Blan.) G72	68	FF19
Alderside Dr. (Udd.) G71	57	GG16
Alexander St., Clyde. G81	5	L7
Alexandra Av. (Stepps) G33	25	CC9
Alexandra Av. (Lenzie) G66	13	CC6
Alexandra Ct. G31	37	Y12
Roebank St.		
Alexandra Cross G31	37	Y12
Duke St.		
Alexandra Dr., Pais. PA2	45	H14
Alexandra Dr., Renf. PA4	17	M10
Alexandra Gdns. (Kirk.) G66	13	CC6
Alexandra Par. G31	37	Y12
Alexandra Pk. (Kirk.) G66	13	CC6
Alexandra Pk. St. G31	37	Y12
Alexandra Rd. (Lenzie) G66	13	CC6
Alford St. G21	22	W10
Alfred La. G12	20	T10
Cecil St.		
Algie St. G41	51	U16
Alice St., Pais. PA2	46	K15
Aline Ct. (Barr.) G78	59	L18
Allan Av., Renf. PA4	32	N11
Allan Glen Gdns. (Bishop.) G64	11	Y6
Allan Pl. G40	53	Y14
Allan St. G40	53	Y15
Allander Gdns. (Bishop.) G64	10	X6
Allander Rd. (Bears.) G61	7	Q6
Allander St. G22	22	W10
Allands Av. (Inch.), Renf. PA4	16	J9
Allanfauld Rd. (Cumb.) G67	70	NN2
Allanton Av., Pais. PA1	48	N14
Allanton Dr. G52	32	P13
Allerdyce Ct. G15	6	N7
Allerdyce Dr. G15	6	N7
Allerdyce Pl. G15	6	N7
Allerdyce Rd. G15	6	N7
Allerton Gdns. (Bail.) G69	55	DD14
Alleysbank Rd. (Ruther.) G73	53	Y15
Allison Dr. (Camb.) G72	66	BB17
Allison Pl. G42	51	V15
Prince Edward St.		
Allison Pl. (Gart.) G69	27	GG10
Allison St. G42	51	V15
Allnach Pl. G34	41	GG12
Alloway Av., Pais. PA2	47	L16
Alloway Cres. (Ruther.) G73	64	X17
Alloway Cres., Pais. PA2	47	L16
Alloway Dr. (Ruther.) G73	64	X17
Alloway Dr., Clyde. G81	5	M6
Alloway Dr., Pais. PA2	47	L16
Alloway Rd. G43	62	T17
Alma St. G40	37	Y13
Almond Av., Renf. PA4	32	N11
Almond Bk. (Bears.) G61	7	Q7
Almond Rd.		
Almond Cres., Pais. PA2	45	G15
Almond Dr. (Kirk.) G66	12	BB5
Almond Rd. G33	25	CC9
Almond Rd. (Bears.) G61	7	Q7
Almond St. G33	37	Z11
Almond Vale (Udd.) G71	57	HH16
Hamilton Vw.		
Alness Cres. G52	49	R14
Alpatrick Gdns. (Elder.), John. PA5	44	E14
Alpine Gro. (Udd.) G71	57	GG16
Alsatian Av., Clyde. G81	5	M7
Alston La. G40	36	X13
Claythorn St.		
Altnacreag Gdns. (Chry.) G69	15	HH6
Great George St.		
Alton Gdns. G12	20	T10
Alton Rd., Pais. PA1	47	M14
Altyre St. G32	54	AA14
Alva Gdns. G52	49	R15
Alva Gate G52	49	R15
Alva Pl. (Lenzie) G66	13	DD6
Alyth Gdns. G52	49	R14
Ambassador Way, Renf. PA4	31	M11
Cockels Ln.		
Amisfield St. G20	21	U9
Amochrie Dr., Pais. PA2	45	H16
Amochrie Rd., Pais. PA2	45	G15
Amochrie Way, Pais. PA2	45	G15
Amulree Pl. G32	54	BB14
Amulree St. G32	38	BB13
Ancaster Dr. G13	19	R9
Ancaster La. G13	19	Q8
Great Western Rd.		
Anchor Av., Pais. PA1	47	L14
Anchor Cres., Pais. PA1	47	L14
Anchor Dr., Pais. PA1	47	L14
Anchor Wynd, Pais. PA1	47	L14
Ancroft St. G20	21	V10
Anderson Dr., Renf. PA4	17	M10
Anderson Gdns. (Blan.) G72	69	GG19
Station Rd.		
Anderson St. G11	34	S11
Anderston Cross Cen. G2	35	V12
Anderston Quay G3	35	U13
Andrew Av. (Lenzie) G66	13	CC6
Andrew Av., Renf. PA4	18	N10
Andrew Dr., Clyde. G81	17	M8
Andrew Sillars Av. (Camb.) G72	67	CC17
Andrews St., Pais. PA3	30	J13
Angle Gate G14	19	Q10
Angus Av. G52	48	P14
Angus Av. (Bishop.) G64	23	Z8
Angus Gdns. (Udd.) G71	57	GG16
Angus La. (Bishop.) G64	11	Z7
Angus Oval G52	48	P14
Angus Pl. G52	48	P14
Angus St. G21	22	X10
Angus St., Clyde. G81	18	N8
Angus Wk. (Udd.) G71	57	HH16
Annan Dr. (Bears.) G61	7	Q6
Annan Dr. (Ruther.) G73	53	Z16
Annan Dr., Pais. PA2	45	G15
Annan Pl., John. PA5	43	C16
Annan St. G42	51	V16
Annandale St. G42	51	V14
Annbank Pl. G31	36	X13
Annbank St.		
Annbank St. G31	36	X13
Anne Av., Renf. PA4	17	M10
Anne Cres. (Lenzie) G66	13	CC6
Annette St. G42	51	V15
Annfield Gdns. (Blan.) G72	68	FF19
Annfield Pl. G31	36	X12
Annick Dr. (Bears.) G61	7	Q7
Annick St. G32	38	BB13
Annick St. (Camb.) G72	67	CC17
Anniesdale Av. (Stepps) G33	25	CC9
Anniesland Cres. G14	18	P9
Anniesland Mans. G13	19	R9
Ancaster Dr.		
Anniesland Rd. G13	19	Q9
Anniesland Rd. G14	18	P9
Anson St. G40	52	X14
Anson Way, Renf. PA4	31	M11
Britannia Way		
Anstruther St. G32	38	AA13
Anthony St. G2	35	V12
Cadogan St.		
Antonine Gdns., Clyde. G81	5	L5
Antonine Rd. (Bears.) G61	6	P5
Anwoth St. G32	54	BB14
Appin Rd. G31	37	Y12
Appin Ter. (Ruther.) G73	65	Z18
Lochaber Dr.		
Appin Way (Both.) G71	69	HH18
Bracken Ter.		
Appleby St. G22	21	V10
Eltham St.		
Applecross Gdns. (Chry.) G69	15	GG6
Applecross St. G22	21	V10
Appledore Cres. (Both.) G71	69	HH18
Apsley La. G11	34	S11
Apsley St. G11	34	S11
Aranthrue Cres., Renf. PA4	17	M10
Aranthrue Dr., Renf. PA4	17	M10
Aray St. G20	20	T9
Arbroath Av. G52	48	P14
Arcadia St. G40	36	X13
Arcan Cres. G15	6	P7
Archerfield Av. G32	54	BB15
Archerfield Cres. G32	54	BB15
Archerfield Dr. G32	54	BB15
Archerfield Gro. G32	54	BB15
Archerhill Av. G13	18	N8
Archerhill Cotts. G13	18	N8
Archerhill Rd.		
Archerhill Cres. G13	18	P8
Archerhill Gdns. G13	18	P8
Archerhill Rd.		
Archerhill Rd. G13	18	P8
Archerhill Sq. G13	18	N8
Kelso St.		
Archerhill St. G13	18	P8
Archerhill Rd.		
Archerhill Ter. G13	18	P8
Archerhill Rd.		
Ard Rd., Renf. PA4	17	L10
Ard St. G32	54	BB14
Ardagie Dr. G32	55	CC16
Ardagie Pl. G32	55	CC16
Ardbeg Av. (Bishop.) G64	11	Z7
Ardbeg Av. (Ruther.) G73	66	AA18
Ardbeg La. G42	51	V15
Coplaw St.		
Ardbeg St. G42	51	V15
Ardconnel St. (Thorn.) G46	61	R18
Arden Av. (Thorn.) G46	61	R19
Arden Dr. (Giff.) G46	62	S19
Arden Pl. (Thorn.) G46	61	R19
Stewarton Rd.		
Ardencraig Cres. G45	64	W19
Ardencraig Dr. G45	64	X19
Ardencraig La. G45	64	W19
Ardencraig Rd.		

Street	Page	Grid
Ardencraig Quad. G45	64	X19
Ardencraig Rd. G45	64	W19
Ardencraig St. G45	65	Y19
Ardencraig Ter. G45	64	X19
Ardenlea Rd. (Udd.) G71	57	GG16
Ardenlea St. G40	53	Y14
Ardery St. G11	34	S11
Apsley St.		
Ardessie Pl. G20	20	T9
Ardessie St. G23	8	T7
Torrin Rd.		
Ardfern St. G32	54	BB14
Ardgay Pl. G32	54	BB14
Ardgay St. G32	54	BB14
Ardgay Way (Ruther.) G73	65	Y18
Ardgour Dr. (Linw.), Pais. PA3	28	E13
Ardgowan Av., Pais. PA2	46	K14
Ardgowan Dr. (Udd.) G71	57	GG16
Ardgowan St., Pais. PA2	46	K15
Ardholm St. G32	38	BB13
Ardhu Pl. G15	6	N6
Ardlamont Sq. (Linw.), Pais. PA3	28	F13
Ardlaw St. G51	33	R13
Ardle Rd. G43	63	U17
Ardlui St. G32	54	AA14
Ardmaleish Cres. G45	64	X19
Ardmaleish Rd. G45	64	W19
Ardmaleish St. G45	64	X19
Ardmaleish Ter. G45	64	X19
Ardmay Cres. G44	52	W16
Ardmillan St. G33	38	AA12
Ardmory Av. G42	52	W16
Ardmory La. G42	52	X16
Ardmory Pl. G42	52	X16
Ardnahoe Av. G42	52	W16
Ardnahoe Pl. G42	52	W16
Ardneil Rd. G51	33	R13
Ardnish St. G51	33	R12
Ardo Gdns. G51	34	S13
Ardoch Gro. (Camb.) G72	66	AA17
Ardoch Rd. (Bears.) G61	8	S5
Ardoch St. G22	22	W10
Ardoch Way (Chry.) G69	15	GG7
Braeside Av.		
Ardshiel Rd. G51	33	R12
Ardsloy La. G14	18	P10
Ardsloy Pl.		
Ardsloy Pl. G14	18	P10
Ardtoe Cres. G33	25	DD9
Ardtoe Pl. G33	25	DD9
Arduthie Rd. G51	33	R12
Ardwell Rd. G52	49	R14
Argosy Way, Renf. PA4	31	M11
Britannia Way		
Argyle St. G2	35	V12
Argyle St. G3	34	T11
Argyle St., Pais. PA1	46	J14
Argyll Arc. G2	35	V12
Argyll Av. (Abbots.), Pais. PA3	30	K11
Argyll Av., Renf. PA4	17	L10
Argyll Rd., Clyde. G81	5	M7
Arisaig Dr. G52	49	R14
Arisaig Dr. (Bears.) G61	8	S6
Arisaig Pl. G52	49	R14
Ark La. G31	36	X12
Arkle Ter. (Camb.) G72	66	AA18
Arkleston Cres., Pais. PA3	31	L12
Arkleston Rd., Pais. PA1	31	L13
Arkleston Rd., Pais. PA3	31	M12
Arkleston Rd., Renf. PA4	31	L12
Arklet Rd. G51	33	R13
Arlington St. G3	35	U11
Armadale Ct. G31	37	Y12
Townmill Rd.		
Armadale Path G31	37	Y12
Armadale Pl. G31	37	Y12
Armadale St. G31	37	Y12
Armaleish Dr. G45	64	X19
Armour Pl., John. PA5	44	E14
Armour St. G31	36	X13
Armour St., John. PA5	44	E14
Armstrong Cres. (Udd.) G71	57	HH16
Arngask Rd. G51	33	R12
Arnhall Pl. G52	49	R14
Arnholm Pl. G52	49	R14
Arnisdale Pl. G34	40	EE12
Arnisdale Rd. G34	40	EE12
Arnisdale Way (Ruther.) G73	65	Y18
Shieldaig Dr.		
Arniston St. G32	38	AA12
Arnol Pl. G33	39	DD12
Arnold Av. (Bishop.) G64	11	Y7
Arnold St. G20	21	V9
Arnott Way (Camb.) G72	66	BB17
Arnprior Cres. G45	64	W18
Arnprior Gdns. (Chry.) G69	15	GG7
Braeside Av.		
Arnprior Quad. G45	64	W18
Arnprior Rd. G45	64	W18
Arnprior St. G45	64	W18
Arnside Av. (Giff.) G46	62	T18
Arnthern St. (Camb.) G72	67	CC17
Arnwood Dr. G12	20	S9
Aron Ter. (Camb.) G72	66	AA18
Aros Dr. G52	49	R15
Aros La. G52	49	Q15
Aros Dr.		
Arran Av. (Abbots.), Pais. PA3	30	K11
Arran Dr. (Giff.) G46	62	S19
Arran Dr. G52	49	R14
Arran Dr. (Cumb.) G67	70	MM4
Arran Dr., John. PA5	43	C15
Arran Dr., Pais. PA2	46	K16
Arran La. (Chry.) G69	15	HH7
Burnbrae Av.		
Arran Pl., Clyde. G81	5	M7
Arran Pl. (Linw.), Pais. PA3	28	E13
Arran Rd., Renf. PA4	31	M11
Arran Ter. (Ruther.) G73	64	X17
Arriochmill Rd. G20	20	T10
Kelvin Dr.		
Arrochar Ct. G23	21	U8
Sunningdale Rd.		
Arrochar Dr. G23	8	T7
Arrochar St. G23	20	T8
Arrol Pl. G40	53	Y14
Arrol St. G52	32	N12
Arrowsmith Av. G13	19	Q8
Arthur Av. (Barr.) G78	59	L19
Arthur Rd., Pais. PA2	46	K16
Arthur St. G3	34	T11
Arthur St., Pais. PA1	30	J13
Arthurlie Av. (Barr.) G78	59	M19
Arthurlie Dr. (Giff.) G46	62	T19
Arthurlie St. G51	33	R12
Arthurlie St. (Barr.) G78	59	M19
Arundel Dr. G42	51	V16
Arundel Dr. (Bishop.) G64	11	Y6
Asbury Ct. (Linw.), Pais. PA3	28	F13
Ascaig Cres. G52	49	R15
Ascog Rd. (Bears.) G61	7	R7
Ascog St. G42	51	V15
Ascot Av. G12	19	R9
Ascot Ct. G12	20	S9
Ash Gro. (Bishop.) G64	11	Y7
Ash Gro. (Kirk.) G66	12	BB5
Ash Gro. (Bail.) G69	41	GG13
Ash Gro. (Udd.) G71	57	HH16
Ash Pl., John. PA5	44	C15
Ash Rd. (Cumb.) G67	71	QQ1
Ash Rd. (Bail.) G69	56	EE14
Ash Rd., Clyde. G81	4	K5
Ash Wk. (Ruther.) G73	65	Z18
Ashburton La. G12	20	S9
Ashburton Rd.		
Ashburton Rd. G12	20	S9
Ashby Cres. G13	7	R7
Ashcroft Dr. G44	64	X17
Ashdale Dr. G52	49	R14
Ashdene Rd. G22	21	V8
Ashfield (Bishop.) G64	11	Y6
Ashfield St. G22	22	W10
Ashgill Pl. G22	22	W9
Ashgill Rd. G22	21	V9
Ashgrove (Mood.) G69	41	GG13
Ashgrove St. G40	53	Y15
Ashkirk Dr. G52	49	R14
Ashlea Dr. (Giff.) G46	62	T18
Ashley Dr. (Both.) G71	69	HH19
Ashley La. G3	35	U11
Woodlands Rd.		
Ashley St. G3	35	U11
Ashmore Rd. G43	63	U17
Ashmore Rd. G44	63	U17
Ashton Gdns. G12	34	T11
University Av.		
Ashton La. G12	34	T11
University Av.		
Ashton La. N. G12	34	T11
University Av.		
Ashton Pl. G12	20	T10
Byres Rd.		
Ashton Rd. G12	34	T11
University Av.		
Ashton Rd. (Ruther.) G73	53	Y15
Ashton Ter. G12	34	T11
University Av.		
Ashton Way, Pais. PA2	45	G16
Ashtree Rd. G43	50	T16
Ashvale Cres. G21	22	X10
Aspen Dr. G21	23	Y10
Foresthall Dr.		
Aspen Pl., John. PA5	44	E15
Aster Dr. G45	65	Y18
Aster Gdns. G53	61	Q18
Waukglen Cres.		
Athelstane Dr. (Cumb.) G67	70	MM4
Athelstane Rd. G13	19	Q8
Athena Way (Udd.) G71	57	HH16
Athol Av. G52	32	N12
Athol Ter. (Udd.) G71	57	GG15
Athole Gdns. G12	20	T10
Athole La. G12	20	T10
Saltoun St.		
Atholl Cres., Pais. PA1	32	N13
Atholl Gdns. (Bishop.) G64	11	Y6
Atholl Gdns. (Ruther.) G73	66	AA18
Atholl La. (Chry.) G69	15	HH7
Atholl Pl. (Linw.), Pais. PA3	28	E13
Atlas Pl. G21	22	X10
Atlas Rd. G21	22	X10
Atlas Sq. G21	22	X10
Ayr St.		
Atlas St., Clyde. G81	17	L8
Cart St.		
Attlee Av., Clyde. G81	5	M7
Attlee Pl., Clyde. G81	5	M7
Attlee Av.		
Attow Rd. G43	62	S17
Auburn Dr. (Barr.) G78	59	M19
Auchans Rd. (Houston), John. PA6	28	E11
Auchencrow St. G34	40	FF12
Auchengeich Rd. (Mood.) G69	14	FF6
Auchenglen Dr. (Chry.) G69	15	GG7
Auchengreoch Av., John. PA5	43	C16
Auchengreoch Rd., John. PA5	43	C16
Auchenlodment Rd., John. PA5	44	E15
Auchentorlie Quad., Pais. PA1	47	L14
Auchentorlie St. G11	33	R11
Dumbarton Rd.		
Auchentoshan Av., Clyde. G81	4	K5
Auchentoshen Ter. G21	36	X11
Auchentoshen Cotts. (Old Kil.) G60	4	J5
Auchinairn Rd. (Bishop.) G64	22	X8
Auchinbee Way (Cumb.) G68	70	MM2
Eastfield Rd.		
Auchingill Path G34	40	FF11
Auchingill Rd.		
Auchingill Pl. G34	40	FF11
Auchingill Rd. G34	40	FF11
Auchinlea Rd. G34	39	DD11
Auchinleck Av. G33	24	AA9
Auchinleck Cres. G33	24	AA9
Auchinleck Dr. G33	24	AA9
Auchinleck Gdns. G33	24	AA9
Auchinleck Rd. G33	24	AA8
Auchinloch Rd. (Lenzie) G66	13	CC6
Auchinloch St. G21	22	X10

Bardowie St. G22   21   V10
Bardrain Av. (Elder.), John.   44   F15
  PA5
Bardrain Rd., Pais. PA2   46   J16
Bardrill Dr. (Bishop.) G64   10   X7
Bardykes Rd. (Blan.) G72   68   FF19
Barfillan Dr. G52   33   R13
Barfillan Rd. G52   33   R13
Bargaran Rd. G53   48   P14
Bargarron Dr., Pais. PA3   31   L12
Bargeddie St. G33   37   Z11
Barholm Sq. G33   39   CC11
Barke Rd. (Cumb.) G67   71   PP2
Barlanark Av. G32   39   CC12
Barlanark Cres. G33   39   CC12
Barlanark Dr. G33   39   CC12
Barlanark Pl. G32   39   CC13
  Hallhill Rd.
Barlanark Rd. G33   39   DD12
Barlanark Rd. G33   39   CC12
Barlia Dr. G45   64   X18
Barlia St. G45   64   X18
Barlia Ter. G45   64   X18
Barloch St. G22   22   W10
Barlogan Av. G52   33   R13
Barlogan Quad. G52   33   R13
Barmill Rd. G43   62   S17
Barmulloch Rd. G21   23   Y10
Barn Grn. (Kilb.), John.   42   B14
  PA10
Barnard Gdns. (Bishop.)   11   Y6
  G64
Barnard Ter. G40   53   Y14
Barnbeth Rd. G53   48   P15
Barnes Rd. G20   21   V9
Barnes St. (Barr.) G78   59   L19
Barnflat St. (Ruther.) G73   53   Y15
Barnhill Dr. G21   23   Y10
  Foresthall Dr.
Barnkirk Av. G15   6   P6
Barns St., Clyde. G81   5   M7
Barnsford Av. (Inch.), Renf.   16   J9
  PA4
Barnsford Rd. (Abbots.),   29   H12
  Pais. PA3
Barnsford Rd. (Inch.), Renf.   29   H12
  PA4
Barnton St. G32   38   AA12
Barnwell Ter. G51   33   R12
Barochan Cres., Pais. PA3   45   H14
Barochan Rd. G53   48   P14
Baron Rd., Pais. PA3   31   L13
Baron St., Renf. PA4   31   M11
Baronald Dr. G12   20   S9
Baronald Gate G12   20   S9
Baronald St. (Ruther.) G73   53   Y15
Baronhill (Cumb.) G67   71   PP2
Barons Gate (Both.) G71   69   GG18
Baronscourt Dr., Pais. PA1   45   G14
Baronscourt Gdns., Pais.   45   G14
  PA1
Baronscourt Rd., Pais. PA1   45   G14
Barony Dr. (Bail.) G69   40   EE13
Barony Gdns. (Bail.) G69   40   EE13
  Barony Dr.
Barony Wynd (Bail.) G69   41   GG13
  Dukes Rd.
Barr Cres., Clyde. G81   5   L5
Barr Gro. (Udd.) G71   57   HH16
Barr Pl., Pais. PA1   46   J14
Barr St. G20   21   V10
Barra Av., Renf. PA4   31   M11
Barra Cres. (Old Kil.) G60   4   J5
Barra Gdns. (Old Kil.) G60   4   J5
  Barra Rd.
Barra Rd. (Old Kil.) G60   4   J5
Barra St. G20   20   T8
Barrachnie Ct. (Bail.) G69   39   DD13
  Barrachnie Cres.
Barrachnie Cres. (Bail.) G69   39   DD13
Barrachnie Rd. (Bail.) G69   39   DD13
Barrack St. G4   36   X13
Barrhead Rd. G43   49   Q16
Barrhead Rd. G53   48   N16
Barrhead Rd., Pais. PA2   47   L14
Barrhill Cres. (Kilb.), John.   42   B15
  PA10
Barrie Quad., Clyde. G81   5   L6
Barrie Rd. G52   32   P12

Barrington Dr. G4   35   U11
Barrisdale Rd. G20   20   T8
Barrisdale Way (Ruther.)   65   Y18
  G73
Barrland Dr. (Giff.) G46   62   T18
Barrland St. G41   51   V14
Barrochan Rd., John. PA5   43   D14
Barrowfield St. G40   37   Y13
Barrwood Pl. (Udd.) G71   57   HH16
Barrwood St. G33   38   AA11
Barscube Ter., Pais. PA2   46   K14
Barshaw Dr., Pais. PA1   31   L13
Barshaw Pl., Pais. PA1   31   M13
Barshaw Rd. G52   32   N13
Barskiven Rd., Pais. PA1   45   G14
Barterholm Rd., Pais. PA2   46   K15
Bartholomew St. G40   53   Y14
Bartiebeith Rd. G33   39   DD12
Basset Av. G13   18   P8
Basset Cres. G13   18   P8
Bath La. G2   35   V12
  Blythswood St.
Bath La. W. G3   35   U12
  North St.
Bath St. G2   35   V12
Bathgate St. G31   37   Y13
Bathgo Av., Pais. PA1   48   N14
Batson St. G42   51   V15
Battle Pl. G41   51   U16
Battleburn St. G32   54   BB14
Battlefield Av. G42   51   V16
Battlefield Cres. G42   51   V16
  Battlefield Gdns.
Battlefield Gdns. G42   51   V16
Battlefield Rd. G42   51   V16
Bavelaw St. G33   39   CC11
Bayfield Av. G15   6   P6
Bayfield Ter. G15   6   P6
Beaconsfield Rd. G12   20   S9
Beard Cres. (Gart.) G69   27   GG9
Beardmore Cotts. (Inch.),   16   K9
  Renf. PA4
Beardmore St., Clyde. G81   4   J6
Beardmore Way, Clyde. G81   4   J7
Bearford Dr. G52   32   P13
Bearsden Rd. G13   19   R9
Bearsden Rd. (Bears.) G61   19   R9
Beaton Rd. G41   51   U15
Beatson Wynd (Udd.) G71   57   HH15
Beattock St. G31   37   Z13
Beatty St., Clyde. G81   4   J6
Beaufort Av. G43   62   T17
Beaufort Gdns. (Bishop.)   10   X7
  G64
Beauly Dr., Pais. PA2   45   G15
Beauly Pl. G20   20   T9
Beauly Pl. (Bishop.) G64   11   Z7
Beauly Pl. (Chry.) G69   14   FF7
Beauly Rd. (Bail.) G69   56   EE14
Beaumont Gate G12   34   T11
Bedale Rd. (Bail.) G69   55   DD14
Bedford Av., Clyde. G81   5   M7
  Onslow Rd.
Bedford La. G5   35   V13
Bedford Row G5   35   V13
  Dunmore St.
Bedford St. G5   35   V13
Bedlay Ct. (Chry.) G69   15   HH6
Bedlay St. G21   22   X10
  Petershill Rd.
Bedlay Vw. (Udd.) G71   57   HH15
Bedlay Wk. (Chry.) G69   15   HH6
Beech Av. G41   50   S14
Beech Av. (Bail.) G69   40   EE13
Beech Av. (Camb.) G72   66   AA17
Beech Av. (Ruther.) G73   65   Z18
Beech Av. (Elder.), John.   44   F15
  PA5
Beech Av., Pais. PA2   47   L15
Beech Dr., Clyde. G81   5   L5
Beech Gdns. (Bail.) G69   40   EE13
Beech Pl. (Bishop.) G64   23   Y8
Beech Rd. (Bishop.) G64   23   Y8
Beech Rd. (Lenzie) G66   13   CC5
Beech Rd., John. PA5   43   C15
Beechcroft Pl. (Blan.) G72   69   GG19
Beeches Av., Clyde. G81   4   K5
Beeches Rd., Clyde. G81   4   K5
Beeches Ter., Clyde. G81   4   K5

Beechgrove St. G40   53   Y15
Beechlands Av. G44   63   U19
Beechmount Cotts. G14   18   N9
  Dumbarton Rd.
Beechmount Rd. (Lenzie)   13   CC6
  G66
Beechwood Av. G11   19   R10
  Beechwood Dr.
Beechwood Av. (Ruther.)   65   Z17
  G73
Beechwood Ct. (Bears.) G61   7   R6
Beechwood Dr. G11   19   R10
Beechwood Dr., Renf. PA4   31   L11
Beechwood Gdns. (Mood.)   15   GG7
  G69
Beechwood Gro. (Barr.)   59   M19
  G78
  Arthurlie Av.
Beechwood La. (Bears.) G61   7   R6
  Beechwood Ct.
Beechwood Pl. G11   19   R10
  Beechwood Dr.
Beechwood Rd. (Cumb.)   70   NN3
  G67
Beil Dr. G13   18   N8
Beith Rd., John. PA5   44   E15
Beith Rd. (Mill.Pk.), John.   42   B16
  PA10
Beith St. G11   34   S11
Belgrave La. G12   21   U10
  Belgrave Ter.
Belgrave Ter. G12   21   U10
Belhaven Cres. La. G12   20   T10
  Lorraine Rd.
Belhaven Ter. G12   20   T10
Belhaven Ter. La. G12   20   T10
Belhaven Ter. W. G12   20   T10
Belhaven Ter. W. La. G12   20   T10
  Westbourne Gdns. S.
Bell Dr. G1   36   W12
Bell St. G4   36   W13
Bell St., Clyde. G81   17   M8
Bell St., Renf. PA4   17   M10
Bellahouston Dr. G52   49   R14
Bellahouston La. G52   49   R14
Bellairs Pl. (Blan.) G72   68   FF19
Belleisle Av. (Udd.) G71   57   GG16
Belleisle St. G42   51   V15
Bellevue Pl. G21   36   X11
Bellfield Ct. (Barr.) G78   59   L18
Bellfield Cres. (Barr.) G78   59   L18
Bellfield St. G31   37   Y13
Bellflower Av. G53   61   Q18
Bellflower Gdns. G53   61   Q18
Bellflower Pl. G53   61   Q18
Bellgrove St. G31   36   X13
Bellhaven Ter.   65   Z17
  (Ruther.) G73
Bellrock Cres. G33   38   BB12
Bellrock St. G33   38   BB12
Bellscroft Av. (Ruther.) G73   52   X16
Bellshaugh Gdns. G12   20   T9
Bellshaugh La. G12   20   T9
Bellshaugh Pl. G12   20   T9
Bellshaugh Rd. G12   20   T9
Bellshill Rd. (Udd.) G71   69   GG17
Belltrees Cres., Pais. PA3   45   H14
Bellwood St. G41   51   U16
Belmar Ct. (Linw.), Pais.   28   F13
  PA3
Belmont Av. (Udd.) G71   57   GG16
Belmont Cres. G12   21   U10
Belmont Dr. (Giff.) G46   62   S18
Belmont Dr. (Ruther.) G73   53   Y16
Belmont Dr. (Barr.) G78   59   M19
Belmont La. G12   21   U10
  Great Western Rd.
Belmont Rd. G21   22   X9
Belmont Rd. (Camb.) G72   66   AA18
Belmont Rd., Pais. PA3   31   L13
Belmont St. G12   21   U10
Belmont St., Clyde. G81   17   L8
Belses Dr. G52   33   Q13
Belses Gdns. G52   33   Q13
Belstane Pl. (Both.) G71   69   HH18
  Appledore Cres.
Belsyde Av. G15   6   P7
Beltane St. G3   35   U12
Beltrees Av. G53   48   P15

Beltrees Cres. G53 48 P15
Beltrees Rd. G53 48 P15
Belvidere Cres. (Bishop.) 11 Y6
 G64
Bemersyde (Bishop.) G64 11 Z7
Bemersyde Av. G43 62 S17
Bemersyde Rd., Pais. PA2 45 G16
Ben Alder Dr., Pais. PA2 47 M15
Ben Buie Way, Pais. PA2 47 M15
Ben Lawers Dr. (Cumb.) 70 MM3
 G68
 Balloch Loop Rd.
Ben Ledi Av., Pais. PA2 47 M15
Ben Lui Dr., Pais. PA2 47 M15
Ben Macdui Gdns. G53 61 Q18
Ben More Dr., Pais. PA2 47 M15
Ben Nevis Rd., Pais. PA2 47 M15
Ben Venue Way, Pais. PA2 47 M15
Ben Wyvis Dr., Pais. PA2 47 M15
Benalder St. G11 34 T11
Benarty Gdns. 11 Y7
 (Bishop.) G64
Bencroft Dr. G44 64 X17
Bengairn St. G31 37 Z12
Bengal Pl. G43 50 T16
 Christian St.
Bengal St. G43 50 T16
 Shawbridge St.
Benhar Pl. G33 38 AA12
Benholm St. G32 54 AA14
Benhope Av., Pais. PA2 47 M15
Benlawers Dr., Pais. PA2 47 M15
Benloyal Av., Pais. PA2 47 M15
Benmore St. G21 22 X9
Bennan Sq. G42 52 W15
Benny Lynch Ct. G5 36 W13
Benston Pl., John. PA5 43 D15
Benston Rd., John. PA5 43 D15
Benthall St. G5 52 W14
Bentinck St. G3 35 U11
Bents Rd. (Bail.) G69 40 EE13
Benvane Av., Pais. PA2 47 M15
Benvie Gdns. (Bishop.) G64 11 Y7
Benview St. G20 21 U10
Benview Ter., Pais. PA2 47 L15
Berelands Cres. (Ruther.) 52 X16
 G73
Berelands Pl. (Ruther.) G73 52 X16
Beresford Av. G14 19 R10
Berkeley St. G3 35 U12
Berkeley Ter. La. G3 35 U11
 Elderslie St.
Berkley Dr. (Blan.) G72 68 FF19
Bernard Path G40 53 Y14
Bernard St. G40 53 Y14
Bernard Ter. G40 53 Y14
Berneray St. G22 22 W8
Berridale Av. G44 63 V17
Berriedale Av. (Bail.) G69 56 EE14
Berryburn Rd. G21 23 Z10
Berryhill Dr. (Giff.) G46 62 S19
Berryhill Rd. (Giff.) G46 62 S19
Berryhill Rd. (Cumb.) G67 70 NN3
Berryknowes Av. G52 33 Q13
Berryknowes La. G52 33 Q13
Berryknowes Rd. G52 49 Q14
Berryknowes Rd. (Chry.) 26 FF8
 G69
Bertram St. G41 51 U15
Bertrohill Ter. G33 39 CC12
 Stepps Rd.
Bervie St. G51 33 R13
Berwick Av. (Cumb.) G68 70 NN1
Berwick Cres. (Linw.), Pais. 28 E12
 PA3
Berwick Dr. G52 48 P14
Berwick Dr. (Ruther.) G73 53 Z16
Betula Dr., Clyde. G81 5 L5
Bevan Gro., John. PA5 43 C15
Beverley Rd. G43 62 T17
Bevin Av., Clyde. G81 5 M7
Bideford Cres. G32 55 CC14
Biggar St. G31 37 Y13
Bigton St. G33 38 BB11
Bilsland Ct. G20 21 V9
 Bilsland Dr.
Bilsland Dr. G20 21 U9
Binend Rd. G53 49 Q16
Binnie Pl. G40 36 X13

Binniehill Rd. (Cumb.) G68 70 MM2
Binns Rd. G33 39 CC11
Birch Cres., John. PA5 44 E15
Birch Dr. (Lenzie) G66 13 CC5
Birch Gro. (Udd.) G71 57 HH16
 Burnhead St.
Birch Knowle (Bishop.) G64 11 Y7
Birch Rd., Clyde. G81 5 L5
Birch St. G5 52 W14
 Silverfir St.
Birch Vw. (Bears.) G61 8 S5
Birchfield Dr. G14 18 P10
Birchlea Dr. (Giff.) G46 62 T18
Birchwood Av. G32 55 DD14
Birchwood Dr., Pais. PA2 45 H15
Birchwood Pl. G32 55 DD14
Birdston Rd. G21 23 Z9
Birgidale Av. G45 64 W19
Birgidale Rd. G45 64 W19
Birgidale Ter. G45 64 W19
Birkdale Ct. (Both.) G71 69 GG19
Birken Rd. (Lenzie) G66 13 DD6
Birkenshaw St. G31 37 Y12
Birkenshaw Way, Pais. PA3 30 K12
 Abbotsburn Way
Birkhall Av. G52 48 N14
Birkhall Av. (Inch.), Renf. 16 J8
 PA4
Birkhall Dr. (Bears.) G61 7 R7
Birkhill Av. (Bishop.) G64 11 Y6
Birkhill Gdns. (Bishop.) G64 11 Z6
Birkmyre Rd. G51 33 R13
Birks Rd., Renf. PA4 31 L11
 Tower Dr.
Birkwood St. G40 53 Y15
Birmingham Rd., Renf. 31 L11
 PA4
Birnam Av. (Bishop.) G64 11 Y6
Birnam Cres. (Bears.) G61 8 S5
Birnam Gdns. (Bishop.) 11 Y7
 G64
Birnam Rd. G31 53 Z14
Birness Dr. G43 50 T16
Birness St. G43 50 T16
Birnie Ct. G21 23 Z10
Birnie Rd. G21 23 Z10
Birnock Av., Renf. PA4 32 N11
Birsay Rd. G22 21 V8
Bishop Gdns. (Bishop.) G64 10 X7
Bishop St. G3 35 V12
Bishopmill Pl. G21 23 Z10
Bishopmill Rd. G21 23 Z10
Bishopsgate Dr. G21 22 X8
Bishopsgate Gdns. G21 22 X8
Bishopsgate Pl. G21 22 X8
Bishopsgate Rd. G21 22 X8
Bisset Cres., Clyde. G81 4 K5
Black St. G4 36 W11
Blackburn Sq. (Barr.) G78 59 M19
Blackburn St. G51 34 T13
Blackbyres Rd. (Barr.) G78 59 M17
Blackcraig Av. G15 6 P6
Blackcroft Gdns. G32 55 CC14
Blackcroft Rd. G32 55 CC14
Blackford Cres. G32 55 CC14
Blackford Pl. G32 55 CC14
Blackford Rd., Pais. PA2 47 L15
Blackfriars St. G1 36 W12
Blackhall La., Pais. PA1 46 K14
Blackhall St., Pais. PA1 46 K14
Blackhill Cotts. G23 9 V7
Blackhill Pl. G33 37 Z11
Blackhill Rd. G23 8 T7
Blackie St. G3 34 T11
Blacklands Pl. (Lenzie) G66 13 DD6
Blacklaw La., Pais. PA3 30 K13
Blackstone Av. G53 49 Q16
Blackstone Cres. G53 49 Q15
Blackstone Rd., Pais. PA3 29 H12
Blackstoun Av. (Linw.), 28 E13
 Pais. PA3
Blackstoun Oval, Pais. PA3 29 H13
Blackstoun Rd., Pais. PA3 29 H13
Blackthorn Av. (Kirk.) G66 12 BB5
Blackthorn Gro. (Kirk.) G66 12 BB5
Blackthorn Rd. 71 QQ2
 (Cumb.) G67

Blackthorn St. G22 22 X9
Blackwood Av. (Linw.), 28 E13
 Pais. PA3
Blackwood St. G13 19 R8
Blackwood St. (Barr.) G78 59 L19
Blackwoods Cres. (Mood.) 15 GG7
 G69
Blacurvie Rd. G34 40 EE11
Bladda La., Pais. PA1 46 K14
Blades Ct. (Gart.) G69 27 HH9
Bladnoch Dr. G15 7 Q7
 Moraine Av.
Blaeloch Av. G45 64 W19
Blaeloch Dr. G45 64 W19
Blaeloch Ter. G45 64 W19
Blair Cres. (Bail.) G69 56 EE14
Blair Rd., Pais. PA1 32 N13
Blair St. G32 38 AA13
Blairatholl Av. G11 20 S10
Blairatholl Gdns. G11 20 S10
Blairbeth Dr. G44 51 V16
Blairbeth Rd. (Ruther.) G73 65 Y17
Blairbeth Ter. (Ruther.) G73 65 Y18
Blairdardie Rd. G13 7 Q7
Blairdardie Rd. G15 6 P7
Blairdenan Av. (Chry.) G69 15 HH6
Blairdenon Dr. (Cumb.) G68 70 MM2
Blairgowrie Rd. G52 49 Q14
Blairhall Av. G41 51 U16
Blairhill Av. (Kirk.) G66 14 EE5
Blairlogie St. G33 38 BB11
Blairston Av. (Both.) G71 69 HH19
Blairston Gdns. (Both.) G71 69 HH19
 Blairston Av.
Blairtum Dr. (Ruther.) G73 65 Y17
Blairtummock Rd. G33 39 CC12
Blake Rd. (Cumb.) G67 71 PP3
Blane St. G4 36 W11
Blantyre Fm. Rd. 68 FF19
 (Blan.) G72
Blantyre Mill Rd. (Both.) 69 GG19
 G71
Blantyre Rd. (Both.) G71 69 HH19
Blantyre St. G3 34 T11
Blaven Ct. (Bail.) G69 56 FF14
 Bracadale Rd.
Blawarthill St. G14 18 N9
Blenheim Av. (Stepps) G33 25 CC9
Blenheim Ct. (Stepps) G33 25 DD9
 Blenheim Av.
Blenheim Ct., Pais. PA1 30 J13
Blenheim La. (Stepps) G33 25 DD9
Blesdale Ct., Clyde. G81 5 L7
Blochairn Rd. G21 37 Y11
Bluebell Gdns. G45 65 Y19
Bluevale St. G31 37 Y13
Blyth Pl. G33 39 CC13
Blyth Rd. G33 39 DD13
Blythswood Av., Renf. PA4 17 M10
Blythswood Ct. G2 35 V12
 Cadogan St.
Blythswood Dr., Pais. PA3 30 J13
Blythswood Rd., Renf. PA4 17 M9
Blythswood Sq. G2 35 V12
Blythswood St. G2 35 V12
Boclair Av. (Bears.) G61 7 R6
Boclair Cres. (Bears.) G61 8 S6
Boclair Cres. (Bishop.) G64 11 Y7
Boclair Rd. (Bears.) G61 8 S6
Boclair Rd. (Bishop.) G64 11 Y7
Boclair St. G13 19 R8
Boden St. G40 53 Y14
Bodmin Gdns. (Chry.) G69 15 GG6
 Gartferry Rd.
Bogany Ter. G45 64 X19
Bogbain Rd. G34 40 EE12
Boggknowe (Udd.) G71 56 FF16
 Old Edinburgh Rd.
Boghall Rd. (Udd.) G71 56 EE15
Boghall St. G33 38 BB11
Boghead Rd. G21 23 Y10
Boghead Rd. (Kirk.) G66 12 BB6
Bogleshole Rd. (Camb.) G72 54 AA16
Bogmoor Rd. G51 33 Q12
Bogside Pl. (Bail.) G69 40 FF12
 Whamflet Av.
Bogside Rd. G33 24 BB9
Bogside St. G40 53 Y14
Bogton Av. G44 63 U18

Bogton Av. La. G44	63	U18
Bogton Av.		
Boleyn Rd. G41	51	U15
Bolivar Ter. G42	52	W16
Bolton Dr. G42	51	V16
Bon Accord Sq., Clyde. G81	17	L8
Bonawe St. G20	21	U10
Boness St. G40	53	Y14
Bonhill St. G22	21	V10
Bonnar St. G40	53	Y14
Bonnaughton Rd. (Bears.) G61	6	P5
Bonnyholm Av. G53	48	P14
Bonnyrigg Dr. G43	62	S17
Bonyton Av. G13	18	N9
Boon Dr. G15	6	P7
Boquhanran Pl., Clyde. G81	5	L6
Albert Rd.		
Boquhanran Rd., Clyde. G81	4	K7
Borden La. G13	19	R9
Borden Rd. G13	19	R9
Boreland Dr. G13	18	P8
Boreland Pl. G13	18	P9
Borgie Cres. (Camb.) G72	66	BB17
Borland Rd. (Bears.) G61	8	S6
Borron St. G4	22	W10
Borthwick St. G33	38	BB11
Boswell Ct. G42	51	U16
Boswell Sq. G52	32	N12
Botanic Cres. G20	20	T10
Bothlyn Cres. (Gart.) G69	27	GG8
Bothlynn Dr. (Stepps) G33	25	CC9
Bothlynn Rd. (Chry.) G69	26	FF8
Bothwell La. G2	35	V12
West Campbell St.		
Bothwell Pk. Rd. (Both.) G71	69	HH19
Bothwell Rd. (Udd.) G71	69	GG17
Bothwell St. G2	35	V12
Bothwell St. (Camb.) G72	66	AA17
Bothwell Ter. G12	35	U11
Bank St.		
Bothwellpark Ind. Est. (Udd.) G71	69	HH18
Bothwick Way, Pais. PA2	45	G16
Boundary Rd. (Ruther.) G73	52	X15
Rutherglen Rd.		
Bourne Ct. (Inch.), Renf. PA4	16	J8
Bourne Cres. (Inch.), Renf. PA4	16	J8
Bourock Sq. (Barr.) G78	60	N19
Bourtree Dr. (Ruther.) G73	65	Z18
Bouverie St. G14	18	N9
Bouverie St. (Ruther.) G73	52	X16
Bowden Dr. G52	32	P13
Bower St. G12	21	U10
Bowerwalls St. (Barr.) G78	60	N18
Bowes Cres. (Bail.) G69	55	DD14
Bowfield Av. G52	32	N13
Bowfield Cres. G52	32	N13
Bowfield Dr. G52	32	N13
Bowfield Pl. G52	32	N13
Bowfield Ter. G52	32	N13
Bowfield Cres.		
Bowhouse Way (Ruther.) G73	65	Y18
Bowling Grn. La. G14	19	Q10
Westland Dr.		
Bowling Grn. Rd. G14	19	Q10
Bowling Grn. Rd. G32	55	CC14
Bowling Grn. Rd. G44	63	V17
Bowling Grn. Rd. (Chry.) G69	26	FF8
Bowman St. G42	51	V15
Bowmont Gdns. G12	20	T10
Bowmont Hill (Bishop.) G64	11	Y6
Bowmont Ter. G12	20	T10
Bowmore Gdns. (Udd.) G71	57	GG16
Bowmore Gdns. (Ruther.) G73	66	AA18
Bowmore Rd. G52	33	R13
Boyd St. G42	51	V15
Boydstone Pl. (Thorn.) G46	61	R17
Boydstone Rd. G43	61	R17
Boydstone Rd. (Thorn.) G46	61	R17
Boydstone Rd. G53	61	R17
Boyle St., Clyde. G81	17	M8
Boylestone Rd. (Barr.) G78	59	L18
Boyndie Path G34	40	EE12
Boyndie St. G34	40	EE12
Brabloch Cres., Pais. PA3	30	K13
Bracadale Dr. (Bail.) G69	56	FF14
Bracadale Gdns. (Bail.) G69	56	FF14
Bracadale Gro. (Bail.) G69	56	FF14
Bracadale Rd. (Bail.) G69	56	FF14
Bracken St. G22	21	V9
Bracken Ter. (Both.) G71	69	HH18
Brackenbrae Av. (Bishop.) G64	10	X7
Brackenbrae Rd. (Bishop.) G64	10	X7
Brackenrig Rd. (Thorn.) G46	61	R19
Brackla Av. G13	18	N8
Brackla Av., Clyde. G81	18	N8
Bracora Pl. G20	20	T9
Glenfinnan Dr.		
Bradan Av. G13	18	N8
Bradan Av., Clyde. G81	18	N8
Bradda Av. (Ruther.) G73	65	Z18
Bradfield Av. G12	20	T9
Brady Cres. (Mood.) G69	15	HH6
Braeface Rd. (Cumb.) G67	70	NN3
Braefield Dr. (Thorn.) G46	62	S18
Braefoot Cres., Pais. PA2	46	K16
Braehead Rd. (Cumb.) G67	71	PP2
Braehead Rd., Pais. PA2	58	J17
Braehead St. G5	52	W14
Braemar Av., Clyde. G81	4	K6
Braemar Cres. (Bears.) G61	7	R7
Braemar Cres., Pais. PA2	46	K16
Braemar Dr. (Elder.), John. PA5	44	E15
Braemar Rd. (Ruther.) G73	66	AA18
Braemar Rd. (Inch.), Renf. PA4	16	J8
Braemar St. G42	51	U16
Braemar Vw., Clyde. G81	4	K5
Braemount Av., Pais. PA2	58	J17
Braes Av., Clyde. G81	17	M8
Braeside Av. (Chry.) G69	15	GG7
Braeside Av. (Ruther.) G73	53	Z16
Braeside Cres. (Bail.) G69	41	GG13
Braeside Cres. (Barr.) G78	60	N19
Braeside Dr. (Barr.) G78	59	M19
Braeside Pl. (Camb.) G72	66	BB18
Braeside St. G20	21	U10
Braeview Av., Pais. PA2	45	H16
Braeview Dr., Pais. PA2	45	H16
Braeview Gdns., Pais. PA2	45	H16
Braeview Rd., Pais. PA2	45	H16
Braid Sq. G4	35	V11
Braid St. G4	35	V11
Braidbar Fm. Rd. (Giff.) G46	62	T18
Braidbar Rd. (Giff.) G46	62	T18
Braidcraft Pl. G53	49	Q16
Braidcraft Rd. G53	49	Q15
Braidfauld Gdns. G32	54	AA14
Braidfauld Pl. G32	54	AA15
Braidfauld St. G32	54	AA15
Braidfield Gro., Clyde. G81	5	L5
Braidfield Rd., Clyde. G81	5	L5
Braidholm Cres. (Giff.) G46	62	T18
Braidholm Rd. (Giff.) G46	62	T18
Braidpark Cres. (Giff.) G46	62	T18
Braidpark Dr. (Giff.) G46	62	T18
Braids Rd., Pais. PA2	46	K15
Bramley Pl. (Lenzie) G66	13	DD6
Branchock Av. (Camb.) G72	67	CC18
Brand Pl. G51	34	T13
Brand St. G51	34	T13
Brandon Gdns. (Camb.) G72	66	AA17
Brandon St. G31	36	X13
Branscroft (Kilb.), John. PA10	42	B14
Brassey St. G20	21	U9
Breadalbane Gdns. (Ruther.) G73	65	Z18
Breadalbane St. G3	35	U12
St. Vincent St.		
Brechin Rd. (Bishop.) G64	11	Z7
Brechin St. G3	35	U12
Breck Av., Pais. PA2	44	F16
Brediland Rd., Pais. PA2	45	G15
Brediland Rd. (Linw.), Pais. PA3	28	E13
Bredisholm Dr. (Bail.) G69	56	FF14
Bredisholm Rd. (Bail.) G69	56	FF14
Bredisholm Ter. (Bail.) G69	56	FF14
Brenfield Av. G44	63	U18
Brenfield Dr. G44	63	U18
Brenfield Rd. G44	63	U18
Brent Av. (Thorn.) G46	61	R17
Brent Dr. (Thorn.) G46	61	R17
Brent Rd. (Thorn.) G46	61	R17
Brentwood Av. G53	60	P18
Brentwood Dr. G53	60	P18
Brentwood Sq. G53	60	P18
Brentwood Dr.		
Brereton St. G42	52	W15
Bressey Rd. G33	39	DD13
Brewery St., John. PA5	43	D14
Brewster Av., Pais. PA3	31	L12
Briar Dr., Clyde. G81	5	L6
Briar Gdns. G43	62	T17
Briar Gro. G43	62	T17
Briar Neuk (Bishop.) G64	23	Y8
Briar Rd. G43	62	T17
Briarcroft Dr. G33	23	Z8
Briarcroft Pl. G33	24	AA9
Briarcroft Rd. G33	23	Z9
Briarlea Dr. (Giff.) G46	62	T18
Briarwood Ct. G32	55	DD15
Briarwood Gdns. G32	55	DD15
Woodend Rd.		
Brick La., Pais. PA3	30	K13
Bridge of Weir Rd. (Linw.), Pais. PA3	28	E13
Bridge St. G5	35	V13
Bridge St. (Camb.) G72	66	BB17
Bridge St., Clyde. G81	4	K6
Bridge St., Pais. PA1	46	K14
Bridge St. (Linw.), Pais. PA3	28	F13
Bridgebar St. (Barr.) G78	60	N18
Bridgeburn Dr. (Chry.) G69	15	GG7
Bridgegate G1	36	W13
Bridgeton Cross G40	36	X13
Brigham Pl. G23	21	U8
Broughton Rd.		
Bright St. G21	36	X11
Brighton Pl. G51	34	S13
Brighton St. G51	34	S13
Brightside Av. (Udd.) G71	69	HH17
Brisbane Ct. (Giff.) G46	62	T18
Braidpark Dr.		
Brisbane St. G42	51	V16
Brisbane St., Clyde. G81	4	J6
Britannia Way, Renf. PA4	31	M11
Briton St. G51	34	S13
Broad Pl. G40	36	X13
Broad St.		
Broad St. G40	36	X13
Broadford St. G4	36	W11
Harvey St.		
Broadholm St. G22	21	V9
Broadleys Av. (Bishop.) G64	10	X6
Broadlie Dr. G13	18	P9
Broadloan, Renf. PA4	31	M11
Broadwood Dr. G44	63	V17
Brock Oval G53	61	Q17
Brock Pl. G53	49	Q16
Brock Rd. G53	49	Q16
Brock Ter. G53	61	Q17
Brock Way (Cumb.) G67	71	PP3
North Carbrain Rd.		
Brockburn Rd. G53	48	P15
Brockburn Ter. G53	49	Q16
Brockville St. G32	38	AA13
Brodick Sq. (Bishop.) G64	23	Y8
Brodick St. G21	37	Y11
Brodie Pk. Av., Pais. PA2	46	K15
Brodie Pk. Cres., Pais. PA2	46	J15
Brodie Pk. Gdns., Pais. PA2	46	K15
Brodie Pl., Renf. PA4	31	L11
Brodie Rd. G21	23	Z8
Brogknowe (Udd.) G71	56	FF16
Glasgow Rd.		
Bron Way (Cumb.) G67	71	PP3
Brook St. G40	36	X13
Brooklands Av. (Udd.) G71	57	GG16
Brooklea Dr. (Giff.) G46	62	T17

Street	Map	Grid
Brookside St. G40	37	Y13
Broom Cres. (Barr.) G78	59	L17
Broom Dr., Clyde. G81	5	L6
Broom Gdns. (Kirk.) G66	12	BB5
Broom Path (Bail.) G69	55	DD14
Tudor St.		
Broom Rd. G43	62	T17
Broom Rd. (Cumb.) G67	71	QQ1
Broom Ter., John. PA5	43	D15
Broomdyke Way, Pais. PA3	30	J12
Broomfield Av. G21	23	Y10
Broomfield Rd.		
Broomfield Av. (Camb.) G72	53	Z16
Broomfield La. G21	22	X9
Broomfield Rd.		
Broomfield Pl. G21	22	X9
Broomfield Rd.		
Broomfield Rd. G21	22	X9
Broomfield Ter. (Udd.) G71	57	GG15
Broomhill Av. G11	33	R11
Broomhill Av. G32	54	BB16
Broomhill Cres. G11	19	R10
Broomhill Dr. G11	19	R10
Broomhill Dr. (Ruther.) G73	65	Y17
Broomhill Gdns. G11	19	R10
Broomhill La. G11	19	R10
Broomhill Path G11	33	R11
Broomhill Ter.		
Broomhill Pl. G11	19	R10
Broomhill Rd. G11	33	R11
Broomhill Ter. G11	33	R11
Broomieknowe Dr. (Ruther.) G73	65	Y17
Broomieknowe Rd. (Ruther.) G73	65	Y17
Broomielaw G1	35	V13
Broomknowe (Cumb.) G68	70	MM2
Broomknowe Pl. (Lenzie) G66	13	DD6
Broomknowes Rd. G21	23	Y10
Broomlands Av., Ersk. PA8	16	J8
Broomlands Cres., Ersk. PA8	16	J8
Broomlands Gdns., Ersk. PA8	16	J8
Broomlands Rd. (Cumb.) G67	71	PP4
Broomlands St., Pais. PA1	46	J14
Broomlands Way, Ersk. PA8	16	K8
Broomlea Cres. (Inch.), Renf. PA4	16	J8
Broomley Dr. (Giff.) G46	62	T19
Broomley La. (Giff.) G46	62	T19
Broomloan Ct. G51	34	S13
Broomloan Pl. G51	34	S13
Broomloan Rd. G51	34	S13
Broompark Circ. G31	36	X12
Broompark Dr. G31	36	X12
Broompark Dr. (Inch.), Renf. PA4	16	J8
Broompark La. G31	36	X12
Craigpark		
Broompark St. G31	36	X12
Broomton Rd. G21	23	Z8
Broomward Dr., John. PA5	44	E14
Brora Dr. (Giff.) G46	62	T19
Brora Dr. (Bears.) G61	8	S6
Brora Dr., Renf. PA4	18	N10
Brora Gdns. (Bishop.) G64	11	Y7
Brora La. G33	37	Z11
Brora St.		
Brora Rd. (Bishop.) G64	11	Y7
Brora St. G33	37	Z11
Broughton Dr. G23	21	U8
Broughton Gdns. G23	9	U7
Broughton Rd. G23	21	U8
Brown Av., Clyde. G81	17	M8
Brown Rd. (Camb.) G72	66	BB17
Allison Dr.		
Brown Rd. (Cumb.) G67	70	NN3
Brown St. G2	35	V12
Brown St., Pais. PA1	30	J13
Brown St., Renf. PA4	31	L11
Brownhill Rd. G43	62	S18
Brownlie St. G42	51	V16
Browns La., Pais. PA1	46	K14
Brownsdale Rd. (Ruther.) G73	52	X16
Brownside Av. (Camb.) G72	66	AA17
Brownside Av. (Barr.) G78	59	L17
Brownside Av., Pais. PA2	46	J16
Brownside Cres. (Barr.) G78	59	L17
Brownside Dr. G13	18	N9
Brownside Dr. (Barr.) G78	59	L17
Brownside Gro. (Barr.) G78	59	L17
Brownside Rd. (Camb.) G72	65	Z17
Brownside Rd. (Ruther.) G73	65	Z17
Bruce Av., John. PA5	43	D16
Bruce Av., Pais. PA3	31	L12
Bruce Rd. G41	51	U14
Bruce Rd., Pais. PA3	31	L13
Bruce Rd., Renf. PA4	31	L11
Bruce St., Clyde. G81	5	L7
Bruce Ter. (Blan.) G72	69	GG19
Brucefield Pl. G34	40	FF12
Brunstane Rd. G34	40	EE11
Brunswick Ho., Clyde. G81	4	J5
Perth Cres.		
Brunswick La. G1	36	W12
Brunswick St.		
Brunswick St. G1	36	W12
Brunton St. G44	63	V17
Brunton Ter. G44	63	U18
Bruntsfield Av. G53	60	P18
Bruntsfield Gdns. G53	60	P18
Bruntsfield Av.		
Brydson Pl. (Linw.), Pais. PA3	28	E13
Fulwood Av.		
Buccleuch Av. G52	32	N12
Buccleuch La. G3	35	V11
Scott St.		
Buccleuch St. G3	35	V11
Buchan St. G5	35	V13
Norfolk St.		
Buchan Ter. (Camb.) G72	66	AA18
Buchanan Cres. (Bishop.) G64	23	Z8
Buchanan Dr. (Bears.) G61	8	S6
Buchanan Dr. (Bishop.) G64	23	Z8
Buchanan Dr. (Lenzie) G66	13	CC6
Buchanan Dr. (Camb.) G72	66	AA17
Buchanan Dr. (Ruther.) G73	65	Y17
Buchanan Gdns. G32	55	DD15
Buchanan Gro. (Bail.) G69	40	EE13
Buchanan St. G1	35	V12
Buchanan St. (Bail.) G69	56	EE14
Buchanan St., John. PA5	43	D15
Buchley (Bishop.) G64	10	W5
Buchlyvie Gdns. (Bishop.) G64	22	X8
Buchlyvie Path G34	40	EE12
Buchlyvie Rd., Pais. PA1	32	N13
Buchlyvie St. G34	40	EE12
Buckingham Bldgs. G12	20	T10
Great Western Rd.		
Buckingham Dr. G32	54	BB16
Buckingham Dr. (Ruther.) G73	53	Z16
Buckingham St. G12	20	T10
Buckingham Ter. G12	20	T10
Bucklaw Gdns. G52	49	Q14
Bucklaw Pl. G52	49	Q14
Bucklaw Ter. G52	49	Q14
Buckley St. G22	22	W9
Bucksburn Rd. G21	23	Z10
Buckthorne Pl. G53	60	P18
Buddon St. G40	53	Z14
Budhill Av. G32	38	BB13
Bulldale Ct. G14	18	N9
Bulldale Rd. G14	18	N9
Bulldale St. G14	18	N9
Bullionslaw Dr. (Ruther.) G73	65	Z17
Bulloch Av. (Giff.) G46	62	T19
Bullwood Av. G53	48	N15
Bullwood Ct. G53	48	N15
Bullwood Dr. G53	48	N15
Bullwood Gdns. G53	48	N15
Bullwood Pl. G53	48	N15
Bunessan St. G52	33	R13
Bunhouse Rd. G3	34	T11
Burgh Hall La. G11	34	S11
Fortrose St.		
Burgh Hall St. G11	34	S11
Burgh La. G12	20	T10
Vinicombe St.		
Burghead Dr. G51	33	R12
Burghead Pl. G51	33	R12
Burgher St. G31	37	Z13
Burleigh Rd. (Both.) G71	69	HH18
Burleigh St. G51	34	S12
Burlington Av. G12	20	S9
Burmola St. G22	21	V10
Burn Gdns. (Blan.) G72	68	FF19
Burn Pl. (Camb.) G72	54	AA16
Burn Ter.		
Burn Ter. (Camb.) G72	54	AA16
Burn Vw. (Cumb.) G67	71	QQ2
Burnacre Gdns. (Udd.) G71	57	GG16
Burnbank Dr. (Barr.) G78	59	M19
Burnbank Gdns. G20	35	U11
Burnbank Pl. G4	36	X12
Drygate		
Burnbank Ter. G20	35	U11
Burnbrae, Clyde. G81	5	L5
Burnbrae Av. (Mood.) G69	15	HH7
Burnbrae Av. (Linw.), Pais. PA3	28	F13
Bridge St.		
Burnbrae Ct. (Lenzie) G66	13	CC6
Auchinloch Rd.		
Burnbrae Dr. (Ruther.) G73	65	Z17
East Kilbride Rd.		
Burnbrae Rd. (Kirk.) G66	13	DD7
Burnbrae Rd. (Chry.) G69	14	EE7
Burnbrae Rd. (Linw.), Pais. PA3	44	F14
Burnbrae St. G21	23	Y10
Burncleuch Av. (Camb.) G72	66	BB18
Burncrooks Ct., Clyde. G81	4	K5
Burndyke Ct. G51	34	T12
Burndyke Sq. G51	34	T12
Burndyke St. G51	34	S12
Burnett Rd. G33	39	DD12
Burnfield Av. (Thorn.) G46	62	S18
Burnfield Cotts. (Thorn.) G46	62	S18
Burnfield Dr. G43	62	S18
Burnfield Gdns. (Giff.) G46	62	T18
Burnfield Rd.		
Burnfield Rd. G43	62	S18
Burnfield Rd. (Thorn.) G46	62	S18
Burnfoot Cres. (Ruther.) G73	65	Z17
Burnfoot Cres., Pais. PA2	46	J16
Burnfoot Dr. G52	32	P13
Burngreen Ter. (Cumb.) G67	71	PP1
Burnham Rd. G14	18	P10
Burnham Ter. G14	18	P10
Burnham Rd.		
Burnhead Rd. G43	63	U17
Burnhead Rd. (Cumb.) G68	70	MM3
Burnhead St. (Udd.) G71	57	HH16
Burnhill Quad. (Ruther.) G73	52	X16
Burnhill St. (Ruther.) G73	52	X16
Burnhouse St. G20	20	T9
Kelvindale Rd.		
Burnmouth Ct. G33	39	DD13
Pendeen Rd.		
Burnmouth Rd. G33	39	DD13
Burnpark Av. (Udd.) G71	56	FF16
Burns Dr., John. PA5	43	D16
Burns Gro. (Thorn.) G46	62	S19
Burns Rd. (Cumb.) G67	71	PP3
Burns St. G4	35	V11
Burns St., Clyde. G81	4	K6
Burnside Av. (Barr.) G78	59	L18
Burnside Ct., Clyde. G81	4	K6
Scott St.		
Burnside Gdns. (Mill.Pk.), John. PA10	42	B10
Burnside Gate (Ruther.) G73	65	Z17
Burnside Gro., John. PA5	43	D15
Quarrelton Rd.		
Burnside Pl., Pais. PA3	29	H12
Burnside Rd. (Ruther.) G73 65	65	Z17

Cardarrach St. G21	23	Y10	Caroline St. G31	38	AA13	Castle Way (Cumb.) G67	71	QQ2
Cardell Av., Pais. PA2	45	H14	Carolside Dr. G15	6	P6	Castle Way (Bail.) G69	41	GG13
Cardell Dr., Pais. PA2	45	H14	Carradale Gdns. (Bishop.)	11	Z7	*Dukes Rd.*		
Cardell Rd., Pais. PA2	45	H14	G64			Castlebank Ct. G13	19	R9
Carding La. G3	35	U12	*Thrums Av.*			Castlebank Cres. G11	34	S11
Argyle St.			Carradale Pl. (Linw.), Pais.	28	E13	*Meadowside St.*		
Cardonald Dr. G52	48	P14	PA3			Castlebank Gdns. G13	19	R9
Cardonald Gdns. G52	48	P14	Carrbridge Dr. G20	20	T9	Castlebank St. G11	33	R11
Cardonald Pl. Rd. G52	48	P14	*Glenfinnan Dr.*			Castlebank Vills. G13	19	R9
Cardow Rd. G21	23	Z10	Carresbrook Av. (Kirk.) G66	14	EE5	Castlebay Dr. G22	10	W7
Cardowan Dr. (Stepps) G33	25	CC9	Carriagehill Av., Pais. PA2	46	K15	Castlebay Pl. G22	22	W8
Cardowan Pk. (Udd.) G71	57	HH15	Carriagehill Dr., Pais. PA2	46	K15	Castlebay St. G22	22	W8
Cardowan Rd. G32	38	AA13	Carrick Cres. (Giff.) G46	62	T19	Castlecroft Gdns. (Udd.)	69	GG17
Cardowan Rd. (Stepps)	25	DD9	Carrick Dr. G32	55	DD14	G71		
G33			Carrick Dr. (Ruther.) G73	65	Y17	Castlefern Rd. (Ruther.)	65	Y18
Cardrona St. G33	24	BB10	Carrick Gro. G32	55	DD14	G73		
Cardross Ct. G31	36	X12	Carrick Rd. (Bishop.) G64	11	Z7	Castlehill Cres., Renf. PA4	17	M10
Cardross St. G31	36	X12	Carrick Rd. (Cumb.) G67	71	PP2	*Ferry Rd.*		
Cardwell St. G41	51	V14	Carrick Rd. (Ruther.) G73	64	X17	Castlehill Rd. (Bears.) G61	6	P5
Cardyke St. G21	23	Y10	Carrick St. G2	35	V12	Castlelaw Gdns. G32	38	BB13
Careston Pl. (Bishop.) G64	11	Z7	Carrickarden Rd. (Bears.)	7	R6	Castlelaw Pl. G32	38	BB13
Carfin St. G42	51	V15	G61			Castlelaw St. G32	38	BB13
Carfrae St. G3	34	T12	Carrickstone Rd. (Cumb.)	70	NN1	Castlemilk Cres. G44	64	X17
Cargill Sq. (Bishop.) G64	23	Y8	G68			Castlemilk Dr. G45	64	X18
Cargill St. G31	54	AA14	Carrickstone Vw. (Cumb.)	70	NN1	Castlemilk Ms. G44	64	X17
Carham Cres. G52	33	Q13	G68			*Castlemilk Rd.*		
Carham Dr. G52	33	Q13	Carriden Pl. G33	39	DD12	Castlemilk Rd. G44	52	X16
Carillon Rd. G51	34	T13	Carrington St. G4	35	U11	Castleton Av. (Bishop.) G64	22	X8
Carisbrooke Cres.	11	Y6	Carroglen Gdns. G32	39	CC13	*Colston Rd.*		
(Bishop.) G64			Carroglen Gro. G32	39	CC13	Castleton Ct. G45	64	X19
Carlaverock Rd. G43	62	T17	Carron Ct. (Camb.) G72	67	CC17	Castleview Av., Pais. PA2	45	H16
Carleith Av., Clyde. G81	4	K5	Carron Cres. G22	22	W9	Castleview Dr., Pais. PA2	45	H16
Carleith Quad. G51	33	Q12	Carron Cres. (Bears.) G61	7	Q6	Castleview Pl., Pais. PA2	45	H16
Carleith Ter., Clyde. G81	4	K5	Carron Cres. (Bishop.) G64	11	Y7	Cathay St. G22	22	W8
Carleith Av.			Carron Cres. (Lenzie) G66	13	DD6	Cathcart Cres., Pais. PA2	47	L14
Carleston St. G21	22	X10	Carron La., Pais. PA3	31	L12	Cathcart Pl. (Ruther.) G73	52	X16
Atlas Rd.			*Kilearn Rd.*			Cathcart Rd. G42	51	V16
Carleton Dr. (Giff.) G46	62	T18	Carron Pl. G22	22	X9	Cathcart Rd. (Ruther.) G73	52	X16
Carleton Gate (Giff.) G46	62	T18	Carron St. G22	22	X9	Cathedral Ct. G4	36	W12
Carlibar Av. G13	18	N9	Carrour Gdns. (Bishop.)	10	X7	*Rottenrow E.*		
Carlibar Dr. (Barr.) G78	59	M18	G64			Cathedral La. G4	36	W12
Carlibar Gdns. (Barr.) G78	59	M18	Carsaig Dr. G52	33	R13	*Cathedral St.*		
Commercial Rd.			Carse Vw. Dr. (Bears.) G61	8	S5	Cathedral Sq. G4	36	X12
Carlibar Rd. (Barr.) G78	59	L18	Carsebrook Av. (Kirk.) G66	14	EE5	Cathedral St. G1	36	W12
Carlile La., Pais. PA3	30	K13	*Chryston Rd.*			Cathedral St. G4	36	W12
New Sneddon St.			Carsegreen Av., Pais. PA2	45	H16	Catherine Pl. G3	35	U12
Carlile Pl., Pais. PA3	30	K13	Carstairs St. G40	53	Y15	*Hydepark St.*		
Carlisle St. G21	22	W10	Carswell Gdns. G41	51	U15	Cathkin Av. (Camb.) G72	66	AA17
Carlisle Ter., Pais. PA3	30	K13	Cart St., Clyde. G81	17	L8	Cathkin Av. (Ruther.) G73	53	Z16
Carlowrie Av. (Blan.) G72	68	FF19	Cartcraigs Rd. G43	62	S17	Cathkin Bypass (Ruther.)	65	Z18
Carlton Ct. G5	35	V13	Cartha Cres., Pais. PA2	47	L14	G73		
Carlton Pl. G5	35	V13	Cartha St. G41	51	U16	Cathkin Ct. G45	64	X19
Carlton Ter. G20	21	U10	Cartside Av., John. PA5	43	C15	Cathkin Gdns. (Udd.) G71	57	GG15
Wilton St.			Cartside Quad. G42	51	V16	Cathkin Pl. (Camb.) G72	66	AA17
Carlyle Av. G52	32	N12	Cartside St. G42	51	U16	Cathkin Rd. G42	51	U16
Carlyle St., Pais. PA3	30	K13	Cartside Ter. (Mill.Pk.),	43	C15	Cathkin Rd. (Udd.) G71	57	GG15
Carlyle Ter. (Ruther.) G73	53	Y16	John. PA10			Cathkin Rd. (Ruther.) G73	65	Y19
Carmaben Rd. G33	39	DD12	*Kilbarchan Rd.*			Cathkin Rd. (Clark.) G76	65	Y19
Carment Dr. G41	50	T16	Cartvale La., Pais. PA3	30	K13	Cathkin Vw. G32	54	BB16
Carment La. G41	50	T16	Cartvale Rd. G42	51	U16	Cathkinview Pl. G42	51	V16
Carmichael Pl. G42	51	U16	Caskie Dr. (Blan.) G72	69	GG19	Cathkinview Rd. G42	51	V16
Carmichael St. G51	34	S13	Cassley Av., Renf. PA4	32	N11	Catrine Ct. G53	48	P16
Carmunnock La. G44	63	V17	Castle Av. (Udd.) G71	69	GG17	Catrine Gdns. G53	48	P16
Madison Av.			Castle Av. (Elder.), John.	44	E15	Catrine Pl. G53	48	P16
Carmunnock Rd. G44	51	V16	PA5			Catrine Rd. G53	48	P16
Carmunnock Rd. G45	64	W17	Castle Chimmins Av.	67	CC18	Causewayside St. G32	54	BB15
Carmunnock Rd. (Clark.)	64	W19	(Camb.) G72			Causeyside St., Pais. PA1	46	K14
G76			Castle Chimmins Rd.	67	CC18	Cavendish Pl. G5	51	V14
Carmyle Av. G32	54	BB15	(Camb.) G72			Cavendish St. G5	51	V14
Carna Dr. G44	64	W17	Castle Cres. N. Ct. G1	36	W12	Cavin Dr. G45	64	X18
Carnarvon St. G3	35	U11	*Royal Ex. Sq.*			Cavin Rd. G45	64	X18
Carnbooth Ct. G45	64	X19	Castle Gait, Pais. PA1	46	J14	Cayton Gdns. (Bail.) G69	55	DD14
Carnbroe St. G20	35	V11	Castle Gdns. (Chry.) G69	15	GG7	Cecil Pl. G51	35	U13
Carnegie Rd. G52	32	P13	Castle Gdns., Pais. PA3	45	H14	*Paisley Rd. W.*		
Carnock Cres. (Barr.) G78	59	L19	Castle Gate (Udd.) G71	69	GG17	Cecil St. G12	20	T10
Carnock Rd. G53	49	Q16	Castle Pl. (Udd.) G71	69	GG17	Cedar Av., Clyde. G81	4	J6
Carnoustie Ct. (Both.) G71	69	GG19	*Ferry Rd.*			Cedar Av., John. PA5	44	E16
Carnoustie Cres. (Bishop.)	11	Z7	Castle Rd. (Elder.), John.	44	F14	Cedar Ct. G20	35	V11
G64			PA5			Cedar Ct. (Kilb.), John.	42	B14
Carnoustie St. G5	35	U13	Castle Sq., Clyde. G81	4	K6	PA10		
Carntyne Gdns. G32	38	AA12	Castle St. G4	36	X12	Cedar Dr. (Lenzie) G66	13	CC5
Abbeyhill St.			Castle St. G11	34	T11	Cedar Gdns. (Ruther.) G73	65	Z18
Carntyne Pl. G32	37	Z12	*Benalder St.*			Cedar Pl. (Blan.) G72	68	FF19
Carntyne Rd. G31	37	Z13	Castle St. (Bail.) G69	56	EE14	Cedar Pl. (Barr.) G78	59	M19
Carntyne Rd. G32	38	AA12	Castle St. (Ruther.) G73	53	Y16	Cedar Rd. (Bishop.) G64	23	Y8
Carntynehall Rd. G32	38	AA12	Castle St., Clyde. G81	4	K6	Cedar Rd. (Cumb.) G67	71	QQ2
Carnwadric Rd. (Thorn.)	61	R18	Castle St., Pais. PA1	46	J14	Cedar St. G20	35	V11
G46			Castle Vw., Clyde. G81	5	L6	Cedar Wk. (Bishop.) G64	23	Y8
Carnwath Av. G43	63	U17	*Granville St.*			Cedric Pl. G13	19	Q8

Cedric Rd. G13	19	Q8
Celtic St. G20	20	T8
Cemetery Rd. G52	49	Q14
Paisley Rd. W.		
Centenary Ct., Clyde. G81	5	L7
Bruce St.		
Central Av. G11	33	R11
Broomhill Ter.		
Central Av. G32	55	CC14
Central Av. (Camb.) G72	66	AA17
Central Av., Clyde. G81	5	L7
Central Chambers G2	35	V12
Hope St.		
Central Gro. (Camb.) G72	66	AA17
Central Path G32	55	DD14
Central Rd., Pais. PA1	30	K13
Central Sta. G1	35	V12
Central Way (Cumb.) G67	70	NN4
Central Way, Pais. PA1	30	K13
Centre, The (Barr.) G78	59	L19
Centre St. G5	35	V13
Centre Way (Barr.) G78	59	L18
Ceres Gdns. (Bishop.) G64	11	Z7
Cessnock Rd. G33	24	BB9
Cessnock St. G51	34	T13
Chachan Dr. G51	33	R12
Skipness Dr.		
Chalmers Ct. G40	36	X13
Chalmers Gate G40	36	X13
Claythorn St.		
Chalmers Pl. G40	36	X13
Claythorn St.		
Chalmers St. G40	36	X13
Chalmers St., Clyde. G81	5	L7
Chamberlain La. G13	19	R9
Chamberlain Rd. G13	19	R9
Chancellor St. G11	34	S11
Chapel Rd., Clyde. G81	5	L5
Chapel St. G20	21	U9
Chapel St. (Ruther.) G73	52	X16
Chapelhill Rd., Pais. PA2	47	L15
Chapelton Av. (Bears.) G61	7	R6
Chapelton Gdns. (Bears.) G61	7	R6
Chapelton St. G22	21	V9
Chaplet Av. G13	19	Q8
Chapman St. G42	51	V15
Allison St.		
Chappell St. (Barr.) G78	59	L18
Charing Cross G2	35	U11
Charing Cross La. G3	35	U12
Granville St.		
Charles Av., Renf. PA4	17	M10
Charles Cres. (Lenzie) G66	13	CC6
Charles St. G21	36	X11
Charlotte La. G1	36	W13
London Rd.		
Charlotte La. S. G1	36	W13
Charlotte St.		
Charlotte Pl., Pais. PA2	46	K15
Charlotte St. G1	36	W13
Chatelherault Av. (Camb.) G72	66	AA17
Chatton St. G23	8	T7
Cheapside St. G3	35	U12
Chelmsford Dr. G12	20	S9
Cherry Bk. (Kirk.) G66	12	BB5
Cherry Cres., Clyde. G81	5	L6
Cherry Pl. (Bishop.) G64	23	Y8
Cherry Pl., John. PA5	44	E15
Cherrybank Rd. G43	63	U17
Cherrywood Rd. (Elder.), John. PA5	44	F15
Chester St. G32	38	BB13
Chesterfield Av. G12	20	S9
Chesters Pl. (Ruther.) G73	53	Y16
Chesters Rd. (Bears.) G61	7	Q6
Chestnut Dr. (Kirk.) G66	12	BB5
Chestnut Dr., Clyde. G81	5	L5
Chestnut Pl., John. PA5	44	E16
Chestnut St. G22	22	W9
Cheviot Av. (Barr.) G78	59	M19
Cheviot Rd. G43	62	T17
Cheviot Rd., Pais. PA2	46	K16
Chirnside Pl. G52	32	P13
Chirnside Rd. G52	32	P13
Chisholm St. G1	36	W13
Crighton Grn. (Udd.) G71	57	HH16
Christian St. G43	50	T16
Christie La., Pais. PA3	30	K13
New Sneddon St.		
Christie Pl. (Camb.) G72	66	BB17
Christie St., Pais. PA1	30	K13
Christopher St. G21	37	Y11
Chryston Rd. (Kirk.) G66	14	FF5
Chryston Rd. (Chry.) G69	26	FF8
Church Av. (Stepps) G33	25	CC9
Church Av. (Ruther.) G73	65	Z17
Church Dr. (Kirk.) G66	13	CC5
Church Hill, Pais. PA1	30	K13
Church La. G42	51	V15
Victoria Rd.		
Church Rd. (Giff.) G46	62	T19
Church Rd. (Muir.) G69	26	FF8
Church St. (Bail.) G69	56	FF14
Church St. (Udd.) G71	69	GG17
Church St., Clyde. G81	5	L6
Church St., John. PA5	43	D14
Church St. (Kilb.), John. PA10	42	B14
Church Vw. (Camb.) G72	54	BB16
Churchill Av., John. PA5	43	C16
Churchill Cres. (Both.) G71	69	HH18
Churchill Dr. G11	19	R10
Churchill Pl. (Kilb.), John. PA10	42	B14
Churchill Way (Bishop.) G64	10	X7
Kirkintilloch Rd.		
Circus Dr. G31	36	X12
Circus Pl. G31	36	X12
Circus Pl. La. G31	36	X12
Circus Pl.		
Cityford Cres. (Ruther.) G73	52	X16
Cityford Dr. (Ruther.) G73	52	X16
Clachan Dr. G51	33	R12
Skipness Dr.		
Claddens Pl. (Lenzie) G66	13	DD6
Claddens Quad. G22	22	W9
Claddens St. G22	21	V9
Claddens Wynd (Kirk.) G66	13	DD6
Claddon Vw., Clyde. G81	5	M6
Kirkoswald Dr.		
Clair Rd. (Bishop.) G64	11	Z7
Clairmont Gdns. G3	35	U11
Clare St. G21	37	Y11
Claremont Pas. G3	35	U11
Claremont Ter.		
Claremont Pl. G3	35	U11
Claremont Ter.		
Claremont St. G3	35	U12
Claremont Ter. G3	35	U11
Claremont Ter. La. G3	35	U11
Clifton St.		
Claremount Av. (Giff.) G46	62	T19
Clarence Dr. G11	20	S10
Clarence Dr. G12	20	S10
Clarence Dr., Pais. PA1	47	L14
Clarence Gdns. G11	20	S10
Clarence La. G12	20	S10
Hyndland Rd.		
Clarence St., Clyde. G81	5	M6
Clarence St., Pais. PA1	31	L13
Clarendon La. G20	35	V11
Clarendon St.		
Clarendon Pl. G20	35	V11
Clarendon St. G20	35	V11
Clarion Cres. G13	18	P8
Clarion Rd. G13	18	P8
Clark St. G41	35	U13
Tower St.		
Clark St., Clyde. G81	4	K6
Clark St., John. PA5	43	D14
Clark St., Pais. PA3	30	J13
Clark St., Renf. PA4	17	L10
Clarkston Av. G44	63	U18
Clarkston Rd. G44	63	U18
Clarkston Rd. (Clark.) G76	63	U19
Clathic Av. (Bears.) G61	8	S6
Claud Av., Pais. PA3	31	L13
Claude Av. (Camb.) G72	67	DD18
Claudhall Av. (Gart.) G69	27	GG8
Clavens Rd. G52	32	N13
Claverhouse Pl., Pais. PA2	47	L14
Claverhouse Rd. G52	32	N12
Clavering St. E., Pais. PA1	30	J13
Well St.		
Clavering St. W., Pais. PA1	30	J13
King St.		
Clayhouse Rd. G33	25	DD9
Claypotts Pl. G33	38	BB11
Claypotts Rd. G33	38	BB11
Clayslaps Rd. G3	34	T11
Argyle St.		
Claythorn Av. G40	36	X13
Claythorn Circ. G40	36	X13
Claythorn Av.		
Claythorn Ct. G40	36	X13
Claythorn Pk.		
Claythorn Pk. G40	36	X13
Claythorn St. G40	36	X13
Claythorn Ter. G40	36	X13
Claythorn Pk.		
Clayton Ter. G31	36	X12
Cleddans Cres., Clyde. G81	5	M5
Cleddans Rd., Clyde. G81	5	M5
Cleddens Ct. (Bishop.) G64	11	Y7
Cleeves Pl. G53	60	P17
Cleeves Quad. G53	60	P17
Cleeves Rd. G53	60	P17
Cleghorn St. G22	21	V10
Cleland La. G5	36	W13
Cleland St.		
Cleland St. G5	36	W13
Clelland Av. (Bishop.) G64	23	Y8
Clerwood St. G32	37	Z13
Cleveden Cres. G12	20	S9
Cleveden Cres. La. G12	20	S9
Cleveden Dr.		
Cleveden Dr. G12	20	S9
Cleveden Dr. (Ruther.) G73	65	Z17
Cleveden Gdns. G12	20	T9
Cleveden La. G12	20	S9
Burlington Av.		
Cleveden Pl. G12	20	S9
Cleveden Rd. G12	20	S9
Cleveland St. G3	35	U12
Cliff Rd. G3	35	U11
Clifford Gdns. G51	34	S13
Clifford La. G51	34	T13
North Gower St.		
Clifford Pl. G51	34	T13
Clifford St.		
Clifford St. G51	34	S13
Clifton Pl. G3	35	U11
Clifton St.		
Clifton Rd. (Giff.) G46	62	S18
Clifton St. G3	35	U11
Clifton Ter. (Camb.) G72	66	AA18
Clifton Ter., John. PA5	44	E15
Clincart Rd. G42	51	V16
Clincarthill Rd. (Ruther.) G73	53	Y16
Clinton Av. (Udd.) G71	69	GG17
Clippens Rd. (Linw.), Pais. PA3	28	E13
Cloan Av. G15	6	P7
Cloan Cres. (Bishop.) G64	11	Y6
Cloberhill Rd. G13	7	Q7
Cloch St. G33	38	BB12
Clochoderick Av. (Mill.Pk.), John. PA10	42	B15
Mackenzie Dr.		
Clonbeith St. G33	39	DD11
Closeburn St. G22	22	W9
Cloth St. (Barr.) G78	59	M19
Clouden Rd. (Cumb.) G67	71	PP3
Cloudhowe Ter. (Blan.) G72	68	FF19
Clouston Ct. G20	21	U10
Clouston La. G20	20	T10
Clouston St.		
Clouston St. G20	20	T10
Clova Pl. (Udd.) G71	69	GG17
Clova St. (Thorn.) G46	61	R18
Clover Av. (Bishop.) G64	10	X7
Cloverbank St. G21	37	Y11
Clovergate (Bishop.) G64	10	X7
Clunie Rd. G52	49	R14
Cluny Av. (Bears.) G61	8	S7
Cluny Dr. (Bears.) G61	8	S7
Cluny Dr., Pais. PA3	31	L13
Cluny Gdns. G14	19	R10
Cluny Gdns. (Bail.) G69	56	EE14
Cluny Vills. G14	19	Q10
Westland Dr.		

Name	Page	Grid
Coulters La. G40	36	X13
Countess Way (Bail.) G69	41	HH13
Park Rd.		
County Av. (Camb.) G72	53	Z16
County Pl., Pais. PA1	30	K13
Moss St.		
County Sq., Pais. PA1	30	K13
Couper St. G4	36	W11
Courthill (Bears.) G61	7	Q5
Courthill Av. G44	63	V17
Coustonhill St. G43	50	T16
Pleasance St.		
Coustonholm Rd. G43	50	T16
Coventry Dr. G31	37	Y12
Cowal Dr. (Linw.), Pais. PA3	28	E13
Cowal Rd. G20	20	T8
Cowal St. G20	20	T8
Cowan Clo. (Barr.) G78	59	M18
Cowan Cres. (Barr.) G78	59	M19
Cowan La. G12	35	U11
Cowan St.		
Cowan Rd. (Cumb.) G68	70	MM3
Cowan St. G12	35	U11
Cowan Wilson Av. (Blan.) G72	68	FF19
Cowan Wynd (Udd.) G71	57	HH16
Cowcaddens Rd. G4	35	V11
Cowcaddens St. G2	35	V12
Renfield St.		
Cowden Dr. (Bishop.) G64	11	Y6
Cowden St. G51	33	Q12
Cowdenhill Circ. G13	19	Q8
Cowdenhill Pl. G13	19	Q8
Cowdenhill Rd. G13	19	Q8
Cowdray Cres., Renf. PA4	17	M10
Cowell Vw., Clyde. G81	5	L6
Granville St.		
Cowglen Pl. G53	49	Q16
Cowglen Rd.		
Cowglen Rd. G53	49	Q16
Cowglen Ter. G53	49	Q16
Cowlairs Rd. G21	22	X10
Coxhill St. G21	22	W10
Coxton Pl. G33	39	CC11
Coylton Rd. G43	63	U17
Craggan Dr. G14	18	N9
Crags Av., Pais. PA2	46	K15
Crags Cres., Pais. PA2	46	K15
Crags Rd., Pais. PA2	46	K15
Craig Rd. G44	63	V17
Craigallian Av. (Camb.) G72	67	CC18
Craiganour La. G43	62	T17
Craiganour Pl. G43	62	T17
Craigard Pl. (Ruther.) G73	66	AA18
Inverclyde Gdns.		
Craigbank Dr. G53	60	P17
Craigbank St. G22	22	W10
Craigbarnet Cres. G33	24	BB10
Craigbo Av. G23	8	T7
Craigbo Ct. G23	20	T8
Craigbo Dr. G23	20	T8
Craigbo Pl. G23	20	T8
Craigbo Rd. G23	20	T8
Craigbo St. G23	8	T7
Craigbog Av., John. PA5	43	C15
Craigdonald Pl., John. PA5	43	D14
Craigellan Rd. G43	62	T17
Craigenbay Cres. (Lenzie) G66	13	CC5
Craigenbay Rd. (Lenzie) G66	13	CC6
Craigenbay St. G21	23	Y10
Craigencart Ct., Clyde. G81	4	K5
Gentle Row		
Craigend Pl. G13	19	R9
Craigend St. G13	19	R9
Craigendmuir Rd. G33	25	DD10
Craigendmuir St. G33	37	Z11
Craigendon Oval, Pais. PA2	58	J17
Craigendon Rd., Pais. PA2	58	J17
Craigends Dr. (Kilb.), John. PA10	42	B14
High Barholm		
Craigenfeoch Av., John. PA5	43	C15
Craigfaulds Av., Pais. PA2	45	H15
Craigflower Gdns. G53	60	P18
Craigflower Rd. G53	60	P18
Craighalbert Rd. (Cumb.) G68	70	MM2
Craighalbert Way (Cumb.) G68	70	MM2
Craighall Rd. G4	35	V11
Craighead Av. G33	23	Z10
Craighead St. (Barr.) G78	59	L19
Craighead Way (Barr.) G78	59	L19
Craighouse St. G33	38	BB11
Craigie Pk. (Lenzie) G66	13	DD5
Craigie St. G42	51	V15
Craigiebar Dr., Pais. PA2	46	J16
Craigieburn Gdns. G20	20	S8
Craigieburn Rd. (Cumb.) G67	70	NN3
Craigiehall Pl. G51	34	T13
Craigiehall St. G51	35	U13
Craigiehall Pl.		
Craigielea Dr., Pais. PA3	29	H13
Craigielea Pk., Renf. PA4	17	L10
Craigielea Rd., Renf. PA4	17	M10
Craigielea St. G31	37	Y12
Craigielinn Av., Pais. PA2	58	J17
Craigievar St. G33	39	DD11
Craigleith St. G32	38	AA13
Craiglockhart St. G33	39	CC11
Craigmaddie Ter. La. G3	35	U12
Derby St.		
Craigmillar Rd. G42	51	V16
Craigmont Dr. G20	21	U9
Craigmont St. G20	21	U9
Craigmore St. G31	37	Z13
Craigmount Av., Pais. PA2	58	J17
Craigmuir Cres. G52	32	N13
Craigmuir Pl. G52	32	N13
Craigmuir Rd.		
Craigmuir Rd. G52	32	N13
Craigneil St. G33	39	DD11
Craignestock Pl. G40	36	X13
London Rd.		
Craignestock St. G40	36	X13
Lawrie St.		
Craignure Rd. (Ruther.) G73	65	Y18
Craigpark G31	37	Y12
Craigpark Dr. G31	37	Y12
Craigpark Ter. G31	37	Y12
Craigpark		
Craigpark Way (Udd.) G71	57	HH16
Newton Dr.		
Craigs Av., Clyde. G81	5	M5
Craigston Pl., John. PA5	43	D15
Craigston Rd., John. PA5	43	D15
Craigton Av. (Barr.) G78	60	N19
Craigton Dr. G51	33	R13
Craigton Dr. (Barr.) G78	60	N19
Craigton Pl. G51	33	R13
Craigton Dr.		
Craigton Pl. (Blan.) G72	68	FF19
Craigton Rd. G51	33	R13
Craigvicar Gdns. G32	39	CC13
Hailes Av.		
Craigview Av., John. PA5	43	C16
Craigwell Av. (Ruther.) G73	65	Z17
Crail St. G31	37	Z13
Cramond Av., Renf. PA4	32	N11
Cramond St. G5	52	W15
Cramond Ter. G32	38	BB13
Cranborne Rd. G12	20	S9
Cranbrooke Dr. G20	20	T8
Cranston St. G3	35	U12
Cranworth La. G12	20	T10
Great George St.		
Cranworth St. G12	20	T10
Crarae Av. (Bears.) G61	7	R7
Crathie Dr. G11	34	S11
Crathie La. G11	34	S11
Exeter Dr.		
Craw Rd., Pais. PA2	46	J14
Crawford Av. (Lenzie) G66	13	DD6
Crawford Ct. (Giff.) G46	62	S19
Milverton Rd.		
Crawford Cres. (Udd.) G71	57	GG16
Crawford Cres. (Blan.) G72	68	FF19
Crawford Dr. G15	6	N7
Crawford La. G11	34	S11
Crawford Path G11	34	S11
Crawford St.		
Crawford St. G11	34	S11
Crawford Dr., Pais. PA3	29	H13
Crawfurd Gdns. (Ruther.) G73	65	Y18
Crawfurd Rd. (Ruther.) G73	65	Y18
Crawriggs Av. (Kirk.) G66	13	CC5
Crebar Dr. (Barr.) G78	59	M19
Crebar St. (Thorn.) G46	61	R18
Credon Gdns. (Ruther.) G73	65	Z18
Cree Av. (Bishop.) G64	11	Z7
Cree Gdns. G32	38	AA13
Kilmany Dr.		
Creran Dr., Renf. PA4	17	L10
Creran St. G40	36	X13
Tobago St.		
Crescent Ct., Clyde. G81	4	K6
Swindon St.		
Crescent Rd. G13	18	P9
Crescent Rd. G14	18	P9
Cresswell La. G12	20	T10
Great George St.		
Cresswell St. G12	20	T10
Cressy St. G51	33	R12
Crest Av. G13	18	P8
Crestlea Av., Pais. PA2	46	K16
Creswell Ter. (Udd.) G71	57	GG16
Kylepark Dr.		
Crichton Ct. G45	64	X19
Crichton Pl. G21	22	X10
Crichton St.		
Crichton St. G21	22	X10
Crieff Ct. G3	35	U12
North St.		
Criffell Gdns. G32	55	CC14
Criffell Rd. G32	55	CC14
Crimea St. G2	35	V12
Crinan Gdns. (Bishop.) G64	11	Y7
Crinan Rd. (Bishop.) G64	11	Y7
Crinan St. G31	37	Y12
Cripps Av., Clyde. G81	5	M7
Croft Rd. (Camb.) G72	66	BB17
Croft Wynd (Udd.) G71	69	HH17
Croftbank Av. (Both.) G71	69	HH19
Croftbank Cres. (Both.) G71	69	HH19
Croftbank Cres. (Udd.) G71	69	GG17
Croftbank St. G21	22	X10
Croftbank St. (Udd.) G71	69	GG17
Croftburn Dr. G44	64	W18
Croftcroighn Rd. G33	38	BB11
Croftend Av. G44	64	X17
Croftfoot Cotts. (Gart.) G69	27	HH9
Croftfoot Cres. G45	65	Y18
Croftfoot Dr. G45	64	X18
Croftfoot Quad. G45	64	X18
Croftfoot Rd. G44	64	W18
Croftfoot Rd. G45	64	W18
Croftfoot St. G45	65	Y18
Croftfoot Ter. G45	64	X18
Crofthead St. (Udd.) G71	69	GG17
Crofthill Av. (Udd.) G71	69	GG17
Crofthill Rd. G44	64	W17
Crofthouse Dr. G44	64	X18
Croftmont Av. G44	64	X18
Croftmoraig Av. (Chry.) G69	15	HH6
Crofton Av. G44	64	W18
Croftpark Av. G44	64	W18
Croftside Av. G44	64	X18
Croftspar Av. G32	39	CC13
Croftspar Dr. G32	39	CC13
Croftspar Gro. G32	39	CC13
Croftspar Pl. G32	39	CC13
Croftwood (Bishop.) G64	11	Y6
Croftwood Av. G44	64	W18
Cromart Pl. (Chry.) G69	14	FF7
Cromarty Av. G43	63	U17
Cromarty Av. (Bishop.) G64	11	Z7
Cromarty Gdns. (Clark.) G76	63	V19
Crombie Gdns. (Bail.) G69	56	EE14
Cromdale St. G51	33	R13
Cromer La., Pais. PA3	30	J12
Abbotsburn Way		
Cromer St. G20	21	U9
Cromer Way, Pais. PA3	30	J12
Mosslands Rd.		
Crompton Av. G44	63	V17

Cromwell La. G20	35	V11
Cromwell St.		
Cromwell St. G20	35	V11
Cronberry Quad. G52	48	N14
Cronberry Ter. G52	48	N14
Crookedshields Rd.	66	BB19
(Camb.) G72		
Crookston Av. G52	48	P14
Crookston Ct. G52	48	P14
Crookston Dr. G52	48	N14
Crookston Dr., Pais. PA1	48	N14
Crookston Gdns. G52	48	N14
Crookston Gro. G52	48	P14
Crookston Pl. G52	48	N14
Crookston Quad. G52	48	N14
Crookston Rd. G52	48	N15
Crookston Rd. G53	48	P15
Crookston Ter. G52	48	P14
Crookston Rd.		
Crosbie Dr., Pais. PA2	45	G16
Crosbie La. G20	20	T8
Crosbie St. G20	20	T8
Crosbie Wds., Pais. PA2	45	H15
Cross, The G1	36	W13
Cross, The, Pais. PA1	30	K13
Cross Arthurlie St. (Barr.)	59	L19
G78		
Cross Rd., Pais. PA2	45	H15
Cross St. G32	55	CC15
Cross St., Pais. PA1	46	J14
Crossbank Av. G42	52	X15
Crossbank Dr. G42	52	X15
Crossbank Rd. G42	52	W15
Crossbank Ter. G42	52	W15
Crossflat Cres., Pais. PA1	31	L13
Crossford Dr. G23	9	U7
Crosshill Av. G42	51	V15
Crosshill Av. (Kirk.) G66	13	CC5
Crosshill Dr. (Ruther.) G73	65	Y17
Crosshill Rd. (Bishop.) G64	11	Z5
Crosshill Rd. (Kirk.) G66	12	BB6
Crosshill Sq. (Bail.) G69	56	FF14
Crosslee St. G52	33	R13
Crosslees Ct. (Thorn.) G46	61	R18
Main St.		
Crosslees Dr. (Thorn.) G46	61	R18
Crosslees Pk. (Thorn.) G46	61	R18
Crosslees Rd. (Thorn.) G46	61	R19
Crossloan Pl. G51	33	R12
Crossloan Rd. G51	33	R12
Crossloan Ter. G51	33	R12
Crossmill Av. (Barr.) G78	59	M18
Crossmyloof Gdns. G41	50	T15
Crosspoint Dr. G23	9	U7
Invershiel Rd.		
Crosstobs Rd. G53	48	P15
Crossview Av. (Bail.) G69	40	FF13
Swinton Av.		
Crossview Pl. (Bail.) G69	40	FF13
Crovie Rd. G53	48	P16
Crow Ct., The (Bishop.) G64	10	X7
Kenmure Av.		
Crow La. G13	19	R9
Crow Rd. G11	19	R10
Crow Rd. G13	19	R10
Crow Wd. Rd. (Chry.) G69	26	EE8
Crow Wd. Ter. (Chry.) G69	26	EE8
Crowflats Rd. (Udd.) G71	69	GG17
Lady Isle Cres.		
Crowhill Rd. (Bishop.) G64	22	X8
Crowhill St. G22	22	W9
Crowlin Cres. G33	38	BB12
Crown Av., Clyde. G81	5	L6
Crown Circ. G12	20	S10
Crown Rd. S.		
Crown Ct. G1	36	W12
Virginia St.		
Crown Gdns. G12	20	S10
Crown Rd. N.		
Crown Mans. G11	20	S10
North Gardner St.		
Crown Rd. N. G12	20	S10
Crown Rd. S. G12	20	S10
Crown St. G5	52	W14
Crown St. (Bail.) G69	55	DD14
Crown Ter. G12	20	S10
Crown Rd. S.		
Crownhall Pl. G32	55	CC14
Crownhall Rd. G32	39	CC13
Crownpoint Rd. G40	36	X13
Crowpoint Rd. G40	37	Y13
Alma St.		
Croy Pl. G21	23	Z9
Croy Rd.		
Croy Rd. G21	23	Z9
Cruachan Av., Renf. PA4	31	M11
Cruachan Cres., Pais. PA2	46	K16
Cruachan Dr. (Barr.) G78	59	M19
Cruachan Rd. (Ruther.) G73	65	Z18
Cruachan St. (Thorn.) G46	61	R18
Cruachan Way (Barr.) G78	59	M19
Cruden St. G51	33	R13
Crum Av. (Thorn.) G46	62	S18
Crusader Av. G13	7	Q7
Cubie St. G40	36	X13
Cuilhill Rd. (Bail.) G69	41	GG12
Cuillin Way (Barr.) G78	59	M19
Cuillins, The (Udd.) G71	56	FF15
Cuillins Rd. (Ruther.) G73	65	Z18
Culbin Dr. G13	18	N8
Cullen Pl. (Udd.) G71	57	HH16
Kingston Av.		
Cullen St. G32	54	BB14
Cullins, The (Mood.) G69	15	HH6
Culloden St. G31	37	Y12
Coventry Dr.		
Culrain Gdns. G32	38	BB13
Culrain St. G32	38	BB13
Culross La. G32	55	CC14
Culross St. G32	55	CC14
Cult Rd. (Lenzie) G66	13	DD6
Cults St. G51	33	R13
Culzean Cres. (Bail.) G69	56	EE14
Huntingtower Rd.		
Culzean Dr. G32	39	CC13
Cumberland Ct. G1	36	W13
Gallowgate		
Cumberland La. G5	51	V14
Cumberland St.		
Cumberland Pl. G5	52	W14
Cumberland Pl., Pais. PA1	46	K14
Causeyside St.		
Cumberland St. G5	35	V13
Cumbernauld Rd. G31	37	Z12
Cumbernauld Rd. G33	24	AA10
Cumbernauld Rd. (Chry.)	26	EE9
G69		
Cumbrae Ct., Clyde. G81	5	L7
Montrose St.		
Cumbrae Rd., Pais. PA2	46	K16
Cumbrae Rd., Renf. PA4	31	M11
Cumbrae St. G33	38	BB12
Cumlodden Dr. G20	20	T8
Cumming Dr. G42	51	V16
Cumnock Dr. (Barr.) G78	59	M19
Cumnock Rd. G33	24	AA9
Cunard St., Clyde. G81	17	L8
Cunningham Dr. (Giff.)	63	U18
G46		
Cunningham Dr., Clyde.	4	K5
G81		
Cunningham Rd. G52	32	N12
Cunningham Rd. (Ruther.)	53	Z16
G73		
Cunninghame Rd. (Kilb.),	42	B14
John. PA10		
Curfew Rd. G13	7	Q7
Curle St. G14	33	Q11
Curlew Pl., John. PA5	43	C16
Curling Cres. G44	52	W16
Currie St. G20	21	U9
Curtis Av. G44	52	W16
Curtis Av. (Ruther.) G73	52	W16
Curzon St. G20	21	U9
Custom Ho. Quay G1	36	W12
Cut, The (Udd.) G71	69	GG17
Cuthbert St. (Udd.) G71	57	HH16
Cuthbertson St. G42	51	V15
Cuthelton Dr. G31	54	AA14
Cuthelton St.		
Cuthelton St. G31	53	Z14
Cuthelton Ter. G31	53	Z14
Cypress Av. (Udd.) G71	57	HH16
Cypress Av. (Blan.) G72	68	FF19
Cypress Ct. (Kirk.) G66	12	BB5
Cypress St. G22	22	W9
Cyprus Av. (Elder.), John.	44	E15
PA5		
Cyprus St., Clyde. G81	17	M8
Cyril St., Pais. PA1	47	L14

D

Daer Av., Renf. PA4	32	N11
Dairsie Gdns. (Bishop.) G64	23	Z8
Dairsie St. G44	63	U18
Daisy St. G42	51	V15
Dakota Way, Renf. PA4	31	M11
Friendship Way		
Dalbeth Rd. G32	54	AA15
Dalcharn Path G34	40	EE12
Dalcharn Pl.		
Dalcharn Pl. G34	40	EE12
Dalcraig Cres. (Blan.) G72	68	FF19
Dalcross La. G11	34	T11
Byres Rd.		
Dalcross St. G11	34	T11
Dalcruin Gdns. (Mood.) G69	15	HH6
Daldowie Av. G32	55	CC14
Dale St. G40	52	X14
Dale Way (Ruther.) G73	65	Y18
Daleview Av. G12	20	S9
Dalfoil Ct., Pais. PA1	48	N14
Dalgarroch Av., Clyde. G81	18	N8
Dalgleish Av., Clyde. G81	4	K5
Dalhouse Rd. (Udd.) G71	56	EE15
Dalhousie Gdns. (Bishop.)	10	X7
G64		
Dalhousie La. G3	35	V11
Scott St.		
Dalhousie La. W. G3	35	V11
Buccleuch St.		
Dalhousie Rd. (Mill.Pk.),	42	B15
John. PA10		
Dalhousie St. G3	35	V11
Dalilea Dr. G34	40	FF11
Dalilea Path G34	40	FF11
Dalilea Dr.		
Dalilea Pl. G34	40	FF11
Dalintober St. G5	35	V13
Dalkeith Av. G41	50	S14
Dalkeith Av. (Bishop.) G64	11	Y6
Dalkeith Rd. (Bishop.) G64	11	Y6
Dalmahoy St. G32	38	AA12
Dalmally St. G20	21	U10
Dalmarnock Bri. G40	53	Y15
Dalmarnock Bri. (Ruther.)	53	Y15
G73		
Dalmarnock Ct. G40	53	Y14
Baltic St.		
Dalmarnock Rd. G40	52	X14
Dalmarnock Rd. (Ruther.)	53	Y15
G73		
Dalmary Dr., Pais. PA1	31	L13
Dalmellington Rd. G53	48	P16
Dalmeny Av. (Giff.) G46	62	T18
Dalmeny Dr. (Barr.) G78	59	L19
Dalmeny St. G5	52	X15
Dalmuir Ct., Clyde. G81	4	K6
Stewart St.		
Dalnair St. G3	34	T11
Dalness Sq. G32	54	BB14
Ochil St.		
Dalness St. G32	54	BB14
Dalreoch Av. (Bail.) G69	40	FF13
Dalriada St. G40	53	Z14
Dalry Rd. (Udd.) G71	57	HH16
Myrtle Av.		
Dalry St. G32	54	BB14
Dalserf Cres. (Giff.) G46	62	S19
Dalserf St. G31	37	Y13
Dalsetter Av. G15	6	N7
Dalsetter Pl. G15	6	P7
Dalsholm Rd. G20	20	S8
Dalskeith Av., Pais. PA3	29	H13
Dalskeith Cres., Pais. PA3	29	H13
Dalskeith Rd., Pais. PA3	45	H14
Dalswinton Pl. G34	40	FF12
Dalswinton St.		
Dalswinton St. G34	40	FF12
Dalton Av., Clyde. G81	6	N7
Dalton St. G31	38	AA13
Dalveen Av. (Udd.) G71	57	GG16
Dalveen Ct. (Barr.) G78	59	M19
Dalveen St. G32	38	AA13
Dalveen Way (Ruther.) G73	65	Z18
Dalwhinnie Av. (Blan.) G72	68	FF19

Daly Gdns. (Blan.) G72	69	GG19
Dalziel Dr. G41	50	T14
Dalziel Quad. G41	50	T14
Dalziel Dr.		
Dalziel Rd. G52	32	N12
Damshot Cres. G53	49	Q15
Damshot Rd. G53	49	Q16
Danby Rd. (Bail.) G69	55	DD14
Danes Av. G14	19	Q10
Danes Cres. G14	18	P9
Danes Dr. G14	18	P9
Danes La. N. G14	19	Q10
Upland Rd.		
Danes La. S. G14	19	Q10
Dargarvel Av. G41	50	S14
Darkwood Cres., Pais. PA3	29	H13
Darkwood Dr., Pais. PA3	29	H13
Darkwood Cres.		
Darleith St. G32	38	AA13
Darley Rd. (Cumb.) G68	70	NN1
Darnaway Av. G33	39	CC11
Darnaway Dr. G33	39	CC11
Darnaway St. G33	39	CC11
Darnick St. G21	23	Y10
Hobden St.		
Darnley Cres. (Bishop.) G64	10	X6
Darnley Gdns. G41	51	U15
Darnley Path (Thorn.) G46	61	R17
Kennisholm Av.		
Darnley Pl. G41	51	U15
Darnley Rd.		
Darnley Rd. G41	51	U15
Darnley Rd. (Barr.) G78	60	N18
Darnley St. G41	51	U15
Darroch Way (Cumb.) G67	71	PP2
Dartford St. G22	21	V10
Darvel Cres., Pais. PA1	47	M14
Darvel St. G53	60	N17
Darwin Pl., Clyde. G81	4	J6
Dava St. G51	34	S12
Davaar Rd., Pais. PA2	46	K16
Davaar Rd., Renf. PA4	31	M11
Davaar St. G40	53	Y14
Daventry Dr. G12	20	S9
David Pl. (Bail.) G69	55	DD14
David Pl., Pais. PA3	31	L12
Killarn Way		
David St. G40	37	Y13
David Way, Pais. PA3	31	L12
Killarn Way		
Davidson Gdns. G14	19	Q10
Westland Dr.		
Davidson Pl. G32	39	CC13
Davidson St. G40	53	Y15
Davidson St., Clyde. G81	18	N8
Davidston Pl. (Kirk.) G66	13	DD6
Davieland Rd. (Giff.) G46	62	S19
Daviot St. G51	33	Q13
Dawes La. N. G14	19	Q10
Upland Rd.		
Dawson Pl. G4	21	V10
Dawson Rd.		
Dawson Rd. G4	21	V10
Dealston Rd. (Barr.) G78	59	L18
Dean Pk. Dr. (Camb.) G72	67	CC18
Dean Pk. Rd., Renf. PA4	32	N11
Dean St., Clyde. G81	5	M7
Deanbrae St. (Udd.) G71	69	GG17
Deanfield Quad. G52	32	N13
Deans Av. (Camb.) G72	67	CC18
Deanside La. G4	36	W12
Rottenrow		
Deanside Rd. G52	32	P12
Deanston Dr. G41	51	U16
Deanwood Av. G44	63	U18
Deanwood Rd. G44	63	U18
Debdale Cotts. G13	19	R9
Whittingehame Dr.		
Dechmont Av. (Camb.) G72	67	CC18
Dechmont Gdns. (Udd.) G71	57	GG15
Dechmont Gdns. (Blan.) G72	68	FF19
Dechmont Pl. (Camb.) G72	67	CC18
Dechmont Rd. (Udd.) G71	57	GG15
Dechmont St. G31	53	Z14
Dechmont Vw. (Udd.) G71	57	HH16
Hamilton Vw.		

Dee Av., Pais. PA2	45	G15
Dee Av., Renf. PA4	18	N10
Dee Dr., Pais. PA2	45	G15
Dee Pl., John. PA5	43	C16
Dee St. G33	37	Z11
Deepdene Rd. (Bears.) G61	7	Q7
Deepdene Rd. (Chry.) G69	15	HH7
Delburn St. G31	53	Z14
Delhi Av., Clyde. G81	4	J6
Delny Pl. G33	39	DD12
Delvin Rd. G44	63	V17
Denbeck St. G32	38	AA13
Denbrae St. G32	38	AA13
Dene Wk. (Bishop.) G64	23	Z8
Denewood Av., Pais. PA2	46	J16
Denham St. G22	21	V10
Denholme Dr. (Giff.) G46	62	T19
Denkenny Sq. G15	6	N6
Denmark St. G22	22	W10
Denmilne Path G34	40	FF12
Denmilne Pl. G34	40	FF12
Denmilne Rd. (Bail.) G69	40	FF12
Denmilne St. G34	40	FF12
Derby St. G3	35	U12
Derby Ter. La. G3	35	U12
Derby St.		
Derwent St. G22	21	V10
Despard Av. G32	55	DD14
Despard Gdns. G32	55	DD14
Deveron Av. (Giff.) G46	62	T19
Deveron Rd. (Bears.) G61	7	Q7
Deveron St. G33	37	Z11
Devol Cres. G53	48	P16
Devon Gdns. G12	20	S10
Hyndland Rd.		
Devon Gdns. (Bishop.) G64	10	X6
Devon Pl. G41	51	V14
Devon St. G5	51	V14
Devondale Av. (Blan.) G72	68	FF19
Devonshire Gdns. G12	20	S10
Devonshire Gdns. La. G12	20	S10
Hyndland Rd.		
Devonshire Ter. G12	20	S10
Devonshire Ter. La. G12	20	S10
Hughenden Rd.		
Dewar Clo. (Udd.) G71	57	HH15
Diana Av. G13	18	P8
Dick St. G20	21	U10
Henderson St.		
Dickens Av., Clyde. G81	4	K6
Dilwara Av. G14	33	R11
Dimity St., John. PA5	43	D15
Dinard Dr. (Giff.) G46	62	T18
Dinart St. G33	37	Z11
Dinduff St. G34	40	FF11
Dingwall St. G3	34	T12
Kelvinhaugh St.		
Dinmont Pl. G41	51	U15
Norham St.		
Dinmont Rd. G41	50	T15
Dinwiddie St. G21	37	Z11
Dipple Pl. G15	6	P7
Dirleton Av. G41	51	U16
Dirleton Dr., Pais. PA2	45	H15
Dirleton Gate (Bears.) G61	7	Q7
Dixon Av. G42	51	V15
Dixon Rd. G42	52	W15
Dixon St. G1	35	V13
Dixon St., Pais. PA1	46	K14
Dobbies Ln. G4	35	V11
Dobbies Ln. Pl. G4	36	W12
Dochart Av., Renf. PA4	32	N11
Dochart St. G33	38	AA11
Dock St., Clyde. G81	17	M8
Dodhill Pl. G13	18	P9
Dodside Gdns. G32	55	CC14
Dodside Pl. G32	55	CC14
Dodside St. G32	55	CC14
Dolan St. (Bail.) G69	40	EE13
Dollar Ter. G20	20	T8
Crosbie St.		
Dolphin Rd. G41	50	T15
Don Av., Renf. PA4	32	N11
Don Dr., Pais. PA2	45	G15
Don Pl., John. PA5	43	C16
Don St. G33	37	Z12
Donald Way (Udd.) G71	57	HH16
Donaldson Dr., Renf. PA4	17	M10
Ferguson St.		

Donaldson Grn. (Udd.)	57	HH16
G71		
Donaldswood Pk., Pais.	46	J16
PA2		
Donaldswood Rd., Pais.	46	J16
PA2		
Doncaster St. G20	21	V10
Doon Cres. (Bears.) G61	7	Q6
Doon Side (Cumb.) G67	71	PP3
Doon St., Clyde. G81	5	M6
Doonfoot Rd. G43	62	T17
Dora St. G40	53	Y14
Dorchester Av. G12	20	S9
Dorchester Ct. G12	20	S9
Dorchester Av.		
Dorchester Pl. G12	20	S9
Dorlin Rd. G33	25	DD9
Dormanside Ct. G53	48	P14
Dormanside Gate G53	48	P14
Dormanside Gro. G53	48	P14
Dormanside Rd. G53	48	P14
Dornal Av. G13	18	N8
Dornford Av. G32	55	CC15
Dornford Rd. G32	55	CC15
Dornie Dr. G32	55	CC16
Dornie Dr. (Thorn.) G46	61	R18
Dornoch Av. (Giff.) G46	62	T19
Dornoch Pl. (Bishop.) G64	11	Z7
Dornoch Pl. (Chry.) G69	14	FF7
Dornoch Rd. (Bears.) G61	7	Q7
Dornoch St. G40	36	X13
Dornoch Way (Cumb.) G68	71	PP1
Dorset Sq. G3	35	U12
Dorset St.		
Dorset St. G3	35	U12
Dosk Av. G13	18	N8
Dosk Pl. G13	18	N8
Dougalston Rd. G23	9	U7
Douglas Av. G32	54	BB15
Douglas Av. (Giff.) G46	62	T19
Douglas Av. (Lenzie) G66	13	CC5
Douglas Av. (Ruther.) G73	65	Z17
Douglas Av. (Elder.), John.	44	E15
PA5		
Douglas Ct. (Lenzie) G66	13	CC5
Douglas Cres. (Udd.) G71	57	HH16
Douglas Dr. G15	6	N7
Douglas Dr. (Bail.) G69	39	DD13
Douglas Dr. (Both.) G71	69	HH19
Douglas Dr. (Camb.) G72	66	AA17
Douglas Gdns. (Giff.) G46	62	T19
Douglas Gdns. (Bears.) G61	7	R6
Douglas Gdns. (Lenzie)	13	CC5
G66		
Douglas Gdns. (Udd.) G71	69	GG17
Douglas La. G2	35	V12
West George St.		
Douglas Pk. Cres. (Bears.)	8	S5
G61		
Douglas Pl. (Bears.) G61	7	R5
Douglas Pl. (Kirk.) G66	13	CC5
Douglas Av.		
Douglas Rd., Renf. PA4	31	L12
Douglas St. G2	35	V12
Douglas St. (Udd.) G71	57	HH16
Douglas St., Pais. PA1	30	J13
Douglas Ter. G41	51	U15
Glencairn Dr.		
Douglas Ter., Pais. PA3	30	K11
Dougray Pl. (Barr.) G78	59	M19
Dougrie Dr. G45	64	W18
Dougrie Pl. G45	64	X18
Dougrie Rd. G45	64	W19
Dougrie St. G45	64	X18
Dougrie Ter. G45	64	W18
Doune Cres. (Bishop.) G64	11	Y6
Doune Gdns. G20	21	U10
Doune Quad. G20	21	U10
Dove St. G53	60	P17
Dovecot G43	50	T16
Shawhill Rd.		
Dovecothall St. (Barr.) G78	59	M18
Dover St. G3	35	U12
Dowanfield Rd. (Cumb.)	70	NN3
G67		
Dowanhill Pl. G11	34	T11
Old Dumbarton Rd.		
Dowanhill St. G11	34	T11
Dowanhill St. G12	34	T11

Street	Page	Grid
Dowanside La. G12	20	T10
Byres Rd.		
Dowanside Rd. G12	20	T10
Dowanvale Ter. G11	34	S11
White St.		
Downcraig Dr. G45	64	W19
Downcraig Gro. G45	64	W19
Downcraig Rd. G45	64	W19
Downcraig Ter. G45	64	W19
Downfield Gdns. (Both.) G71	69	GG19
Downfield St. G32	54	AA14
Downie Clo. (Udd.) G71	57	HH16
Downiebrae Rd. (Ruther.) G73	53	Y15
Downs St. G21	22	X10
Dowrie Cres. G53	48	P15
Dows Pl. G4	21	V10
Possil Rd.		
Drainie St. G34	40	EE12
Westerhouse Rd.		
Drake St. G40	36	X13
Drakemire Av. G45	64	W18
Drakemire Dr. G44	64	W18
Drakemire Dr. G45	64	W18
Dreghorn St. G31	37	Z12
Drem Pl. G11	34	S11
Merkland St.		
Drimnin Rd. G33	25	DD9
Drive Rd. G51	33	R12
Drochil St. G34	40	EE11
Drumbeg Dr. G53	60	P17
Drumbeg Pl. G53	60	P17
Drumbottie Rd. G21	23	Y9
Drumby Cres. (Clark.) G76	62	T19
Drumcavel Rd. (Muir.) G69	26	FF8
Drumchapel Gdns. G15	6	P7
Drumchapel Pl. G15	6	P7
Drumchapel Rd. G15	6	P7
Drumclog Gdns. G33	24	AA9
Drumcross Rd. G53	49	Q15
Drumhead Pl. G32	54	AA15
Drumhead Rd. G32	54	AA15
Drumilaw Rd. (Ruther.) G73	65	Y17
Drumilaw Way (Ruther.) G73	65	Y17
Drumlaken Av. G23	8	T7
Drumlaken Ct. G23	8	T7
Drumlaken St. G23	8	T7
Drumlanrig Av. G34	40	FF11
Drumlanrig Pl. G34	40	FF11
Drumlanrig Quad. G34	40	FF11
Drumlochy Rd. G33	38	BB11
Drummond Av. (Ruther.) G73	52	X16
Drummond Dr., Pais. PA1	47	M14
Drummond Gdns. G13	19	R9
Crow Rd.		
Drummore Rd. G15	6	P5
Drumover Dr. G31	54	AA14
Drumoyne Av. G51	33	R12
Drumoyne Circ. G51	33	R13
Drumoyne Dr. G51	33	R12
Drumoyne Pl. G51	33	R13
Drumoyne Circ.		
Drumoyne Quad. G51	33	R13
Drumoyne Rd. G51	33	R13
Drumoyne Sq. G51	33	R12
Drumpark St. (Thorn.) G46	61	R18
Drumpark St., Coat. ML5	57	HH14
Dunnachie Dr.		
Drumpellier Av. (Bail.) G69	56	EE14
Drumpellier Pl. (Bail.) G69	56	EE14
Drumpellier Rd. (Bail.) G69	56	EE14
Drumpellier St. G33	37	Z11
Drumreoch Dr. G42	52	X16
Drumreoch Pl. G42	52	X16
Drumry Pl. G15	6	N7
Drumry Rd., Clyde. G81	5	L6
Drumry Rd. E. G15	5	M7
Drums Av., Pais. PA3	29	H13
Drums Cres., Pais. PA3	30	J13
Drums Rd. G53	48	P14
Drumsack Av. (Chry.) G69	26	FF8
Drumsargard Rd. (Ruther.) G73	65	Z17
Drumshaw Dr. G32	55	CC16
Drumvale Dr. (Chry.) G69	15	GG7
Drury St. G2	35	V12
Dryad St. (Thorn.) G46	61	R17
Dryborough Av., Pais. PA2	45	H15
Dryburgh Av. (Ruther.) G73	53	Y16
Dryburgh Gdns. G20	21	U10
Dryburgh Rd. (Bears.) G61	7	Q5
Dryburgh Wk. (Mood.) G69	15	HH6
Dryburn Av. G52	32	P13
Drygate G4	36	X12
Drygrange Rd. G33	39	CC11
Drymen Pl. (Lenzie) G66	13	CC6
Drymen Rd. (Bears.) G61	7	Q5
Drymen St. G52	33	R13
Morven St.		
Drymen Wynd (Bears.) G61	7	R6
Drynoch Pl. G22	21	V8
Drysdale St. G14	18	N9
Duart Dr. (Elder.), John. PA5	44	E15
Duart St. G20	20	T8
Dubs Rd. (Barr.) G78	60	N18
Dubton Path G34	40	EE11
Dubton St. G34	40	EE11
Duchall Pl. G14	18	P10
Duchess Pl. (Ruther.) G73	53	Z16
Duchess Rd. (Ruther.) G73	53	Z15
Duchess Way (Bail.) G69	41	GG13
Park Rd.		
Duchray Dr., Pais. PA1	48	N14
Duchray La. G33	37	Z11
Duchray St.		
Duchray St. G33	37	Z11
Dudhope St. G33	39	CC11
Dudley Dr. G12	20	S10
Dudley La. G12	20	S10
Clarence Dr.		
Duffus Pl. G32	55	CC16
Duffus St. G34	40	EE11
Duffus Ter. G32	55	CC16
Duich Gdns. G23	9	U7
Duisdale Rd. G32	55	CC16
Duke St. G4	36	X12
Duke St. G31	36	X12
Duke St., Pais. PA2	46	K15
Duke St. (Linw.), Pais. PA3	28	F13
Dukes Gate (Both.) G71	69	GG18
Dukes Rd. (Bail.) G69	41	GG13
Dukes Rd. (Camb.) G72	65	Z17
Dukes Rd. (Ruther.) G73	65	Z17
Dulnain St. (Camb.) G72	67	DD17
Dulsie Rd. G21	23	Z9
Dumbarton Rd. G11	34	S11
Dumbarton Rd. G14	18	N9
Dumbarton Rd. (Old Kil.) G60	4	J6
Dumbarton Rd., Clyde. G81	4	J6
Dumbarton Rd. (Dunt.), Clyde. G81	4	K5
Dumbreck Av. G41	50	S14
Dumbreck Ct. G41	50	S14
Dumbreck Pl. (Kirk.) G66	13	DD6
Dumbreck Rd. G41	50	S14
Dumbreck Sq. G41	50	S14
Dumbreck Av.		
Dunagoil Rd. G45	64	W19
Dunagoil St. G45	64	X19
Dunagoil Ter. G45	64	X19
Dunalistair Dr. G33	24	BB9
Dunan Pl. G33	39	DD11
Dunard Rd. (Ruther.) G73	53	Y16
Dunard St. G20	21	U10
Dunard Way, Pais. PA3	30	J12
Mosslands Rd.		
Dunaskin St. G11	34	T11
Dunbar Av. (Ruther.) G73	53	Z16
Dunbar Av., John. PA5	43	D16
Dunbar Rd., Pais. PA2	45	H15
Dunbeith Pl. G20	20	T9
Dunblane St. G4	35	V11
Dunbrach Rd. (Cumb.) G68	70	MM2
Duncan Av. G14	19	Q10
Duncan La. G14	19	Q10
Duncan Av.		
Duncan La. N. G14	19	Q10
Ormiston Av.		
Duncan La. S. G14	19	Q10
Duncan Av.		
Duncan St., Clyde. G81	5	L6
Duncansby Rd. G33	39	CC13
Dunchattan Pl. G31	36	X12
Duke St.		
Dunchattan St. G31	36	X12
Dunchurch Rd., Pais. PA1	31	M13
Dunclutha Dr. (Both.) G71	69	HH19
Dunclutha St. G40	53	Y15
Duncombe St. G20	20	T8
Duncombe Vw., Clyde. G81	5	M6
Kirkoswald Dr.		
Duncraig Cres., John. PA5	43	C16
Duncrub Dr. (Bishop.) G64	10	X7
Duncruin St. G20	20	T8
Duncryne Av. G32	55	CC14
Duncryne Gdns. G32	55	DD14
Duncryne Pl. (Bishop.) G64	22	X8
Dundas La. G1	36	W12
Dundas St. G1	36	W12
Dundasvale Ct. G4	35	V11
Maitland St.		
Dundasvale Rd. G4	35	V11
Maitland St.		
Dundee Dr. G52	48	P14
Dundee Path G52	49	Q14
Dundee Dr.		
Dundonald Av., John. PA5	43	C15
Dundonald Rd. G12	20	T10
Dundonald Rd., Pais. PA3	31	L12
Dundrennan Rd. G42	51	U16
Dunearn Pl., Pais. PA2	47	L14
Dunearn St. G4	35	U11
Dunellan St. G52	33	R13
Dungeonhill Rd. G34	40	FF12
Dunglass Av. G14	19	Q10
Dunglass La. G14	19	Q10
Dunglass Av.		
Dunglass La. N. G14	19	Q10
Verona Av.		
Dunglass La. S. G14	19	Q10
Dunglass Av.		
Dungoil Av. (Cumb.) G68	70	LL2
Dungoil Rd. (Lenzie) G66	13	DD6
Dungoyne St. G20	20	T8
Dunira St. G32	54	AA14
Dunivaig St. G33	39	DD12
Dunkeld Av. (Ruther.) G73	53	Y16
Dunkeld Dr. (Bears.) G61	8	S6
Dunkeld Gdns. (Bishop.) G64	11	Y7
Dunkeld La. (Chry.) G69	15	HH7
Burnbrae Av.		
Dunkeld St. G31	53	Z14
Dunkenny Pl. G15	6	N6
Dunkenny Rd. G15	6	N6
Dunkenny Sq. G15	6	N6
Dunlop Cres. (Both.) G71	69	HH19
Dunlop Cres., Renf. PA4	17	M10
Fulbar St.		
Dunlop Gro. (Udd.) G71	57	HH15
Dunlop St. G1	36	W13
Dunlop St. (Camb.) G72	67	DD17
Dunlop St. (Linw.), Pais. PA3	28	F13
Dunlop St., Renf. PA4	17	M10
Fulbar St.		
Dunmore La. G5	35	V13
Norfolk St.		
Dunmore St. G5	35	V13
Dunmore St., Clyde. G81	17	M8
Dunn St. G40	53	Y14
Dunn St., Clyde. G81	4	K6
Dunn St. (Dunt.), Clyde. G81	4	K5
Dunn St., Pais. PA1	47	L14
Dunnachie Dr., Coat. ML5	57	HH14
Dunnichen Pl. (Bishop.) G64	11	Z7
Dunning St. G31	53	Z14
Dunolly St. G21	37	Y11
Dunottar St. G33	38	BB11
Dunottar St. (Bishop.) G64	11	Z7
Dunphail Dr. G34	40	FF12
Dunphail Rd. G34	40	FF12
Dunragit St. G31	37	Z12
Dunrobin Av. (Elder.), John. PA5	44	F15
Dunrobin St. G31	37	Y13
Dunrod St. G32	54	BB14
Dunside Dr. G53	60	P17
Dunskaith Pl. G34	40	FF12
Dunskaith St. G34	40	FF12

Name	Map	Ref
Dunsmuir St. G51	34	S12
Dunster Gdns. (Bishop.) G64	11	Y6
Dunswin Av., Clyde. G81	4	K6
Dunswin Ct., Clyde. G81	4	K6
Dunswin Av.		
Dunsyre Pl. G23	9	U7
Dunsyre St. G33	38	AA12
Duntarvie Cres. G34	40	FF12
Duntarvie Dr. G34	40	EE12
Duntarvie Pl. G34	40	EE12
Duntarvie Quad. G34	40	FF12
Duntarvie Rd. G34	40	EE12
Dunterle Ct. (Barr.) G78	59	M18
Dunterlie Av. G13	18	P9
Duntiglennan Rd., Clyde. G81	5	L5
Duntocher Rd. (Bears.) G61	6	P5
Duntocher Rd., Clyde. G81	4	K6
Duntocher Rd. (Dunt.), Clyde. G81	5	L5
Duntocher St. G21	22	X10
Northcroft Rd.		
Duntreath Av. G13	18	N8
Duntreath Av. G15	18	N8
Duntreath Dr. G15	6	N7
Duntreath Gdns. G15	6	N7
Duntreath Gro. G15	6	N7
Duntroon St. G31	37	Y12
Dunure Dr. (Ruther.) G73	64	X17
Dunure St. G20	20	T8
Dunvegan Av. (Elder.), John. PA5	44	F15
Dunvegan Ct. G13	18	P9
Kintillo Dr.		
Dunvegan Dr. (Bishop.) G64	11	Y6
Dunvegan Quad., Renf. PA4	17	L10
Kirklandneuk Rd.		
Dunwan Av. G13	18	N8
Dunwan Pl. G13	18	N8
Durban Av., Clyde. G81	4	J6
Durham St. G41	34	T13
Durness Av. (Bears.) G61	8	S5
Durno Path G33	39	DD12
Duror St. G32	38	BB13
Durris Gdns. G32	55	CC14
Durrockstock Cres., Pais. PA2	45	G16
Durrockstock Rd., Pais. PA2	45	G16
Durward Av. G41	50	T15
Durward Cres., Pais. PA2	45	G15
Durwood Ct. G41	50	T15
Duthil St. G51	33	Q13
Dyce La. G11	34	S11
Dyers La. G1	36	W13
Turnbull St.		
Dyers Wynd, Pais. PA1	30	K13
Gilmour St.		
Dyke Pl. G13	18	P8
Dyke Rd. G13	18	N9
Dyke Rd. G14	18	N9
Dyke St. (Bail.) G69	40	FF13
Dykebar Av. G13	18	P9
Dykebar Cres., Pais. PA2	47	L15
Dykefoot Dr. G53	49	Q16
Dykehead La. G33	39	CC12
Dykehead Rd. (Bail.) G69	41	GG13
Dykehead St. G33	39	CC12
Dykemuir Pl. G21	23	Y10
Dykemuir Quad. G21	23	Y10
Dykemuir St.		
Dykemuir St. G21	23	Y10

E

Name	Map	Ref
Eagle Cres. (Bears.) G61	6	P5
Eagle St. G4	36	W11
Eaglesham Ct. G51	35	U13
Blackburn St.		
Eaglesham Pl. G51	35	U13
Earl Haig Rd. G52	32	N12
Earl La. G14	19	Q10
Harland St.		
Earl Pl. G14	19	Q10
Earl St. G14	18	P10
Earlbank Av. G14	19	Q10
Earlbank La. N. G14	19	Q10
Dunglass Av.		
Earlbank La. S. G14	19	Q10
Verona Av.		
Earls Ct. (Mood.) G69	15	GG7
Longdale Rd.		
Earls Gate (Both.) G71	69	GG18
Earls Hill (Cumb.) G68	70	LL2
Earlsburn Rd. (Lenzie) G66	13	DD6
Earlspark Av. G43	51	U16
Earn Av. (Bears.) G61	8	S6
Earn Av., Renf. PA4	32	N11
Almond Av.		
Earn St. G33	38	AA11
Earnock St. G33	23	Z10
Earnside St. G32	38	BB13
Easdale Dr. G32	54	BB14
East Av., Renf. PA4	17	M10
East Barns St., Clyde. G81	17	M8
East Bath La. G2	35	V12
Sauchiehall St.		
East Buchanan St., Pais. PA1	30	K13
East Campbell St. G1	36	X13
East Greenlees Av. (Camb.) G72	67	CC18
East Greenlees Cres. (Camb.) G72	66	BB18
East Greenlees Dr. (Camb.) G72	66	BB18
East Greenlees Gro. (Camb.) G72	66	BB18
East Greenlees Rd. (Camb.) G72	66	BB18
East Hallhill Rd. (Bail.) G69	40	EE13
East Kilbride Expressway (Camb.) G72	66	BB19
East Kilbride Rd. (Ruther.) G73	65	Z17
East La., Pais. PA1	47	L14
East Reid St. (Ruther.) G73	53	Z16
East Rd. (Kilb.), John. PA10	42	B14
East Springfield Ter. (Bishop.) G64	23	Y8
East Thomson St., Clyde. G81	5	L6
East Wellington St. G31	37	Z13
East Whitby St. G31	53	Z14
Eastburn Rd. G21	23	Y9
Eastcote Av. G14	19	R10
Eastcroft (Ruther.) G73	53	Y16
Eastcroft Ter. G21	23	Y10
Easter Av. (Udd.) G71	69	GG17
Easter Garngaber Rd. (Lenzie) G66	13	DD5
Easter Ms. (Udd.) G71	69	GG17
Church St.		
Easter Queenslie Rd. G33	39	DD12
Eastercraigs G31	37	Y12
Easterhill Pl. G32	54	AA14
Easterhill St. G32	54	AA14
Easterhouse Path G34	40	FF12
Easterhouse Pl. G34	40	FF12
Easterhouse Quad. G34	40	FF12
Easterhouse Rd. G34	40	FF12
Easterhouse Rd. (Bail.) G69	40	FF12
Eastfield Av. (Camb.) G72	66	AA17
Eastfield Rd. G21	22	X10
Eastfield Rd. (Cumb.) G68	70	MM2
Eastgate (Gart.) G69	27	HH9
Easthall Pl. G33	39	DD12
Eastmuir St. G32	38	BB13
Eastvale Pl. G3	34	T12
Eastwood Av. G41	50	T16
Eastwood Av. (Giff.) G46	62	T19
Eastwood Ct. (Thorn.) G46	61	R18
Main St.		
Eastwood Cres. (Thorn.) G46	61	R18
Eastwood Rd. (Chry.) G69	15	GG7
Eastwood Vw. (Camb.) G72	67	DD17
Eastwoodmains Rd. (Giff.) G46	62	S19
Eastwoodmains Rd. (Clark.) G76	62	S19
Easwald Bk. (Mill.Pk.), John. PA10	42	B15
Eccles St. G22	22	X9
Eckford St. G32	54	BB14
Eday St. G22	22	W9
Edderton Pl. G34	40	EE12
Eddleston Pl. (Camb.) G72	67	DD17
Eddlewood Path G33	39	DD12
Eddlewood Pl. G33	39	DD12
Eddlewood Rd. G33	39	DD12
Edelweiss Ter. G11	34	S11
Gardner St.		
Eden La. G33	37	Z11
Eden Pk. (Both.) G71	69	GG19
Eden Pl. (Camb.) G72	67	CC17
Eden Pl., Renf. PA4	32	N11
Eden St. G33	37	Z11
Edenwood St. G31	38	AA13
Edgam Dr. G52	33	Q13
Edgefauld Av. G21	22	X10
Edgefauld Dr. G21	22	X10
Edgefauld Pl. G21	22	X9
Balgrayhill Rd.		
Edgefauld Rd. G21	22	X10
Edgehill La. G11	20	S10
Marlborough Av.		
Edgehill Rd. G11	20	S10
Edgehill Rd. (Bears.) G61	7	R5
Edgemont St. G41	51	U16
Edinbeg Av. G42	52	X16
Edinbeg Pl. G42	52	X16
Edinburgh Rd. G33	37	Z12
Edinburgh Rd. (Bail.) G69	39	DD12
Edington Gdns. (Chry.) G69	15	GG6
Edington St. G4	35	V11
Edison St. G52	32	N12
Edmiston Dr. G51	33	R13
Edmiston Dr. (Linw.), Pais. PA3	28	E13
Edmiston St. G31	53	Z14
Edmondstone Ct., Clyde. G81	17	M8
Yokerburn Ter.		
Edrom Path G32	38	AA13
Edrom St.		
Edrom St. G32	38	AA13
Edward Av., Renf. PA4	18	N10
Edward St. G3	34	T12
Lumsden St.		
Edward St. (Bail.) G69	41	GG14
Edward St., Clyde. G81	17	M8
Edwin St. G51	34	T13
Edzell Ct. G14	33	Q11
Edzell Dr. (Elder.), John. PA5	44	F15
Edzell Gdns. (Bishop.) G64	23	Z8
Edzell Pl. G14	33	Q11
Edzell St. G14	33	Q11
Egidia Av. (Giff.) G46	62	S19
Egilsay Cres. G22	22	W8
Egilsay Pl. G22	22	W8
Egilsay St. G22	22	W8
Egilsay Ter. G22	22	W8
Eglinton Ct. G5	35	V13
Eglinton Dr. (Giff.) G46	62	T19
Eglinton La. G5	51	V14
Eglinton St.		
Eglinton St. G5	51	V14
Eighth St. (Udd.) G71	57	GG15
Eildon Dr. (Barr.) G78	59	M19
Eileen Gdns. (Bishop.) G64	11	Y7
Elba La. G31	37	Z13
Elcho St. G40	36	X13
Elder Gro. (Udd.) G71	57	HH16
Elder St. G51	33	R12
Elderbank (Bears.) G61	7	R6
Elderpark Gdns. G51	33	R12
Elderpark Gro. G51	33	R12
Elderpark St. G51	33	R12
Elderslie St. G3	35	U11
Eldin Pl. (Elder.), John. PA5	44	E15
Eldon Gdns. (Bishop.) G64	10	X7
Eldon St. G3	35	U11
Eldon Ter. G11	34	S11
Caird Dr.		
Elgin St. G40	37	Y13
Elibank St. G33	38	BB11
Elie St. G11	34	T11
Elizabeth Cres. (Thorn.) G46	62	S18
Elizabeth St. G51	34	T13
Elizabethan Way, Renf. PA4	31	M11
Cockels Ln.		
Ellangowan Rd. G41	50	T16
Ellergreen Rd. (Bears.) G61	7	R6

Ellerslie St., John. PA5 44 E14
Ellesmere St. G22 21 V10
Ellinger Ct., Clyde. G81 4 K6
Scott St.
Elliot Av. (Giff.) G46 62 T19
Elliot Av., Pais. PA2 45 G16
Elliot Dr. (Giff.) G46 62 T18
Elliot La. G3 35 U12
Elliot St.
Elliot Pl. G3 35 U12
Elliot St. G3 35 U12
Ellisland Av., Clyde. G81 5 M6
Ellisland Cres. (Ruther.) 64 X17
G73
Ellisland Rd. G43 62 T17
Ellisland Rd. (Cumb.) G67 71 PP3
Ellismuir Fm. Rd. (Bail.) 56 FF14
G69
Ellismuir Pl. (Bail.) G69 56 FF14
Ellismuir Rd. (Bail.) G69 56 FF14
Elliston Av. G53 61 Q17
Elliston Cres. G53 61 Q17
Elliston Dr. G53 61 Q17
Elliston Pl. G53 61 Q17
Ravenscraig Dr.
Ellon Dr. (Linw.), Pais. PA3 28 E13
Elm Av. (Lenzie) G66 13 CC5
Elm Av., Renf. PA4 17 M10
Elm Bk. (Bishop.) G64 11 Y7
Elm Dr., John. PA5 43 D16
Elm Gdns. (Bears.) G61 7 R5
Elm La. E. G14 19 Q10
Elm St.
Elm La. W. G14 19 Q10
Elm St.
Elm Rd. (Ruther.) G73 65 Y18
Elm Rd., Clyde. G81 5 L5
Elm Rd., Pais. PA2 47 L15
Elm St. G14 19 Q10
Elm Wk. (Bears.) G61 7 R5
Elmbank Av. (Udd.) G71 57 HH16
Elmbank Cres. G2 35 V12
Elmbank St.
Elmbank La. G3 35 U12
North St.
Elmbank St. G2 35 V12
Elmbank St. La. G2 35 V12
Elmbank St.
Elmfoot St. G5 52 W15
Elmira Rd. (Muir.) G69 26 FF8
Elmore Av. G44 63 V17
Elmore La. G44 63 V17
Elmslie Ct. (Bail.) G69 56 EE14
Elmvale Row G21 22 X10
Elmvale Row E. G21 22 X10
Elmvale Row
Elmvale Row W. G21 22 X10
Elmvale Row
Elmvale St. G21 22 X9
Elmwood Av. G11 19 R10
Elmwood Ct. (Both.) G71 69 HH19
Blantyre Mill Rd.
Elmwood Gdns. G11 19 R10
Randolph Rd.
Elmwood Gdns. (Kirk.) 12 BB5
G66
Elmwood La. G11 19 R10
Elmwood Av.
Elmwood Ter. G11 19 R10
Crow Rd.
Elphin St. G23 8 T7
Invershiel Rd.
Elphinstone Pl. G51 34 T12
Elrig Rd. G44 63 V17
Elspeth Gdns. (Bishop.) 11 Y7
G64
Eltham St. G22 21 V10
Elvan Ct. G32 38 AA13
Edrom St.
Elvan St. G32 38 AA13
Embo Dr. G13 18 P9
Emerson Rd. (Bishop.) G64 11 Y7
Emerson St. G20 21 V9
Emily Pl. G31 36 X13
Endfield Av. G12 20 S9
Endrick Bk. (Bishop.) G64 11 Y6
Endrick Dr. (Bears.) G61 7 R6
Endrick Dr., Pais. PA1 31 L13
Endrick St. G21 22 W10

Endsleigh Gdns. G11 20 S10
Partickhill Rd.
Ensay St. G22 22 W8
Enterkin St. G32 54 AA14
Ericht Rd. G43 62 T17
Eriska Av. G14 18 P9
Erradale St. G22 21 V8
Erriboll Pl. G22 21 V8
Erriboll St. G22 21 V8
Errogie St. G34 40 EE12
Errol Gdns. G5 52 W14
Erskine Av. G41 50 S14
Erskine Sq. G52 32 N12
Erskine Vw., Clyde. G81 5 L6
Singer St.
Erskinefauld Rd. (Linw.), 28 E13
Pais. PA3
Ervie St. G34 40 FF12
Esk Av., Renf. PA4 32 N11
Esk Dr., Pais. PA2 45 G15
Esk St. G14 18 N9
Esk Way, Pais. PA2 45 G15
Eskbank St. G32 38 BB13
Eskdale Dr. (Ruther.) G73 53 Z16
Eskdale (Bears.) G61 7 Q7
Eskdale St. G42 51 V15
Esmond St. G3 34 T11
Espedair St., Pais. PA2 46 K14
Essenside Av. G15 7 Q7
Essex Dr. G14 19 R10
Essex La. G14 19 R10
Esslemont Av. G14 18 P9
Estate Quad. G32 55 CC16
Estate Rd. G32 55 CC16
Etive Av. (Bears.) G61 8 S6
Etive Cres. (Bishop.) G64 11 Y7
Etive Ct., Clyde. G81 5 M5
Etive Dr. (Giff.) G46 62 T19
Etive St. G32 38 BB13
Eton Gdns. G12 35 U11
Oakfield Av.
Eton La. G12 35 U11
Great George St.
Eton Pl. G12 35 U11
Oakfield Av.
Eton Ter. G12 35 U11
Oakfield Av.
Ettrick Av., Renf. PA4 32 N11
Ettrick Ct. (Camb.) G72 67 DD18
Gateside Av.
Ettrick Cres. (Ruther.) G73 53 Z16
Ettrick Oval, Pais. PA2 45 G16
Ettrick Pl. G43 50 T16
Ettrick Ter., John. PA5 43 C16
Ettrick Way, Renf. PA4 32 N11
Evan Cres. (Giff.) G46 62 T19
Evan Dr. (Giff.) G46 62 T19
Evanton Dr. (Thorn.) G46 61 R18
Evanton Pl. (Thorn.) G46 61 R18
Evanton Dr.
Everard Ct. G21 22 X8
Everard Dr. G21 22 X8
Everard Pl. G21 22 X8
Everard Quad. G21 22 X8
Everglades, The (Chry.) 26 EE8
G69
Eversley St. G32 54 BB14
Everton Rd. G53 49 Q15
Ewart Pl. G3 34 T12
Kelvinhaugh St.
Ewing St. G31 37 Z13
Ewing St. (Ruther.) G73 53 Y16
Ewing St. (Kilb.), John. 42 B14
PA10
Exchange Pl. G1 36 W12
Buchanan St.
Exeter Dr. G11 34 S11
Exeter La. G11 34 S11
Exeter Dr.
Exhibition Way G3 35 U12
Eynort St. G22 21 V8

F

Fagan Ct. (Blan.) G72 69 GG19
Faifley Rd., Clyde. G81 5 L5
Fairbairn Cres. (Thorn.) G46 62 S19
Fairbairn Path G40 53 Y14
Ruby St.

Fairbairn St. G40 53 Y14
Dalmarnock Rd.
Fairburn St. G32 54 AA14
Fairfax Av. G44 64 W17
Fairfield Gdns. G51 33 R12
Fairfield Pl. G51 33 R12
Fairfield Pl. (Both.) G71 69 HH19
Fairfield St. G51 33 R12
Fairhaven Dr. G23 20 T8
Fairhill Av. G53 49 Q16
Fairholm St. G32 54 AA14
Fairley St. G51 34 S13
Fairlie Pk. Dr. G11 34 S11
Fairway Av., Pais. PA2 46 J16
Fairways (Bears.) G61 6 P5
Fairways Vw., Clyde. G81 5 M5
Fairyknowe Gdns. (Both.) 69 HH19
G71
Falcon Cres., Pais. PA3 29 H13
Falcon Rd., John. PA5 43 C16
Falcon Ter. G20 20 T8
Falcon Ter. La. G20 20 T8
Falfield St. G5 51 V14
Falkland Cres. (Bishop.) 23 Z8
G64
Falkland La. G12 20 S10
Clarence Dr.
Falkland Mans. G12 20 S10
Clarence Dr.
Falkland St. G12 20 S10
Falloch Rd. G42 51 V16
Falloch Rd. (Bears.) G61 7 Q7
Fallside Rd. (Both.) G71 69 HH19
Falside Av., Pais. PA2 46 K15
Falside Rd. G32 54 BB14
Falside Rd., Pais. PA2 46 J15
Fara St. G23 21 U8
Farie St. (Ruther.) G73 53 Y16
Farm Ct. (Both.) G71 69 HH18
Farm La. (Udd.) G71 69 HH17
Myers Cres.
Farm Pk. (Lenzie) G66 13 CC6
Farm Rd. G41 50 S14
Farm Rd. (Blan.) G72 68 FF19
Farm Rd. (Dalmuir), Clyde. 4 J6
G81
Farm Rd. (Dunt.), Clyde. 5 L5
G81
Farme Cross (Ruther.) G73 53 Y15
Farmeloan Rd. (Ruther.) 53 Y16
G73
Farmington Av. G32 39 CC13
Farmington Gdns. G32 39 CC13
Farmington Gate G32 39 CC13
Farmington Gro. G32 39 CC13
Farne Dr. G44 63 V18
Farnell St. G4 35 V11
Farrier Ct., John. PA5 43 D14
Faskally Av. (Bishop.) G64 10 X6
Faskin Cres. G53 48 N16
Faskin Pl. G53 48 N16
Faskin Rd. G53 48 N16
Fasque Pl. G15 6 N6
Fastnet St. G33 38 BB12
Fauldhouse St. G5 52 W14
Faulds (Bail.) G69 40 FF13
Faulds Gdns. (Bail.) G69 40 FF13
Fauldshead Rd., Renf. PA4 17 M10
Fauldspark Cres. (Bail.) G69 40 FF13
Fauldswood Cres., Pais. 45 H15
PA2
Fauldswood Dr., Pais. PA2 45 H15
Fearnmore Rd. G20 20 T8
Felton Pl. G13 18 N8
Fendoch St. G32 54 BB14
Fenella St. G32 38 BB13
Fennsbank Av. (Ruther.) 65 Z18
G73
Fenwick Dr. (Barr.) G78 59 M19
Fenwick Pl. (Giff.) G46 62 S19
Fenwick Rd. (Giff.) G46 62 T18
Fereneze Av. (Barr.) G78 59 L18
Fereneze Av., Renf. PA4 31 L12
Fereneze Cres. G13 18 P8
Fereneze Dr., Pais. PA2 46 J16
Fereneze Rd. (Barr.) G78 58 J19
Fergus Av., Pais. PA3 29 H13
Westburn Av.
Fergus Ct. G20 21 U10

111

Fergus Dr. G20 — 21 U10
Fergus Dr., Pais. PA3 — 29 H13
Woodvale Dr.
Ferguslie, Pais. PA1 — 45 H14
Ferguslie Pk. Av., Pais. PA3 — 29 H13
Ferguslie Pk. Cres., Pais. PA3 — 45 H14
Ferguslie Pk. Av.
Ferguslie Wk., Pais. PA1 — 45 H14
Ferguson Av., Renf. PA4 — 17 M10
Ferguson St., John. PA5 — 43 D14
Ferguson St., Renf. PA4 — 17 M10
Fergusson Rd. (Cumb.) G67 70 NN3
Ferguston Rd. (Bears.) G61 — 7 R6
Fern Av. (Bishop.) G64 — 23 Y8
Fern Av. (Lenzie) G66 — 13 CC5
Fern Dr. (Barr.) G78 — 59 L18
Fern La. G13 — 19 R9
Whittinghame Dr.
Fernan St. G32 — 38 AA13
Fernbank Av. (Camb.) G72 — 67 CC18
Fernbank St. G21 — 22 X9
Fernbank St. G22 — 22 X9
Fernbrae Rd. (Ruther.) G73 65 Z18
Fernbrae Way (Ruther.) — 65 Y18
G73
Ferncroft Dr. G44 — 64 W17
Ferndale Ct. G23 — 20 T8
Ferndale Dr. G23 — 20 T8
Ferndale Gdns. G23 — 20 T8
Ferndale Pl. G23 — 20 T8
Ferness Oval G21 — 23 Z8
Ferness Pl. G21 — 23 Z8
Ferness Rd. G21 — 23 Z9
Ferngrove Av. G12 — 20 S9
Fernhill Gra. (Both.) G71 69 HH19
Fernhill Rd. (Ruther.) G73 65 Y18
Fernie Gdns. G20 — 21 U8
Fernlea (Bears.) G61 — 7 R6
Fernleigh Pl. (Chry.) G69 15 GG7
Fernleigh Rd. G43 — 62 T17
Ferry Rd. G3 — 34 S12
Ferry Rd. (Both.) G71 69 HH19
Ferry Rd. (Udd.) G71 68 FF17
Ferry Rd., Renf. PA4 — 17 M10
Ferry Vw. Cres. G14 — 18 N9
Ferryden St. G14 — 33 R11
Fersit St. G43 — 62 T17
Fetlar Dr. G44 — 64 W17
Fettercairn Av. G15 — 6 N6
Fettercairn Gdns. (Bishop.) 11 Z7
G64
Fettes St. G33 — 38 AA12
Fidra St. G33 — 38 AA12
Fielden Pl. G40 — 37 Y13
Fielden St. G40 — 37 Y13
Fieldhead Dr. G43 — 62 S17
Fieldhead Sq. G43 — 62 S17
Fife Av. G52 — 48 P14
Fife Cres. (Both.) G71 69 HH19
Fife Way (Bishop.) G64 — 23 Z8
Fifth Av. G12 — 19 R9
Fifth Av. (Stepps) G33 — 24 BB9
Fourth Av.
Fifth Av. (Kirk.) G66 — 13 CC7
Fifth Av., Renf. PA4 — 31 M11
Finch Dr. G13 — 18 N8
Finch Pl., John. PA5 — 43 C16
Findhorn Av., Pais. PA2 45 G15
Findhorn Av., Renf. PA4 — 18 N10
Findhorn St. G33 — 37 Z12
Findochty St. G33 — 39 CC11
Fingal La. G20 — 20 T8
Fingal St.
Fingal St. G20 — 20 T8
Fingask St. G32 — 55 CC14
Finglas Av., Pais. PA2 — 47 L15
Fingleton Av. (Barr.) G78 59 M19
Finhaven St. G32 — 54 AA14
Finlarig St. G34 — 40 FF12
Finlas St. G22 — 22 W10
Finlay Dr. G31 — 37 Y12
Finnart Dr., Pais. PA2 — 47 L15
Finnart Sq. G40 — 52 X14
Finnart St. G40 — 52 X14
Finnieston Pl. G3 — 35 U12
Finnieston St.
Finnieston Sq. G3 — 35 U12
Houldsworth St.

Finnieston St. G3 — 35 U12
Finsbay St. G51 — 33 R13
Fintry Av., Pais. PA2 — 46 K16
Fintry Cres. (Bishop.) G64 11 Z7
Fintry Cres. (Barr.) G78 59 M19
Fintry Dr. G44 — 52 W16
Fir Pl. (Bail.) G69 — 56 EE14
Fir Pl. (Camb.) G72 — 67 CC17
Caledonian Circuit
Fir Pl., John. PA5 — 44 E15
Firbank Ter. (Barr.) G78 — 60 N19
Firdon Cres. G15 — 6 P7
Firhill Rd. G20 — 21 V10
Firhill St. G20 — 21 V10
Firpark Pl. G31 — 36 X12
Firpark St.
Firpark Rd. (Bishop.) G64 23 Y8
Firpark St. G31 — 36 X12
Firpark Ter. G31 — 36 X12
Ark La.
First Av. (Millerston) G33 24 BB10
First Av. G44 — 63 U19
First Av. (Bears.) G61 — 8 S6
First Av. (Kirk.) G66 — 13 CC7
First Av. (Udd.) G71 — 57 GG16
First Gdns. G41 — 50 S14
First St. (Udd.) G71 — 57 GG16
First Ter., Clyde. G81 — 5 L6
Firwood Dr. G44 — 64 W17
Fischer Gdns., Pais. PA1 29 G13
Fisher Av., Pais. PA1 — 45 G14
Fisher Ct. G31 — 36 X12
Fisher Cres., Clyde. G81 — 5 L5
Fisher Dr., Pais. PA1 — 45 G14
Fisher Way, Pais. PA1 — 45 G14
Fisher Dr.
Fishers Rd., Renf. PA4 — 17 M9
Fishescoates Av. (Ruther.) 65 Z18
G73
Fishescoates Gdns. — 65 Z17
(Ruther.) G73
Fishescoates Rd.
Fishescoates Rd. (Ruther.) 65 Z17
G73
Fitzalan Dr., Pais. PA3 — 31 L13
Fitzalan Rd., Renf. PA4 — 31 L11
Fitzroy La. G3 — 35 U12
North Claremont St.
Fitzroy Pl. G3 — 35 U12
North Claremont St.
Flax Rd. (Udd.) G71 — 69 HH17
Fleet Av., Renf. PA4 — 32 N11
Fleet St. G32 — 54 BB14
Fleming Av. (Chry.) G69 26 FF8
Fleming Av., Clyde. G81 — 17 M8
Fleming Rd. (Cumb.) G67 70 NN3
Fleming St. G31 — 37 Y13
Fleming St., Pais. PA3 — 30 K12
Flemington Rd. (Camb.) 67 DD19
G72
Flemington St. G21 — 22 X10
Fleurs Av. G41 — 50 S14
Fleurs Rd. G41 — 50 S14
Floors St., John. PA5 — 43 D15
Floorsburn Cres., John. — 43 D15
PA5
Flora Gdns. (Bishop.) G64 11 Z7
Florence Dr. (Giff.) G46 62 T19
Florence Gdns. (Ruther.) 65 Z18
G73
Florence St. G5 — 36 W13
Florentine Pl. G12 — 35 U11
Gibson St.
Florentine Ter. G12 — 35 U11
Southpark Av.
Florida Av. G42 — 51 V16
Florida Cres. G42 — 51 V16
Florida Dr. G42 — 51 V16
Florida Gdns. (Bail.) G69 40 EE13
Florida Sq. G42 — 51 V16
Florida St. G42 — 51 V16
Flowerdale Pl. G53 — 60 P19
Waukglen Dr.
Flures Av., Ersk. PA8 — 16 K8
Flures Cres., Ersk. PA8 — 16 K8
Flures Dr., Ersk. PA8 — 16 K8
Flures Pl., Ersk. PA8 — 16 K8
Fochabers Dr. G52 — 33 Q13

Fogo Pl. G20 — 20 T9
Forbes Dr. G40 — 36 X13
Forbes Pl., Pais. PA1 — 46 K14
Forbes St. G40 — 36 X13
Ford Rd. G12 — 20 T10
Fordneuk St. G40 — 37 Y13
Fordoun St. G34 — 40 FF12
Fordyce St. G11 — 34 S11
Fore St. G14 — 19 Q10
Forehouse Rd. (Kilb.), — 42 A14
John. PA10
Foremount Ter. La. G12 — 20 T10
Hyndland Rd.
Forest Dr. (Both.) G71 — 69 HH18
Forest Gdns. (Kirk.) G66 12 BB6
Forest Pl. (Kirk.) G66 — 12 BB6
Forest Pl., Pais. PA2 — 46 K15
Brodie Pk. Av.
Forest Rd. (Cumb.) G67 71 QQ3
Forest Vw. (Cumb.) G67 71 QQ2
Foresthall Cres. G21 — 23 Y10
Foresthall Dr. G21 — 23 Y10
Forfar Av. G52 — 48 P14
Forfar Cres. (Bishop.) G64 23 Z8
Forgan Gdns. (Bishop.) G64 23 Z8
Forge, The (Giff.) G46 — 62 T18
Braidpark Dr.
Forge Pl. G21 — 37 Y11
Forge St. G21 — 37 Y11
Forglen St. G34 — 40 EE11
Formby Dr. G23 — 8 T7
Forres Av. (Giff.) G46 — 62 T18
Forres Gate (Giff.) G46 — 62 T19
Forres Av.
Forres St. G23 — 9 U7
Tolsta St.
Forrest Gate (Udd.) G71 57 HH15
Forrest St. G40 — 37 Y13
Forrester Ct. (Bishop.) G64 22 X8
Crowhill Rd.
Forrestfield St. G21 — 37 Y11
Forteviot Av. (Bail.) G69 40 FF13
Forteviot Pl. (Bail.) G69 40 FF13
Forth Av., Pais. PA2 — 45 G15
Forth Pl., John. PA5 — 43 C16
Forth Rd. (Bears.) G61 — 7 Q7
Forth St. G41 — 51 U14
Forth St., Clyde. G81 — 17 M8
Forties Cres. (Thorn.) G46 61 R17
Forties Way (Thorn.) G46 62 S17
Fortingall Av. G12 — 20 T9
Grandtully Dr.
Fortingall Pl. G12 — 20 T9
Fortrose St. G11 — 34 S11
Foswell Pl. G15 — 6 N5
Fotheringay La. G41 — 51 U15
Beaton Rd.
Fotheringay Rd. G41 — 50 T15
Foulis La. G13 — 19 R9
Herschell St.
Foulis St. G13 — 19 R9
Herschell St.
Foundary St. G21 — 22 X10
Foundry La. (Barr.) G78 59 L19
Main St.
Fountain Cres. (Inch.), — 16 J9
Renf. PA4
Fountain Dr. (Inch.), Renf. 16 J9
PA4
Fountain St. G31 — 36 X13
Fountainwell Av. G21 — 36 W11
Fountainwell Dr. G21 — 36 W11
Fountainwell Pl. G21 — 36 W11
Fountainwell Rd. G21 — 36 W11
Fountainwell Sq. G21 — 36 X11
Fountainwell Ter. G21 — 36 X11
Fourth Av. G33 — 24 BB9
Fourth Av. (Kirk.) G66 — 13 CC7
Fourth Av., Renf. PA4 — 31 M11
Third Av.
Fourth Gdns. G41 — 50 S14
Fourth St. (Udd.) G71 — 57 GG13
Fox La. G1 — 36 W13
Fox St. G1 — 35 V13
Foxbar Cres., Pais. PA2 45 G16
Foxbar Dr. G13 — 18 P9
Foxbar Dr., Pais. PA2 — 45 G16
Foxbar Rd. (Elder.), John. 45 G16
PA5

Street	Page	Grid
Foxbar Rd., Pais. PA2	45	G16
Foxes Gro. (Lenzie) G66	13	DD5
Foxglove Pl. G53	60	P18
Foxhills Pl. G23	9	U7
Foxley St. G32	55	CC15
Foyers Ct. G13	18	P9
Kirkton Av.		
Foyers Ter. G21	23	Y10
Francis St. G5	51	V14
Frankfield Rd. G33	25	DD9
Frankfield St. G33	37	Z11
Frankfort St. G41	51	U15
Franklin St. G40	52	X14
Fraser Av. (Ruther.) G73	53	Z16
Fraser Av., John. PA5	44	E15
Fraser St. (Camb.) G72	66	AA17
Fraserbank St. G21	22	W10
Keppochhill Rd.		
Frazer St. G40	37	Y13
Freeland Ct. G53	60	P17
Freeland Dr. G53	60	P17
Freeland Dr. (Inch.), Renf. PA4	16	J9
Freelands Ct. (Old Kil.) G60	4	J5
Freelands Pl. (Old Kil.) G60	4	J6
Freelands Rd. (Old Kil.) G60	4	J5
French St. G40	52	X14
French St., Clyde. G81	4	K6
French St., Renf. PA4	31	L11
Freuchie St. G34	40	EE12
Friar Av. (Bishop.) G64	11	Y6
Friars Ct. Rd. (Chry.) G69	14	EE7
Friars Pl. G13	19	Q8
Friarscourt Av. G13	7	Q7
Friarscourt La. G13	19	Q8
Arrowsmith Av.		
Friarton Rd. G43	63	U17
Friendship Way, Renf. PA4	31	M11
Fruin Pl. G22	22	W10
Fruin Rd. G15	6	N7
Fruin St. G22	22	W10
Fulbar Av., Renf. PA4	17	M10
Fulbar Ct., Renf. PA4	17	M10
Fulbar Av.		
Fulbar Cres., Pais. PA2	45	G15
Fulbar Gdns., Pais. PA2	45	G15
Peacock Dr.		
Fulbar La., Renf. PA4	17	M10
Fulbar Rd. G51	33	Q12
Fulbar Rd., Pais. PA2	45	G15
Fulbar St., Renf. PA4	17	M10
Fullarton Av. G32	54	BB15
Fullarton La. G32	54	BB15
Fullarton Rd. G32	54	AA16
Fullarton Rd. (Cumb.) G68	70	NN1
Fullerton St., Pais. PA3	30	J12
Fullerton Ter., Pais. PA3	30	K12
Fulmar Ct. (Bishop.) G64	22	X8
Fulmar Pl., John. PA5	43	C16
Fulton Cres. (Kilb.), John. PA10	42	B14
Fulton St. G13	19	Q8
Fulwood Av. G13	18	N8
Fulwood Av. (Linw.), Pais. PA3	28	E13
Fulwood Pl. G13	18	N8
Fyvie Av. G43	62	S17

G

Street	Page	Grid
Gadie Av., Renf. PA4	32	N11
Gadie St. G33	37	Z12
Gadloch Av. (Kirk.) G66	13	CC7
Gadloch Gdns. (Kirk.) G66	13	CC6
Gadloch St. G22	22	W9
Gadloch Vw. (Kirk.) G66	13	CC7
Gadsburn Ct. G21	23	Z9
Wallacewell Quad.		
Gadshill St. G21	36	X11
Gailes Pk. (Both.) G71	69	GG19
Gailes Rd. (Cumb.) G68	70	NN1
Gailes St. G40	53	Y14
Gairbraid Av. G20	20	T9
Gairbraid Ct. G20	20	T9
Gairbraid Pl. G20	20	T9
Gairbraid Ter. (Bail.) G69	41	HH13
Gairn St. G11	34	S11
Castlebank St.		
Gala Av., Renf. PA4	32	N11
Gala St. G33	38	AA11
Galbraith Av. G51	33	R12
Burghead Dr.		
Galbraith St. G51	33	Q12
Moss Rd.		
Galdenoch St. G33	38	BB11
Gallacher Av., Pais. PA2	45	H15
Gallan Av. G23	9	U7
Galloway Dr. (Ruther.) G73	65	Y18
Galloway St. G21	22	X9
Gallowflat St. (Ruther.) G73	53	Y16
Reid St.		
Gallowgate G1	36	W13
Gallowgate G4	36	W13
Gallowgate G31	37	Y13
Gallowgate G40	37	Y13
Gallowhill Av. (Lenzie) G66	13	CC5
Gallowhill Gro. (Kirk.) G66	13	CC5
Gallowhill Rd. (Kirk.) G66	13	CC5
Gallowhill Rd., Pais. PA3	30	K13
Galston St. G53	60	N17
Gamrie Dr. G53	48	P16
Gamrie Gdns. G53	48	P16
Gamrie Rd. G53	48	P16
Gannochy Dr. (Bishop.) G64	11	Z7
Gantock Cres. G33	38	BB12
Gardenside Av. G32	54	BB16
Gardenside Av. (Udd.) G71	69	GG17
Gardenside Cres. G32	54	BB16
Gardenside Gro. G32	54	BB16
Gardenside Pl. G32	54	BB16
Gardenside St. (Udd.) G71	69	GG17
Gardner Gro. (Udd.) G71	57	HH16
Gardner La. (Bail.) G69	56	FF14
Church St.		
Gardner St. G11	34	S11
Gardyne St. G34	40	EE11
Garfield St. G31	37	Y13
Garforth Rd. (Bail.) G69	55	DD14
Gargrave Av. (Bail.) G69	55	DD14
Garion Dr. G13	18	P9
Talbot Dr.		
Garlieston Rd. G33	39	DD13
Garmouth Ct. G51	33	R12
Garmouth St.		
Garmouth Gdns. G51	33	R12
Garmouth St. G51	33	R12
Garnet La. G3	35	V11
Garnet St.		
Garnet St. G3	35	V11
Garnethill St. G3	35	V11
Garngaber Av. (Lenzie) G66	13	CC5
Garngaber Ct. (Kirk.) G66	13	DD5
Woodilee Rd.		
Garnie Av., Ersk. PA8	4	J7
Garnie Cres., Ersk. PA8	4	J7
Garnie La., Ersk. PA8	4	J7
Garnie Oval, Ersk. PA8	4	J7
Garnie Pl., Ersk. PA8	4	J7
Garnieland Rd., Ersk. PA8	4	J7
Garnkirk La. G33	25	DD9
Garnkirk St. G21	36	X11
Garnock St. G21	36	X11
Garrell Way (Cumb.) G67	70	NN3
Garrioch Cres. G20	20	T9
Garrioch Dr. G20	20	T9
Garrioch Gate G20	20	T9
Garrioch Quad. G20	20	T9
Garrioch Rd. G20	20	T10
Garriochmill Rd. G20	21	U10
Raeberry St.		
Garriochmill Way G20	21	U10
Woodside Rd.		
Garrowhill Dr. (Bail.) G69	55	DD14
Garry Av. (Bears.) G61	8	S7
Garry Dr., Pais. PA2	45	H15
Garry St. G44	51	V16
Garscadden Rd. G15	6	P7
Garscadden Rd. S. G13	18	P8
Garscadden Vw., Clyde. G81	5	M6
Kirkoswald Dr.		
Garscube Cross G4	35	V11
Garscube Mill (Bears.) G61	8	S7
Maryhill Rd.		
Garscube Rd. G4	21	V10
Garscube Rd. G20	21	V10
Gartartan Rd., Pais. PA1	32	N13
Gartcarron Hill (Cumb.) G68	70	MM2
Dunbrach Rd.		
Gartconnell Dr. (Bears.) G61	7	R5
Gartconnell Gdns. (Bears.) G61	7	R5
Gartconnell Rd. (Bears.) G61	7	R5
Gartcosh Rd. (Gart.) G69	41	HH12
Gartcraig Path G33	38	AA11
Gartcraig Pl.		
Gartcraig Pl. G33	38	AA11
Gartcraig Rd. G33	38	AA12
Gartferry Av. (Chry.) G69	15	GG7
Gartferry Rd. (Mood.) G69	15	GG7
Gartferry St. G21	23	Y10
Garth St. G1	36	W12
Garthamlock Rd. G33	39	DD11
Garthland Dr. G31	37	Y12
Garthland La., Pais. PA1	30	K13
Gartliston Ter. (Bail.) G69	41	HH13
Gartloch Cotts. (Gart.) G69	27	GG10
Gartloch Cotts. (Muir.) G69	26	EE9
Gartloch Rd. G33	38	AA11
Gartloch Rd. G34	39	CC11
Gartloch Rd. (Gart.) G69	26	EE10
Gartly St. G44	63	U18
Clarkston Rd.		
Gartmore Gdns. (Udd.) G71	57	GG16
Gartmore La. (Chry.) G69	15	HH7
Gartmore Rd., Pais. PA1	47	L14
Gartmore Ter. (Camb.) G72	66	AA18
Gartness St. G31	37	Y12
Gartocher Dr. G32	39	CC13
Gartocher Rd. G32	39	CC13
Gartochmill Rd. G20	21	U10
Gartons Rd. G21	23	Z10
Gartshore Rd. (Kirk.) G66	15	GG5
Gartshore Rd. (Chry.) G69	15	GG5
Garturk St. G42	51	V15
Garvald Ct. G40	53	Y14
Baltic St.		
Garvald St. G40	53	Y14
Garve Av. G44	63	V18
Garvel Cres. G33	39	DD13
Garvel Rd. G33	39	DD13
Garvock Dr. G43	62	S17
Gas St., John. PA5	44	E14
Gask Pl. G13	18	N8
Gaskin Path G33	25	DD9
Clayhouse Rd.		
Gatehouse St. G32	38	BB13
Gateside Av. (Camb.) G72	67	CC17
Gateside Cres. (Barr.) G78	59	L19
Gateside Pl. (Kilb.), John. PA10	42	B14
Gateside Rd. (Barr.) G78	59	L19
Gateside St. G31	37	Y13
Gauldry Av. G52	49	Q14
Gauze St., Pais. PA1	30	K13
Gavins Rd., Clyde. G81	5	L5
Gavinton St. G44	63	U18
Gear Ter. G40	53	Y15
Geary St. G23	8	T7
Torrin Rd.		
Geddes Rd. G21	23	Z8
Gelston St. G32	54	BB14
General Terminus Quay G51	35	U13
Generals Gate (Udd.) G71	69	GG17
Cobblerigg Way		
Gentle Row, Clyde. G81	4	K5
George Av., Clyde. G81	5	M6
Robert Burns Av.		
George Cres., Clyde. G81	5	M6
George Gray St. (Ruther.) G73	53	Z16
George La., Pais. PA1	46	K14
George St.		
George Mann Ter. (Ruther.) G73	65	Y17
George Pl., Pais. PA1	46	K14
George Reith Av. G12	19	R9
George Sq. G2	36	W12
George St. G1	36	W12
George St. (Bail.) G69	56	EE14
George St. (Barr.) G78	59	L18
George St., John. PA5	43	D14
George St., Pais. PA1	46	J14
Gertrude Pl. (Barr.) G78	59	L19
Gibb St. G21	36	X11
Royston Rd.		

Gibson Cres., John. PA5 43 D15
Gibson Rd., Renf. PA4 31 L11
Gibson St. G12 34 T11
Gibson St. G40 36 X13
Giffnock Pk. Av. (Giff.) G46 62 T18
Gifford Dr. G52 32 P13
Gifford Wynd, Pais. PA2 45 G15
Gilbert St. G3 34 T12
Gilbertfield Pl. G33 38 BB11
Gilbertfield Rd. (Camb.) 67 CC18
G72
Gilbertfield St. G33 38 BB11
Gilfillan Way, Pais. PA2 45 G16
Gilhill St. G20 20 T8
Gilia St. (Camb.) G72 66 AA17
Gillies La. (Bail.) G69 56 FF14
Bredisholm Rd.
Gilmerton St. G32 54 BB14
Gilmour Av., Clyde. G81 5 L5
Gilmour Cres. (Ruther.) 52 X16
G73
Gilmour Pl. G5 52 W14
Gilmour St., Clyde. G81 5 M6
Gilmour St., Pais. PA1 30 K13
Girthon St. G32 55 CC14
Girvan St. G33 37 Z11
Gladney Av. G13 18 N8
Gladsmuir Rd. G52 32 P13
Gladstone Av. (Barr.) G78 59 L19
Gladstone Av., John. PA5 43 C16
Gladstone St. G4 35 V11
Glaive Rd. G13 7 Q7
Glamis Av. (Elder.), John. 44 E15
PA5
Glamis Gdns. (Bishop.) G64 11 Y6
Glamis Pl. G31 53 Z14
Glamis Rd.
Glamis Rd. G31 53 Z14
Glanderston Av. (Barr.) 60 N19
G78
Glanderston Dr. G13 18 P8
Glaselune St. G34 40 FF12
Lochdochart Rd.
Glasgow Airport (Abbots.), 30 J11
Pais. PA3
Glasgow Bri. G1 35 V13
Glasgow Bri. G5 35 V13
Glasgow Grn. G1 36 W13
Glasgow Grn. G40 36 W13
Glasgow Rd. G53 60 N18
Glasgow Rd. (Cumb.) G67 70 MM4
Glasgow Rd. (Cumb.V.) 71 PP2
G67
Glasgow Rd. (Bail.) G69 55 DD14
Glasgow Rd. (Udd.) G71 56 FF16
Glasgow Rd. (Blan.) G72 68 FF19
Glasgow Rd. (Camb.) G72 54 AA16
Glasgow Rd. (Turnlaw) G72 66 AA16
Glasgow Rd. (Ruther.) G73 52 X15
Glasgow Rd. (Barr.) G78 59 M18
Glasgow Rd., Clyde. G81 17 L8
Glasgow Rd. (Hardgate), 5 L5
Clyde. G81
Glasgow Rd., Pais. PA1 31 L13
Glasgow Rd., Renf. PA4 18 N10
Glasgow St. G12 21 U10
Glassel Rd. G34 40 FF11
Glasserton Pl. G43 63 U17
Glasserton Rd. G43 63 U17
Glassford St. G1 36 W12
Glebe, The (Both.) G71 69 HH19
Glebe Av. (Both.) G71 69 HH19
Green St.
Glebe Ct. G4 36 W12
Glebe Hollow (Both.) G71 69 HH19
Glebe Wynd
Glebe Pl. (Camb.) G72 66 BB17
Glebe Pl. (Ruther.) G73 52 X16
Glebe St. G4 36 W11
Glebe St., Renf. PA4 17 M10
Glebe Wynd (Both.) G71 69 HH19
Gleddoch Rd. G52 32 N13
Glen Affric Av. G53 61 Q18
Glen Affric Dr. G53 61 Q18
Glen Affric Pl. G53 61 Q18
Glen Alby Pl. G53 61 Q18
Glen Av. G32 38 BB13
Glen Av. (Chry.) G69 15 GG7
Glen Clunie Av. G53 61 Q18

Glen Clunie Dr. G53 61 Q18
Glen Clunie Pl. G53 61 Q18
Glen Cona Dr. G53 61 Q17
Glen Cres. G13 18 N8
Glen Douglas Dr. (Cumb.) 70 MM2
G68
Glen Esk Cres. G53 61 Q18
Glen Esk Dr. G53 61 Q18
Glen Etive Pl. (Ruther.) G73 66 AA19
Glen Fyne Rd. (Cumb.) G68 70 LL2
Glen Gdns. (Elder.), John. 44 F14
PA5
Glen La., Pais. PA3 30 K13
Glen Lednock Dr. (Cumb.) 70 MM2
G68
Glen Livet Pl. G53 61 Q18
Glen Loy Pl. G53 61 Q18
Glen Mallie Dr. G53 61 Q18
Glen Markie Dr. G53 61 Q18
Glen Moriston Rd. G53 61 Q18
Glen Nevis Pl. (Ruther.) G73 65 Q19
Glen Ogle St. G32 55 CC14
Glen Orchy Dr. G53 61 Q18
Glen Orchy Pl. G53 61 Q18
Glen Pk. Av. (Thorn.) G46 61 R19
Glen Rd. G32 38 BB12
Glen Sax Dr., Renf. PA4 32 N11
Glen St. (Camb.) G72 67 CC18
Glen St. (Barr.) G78 59 M18
Glen St., Pais. PA3 30 J13
Glen Vw. (Cumb.) G67 71 QQ2
Glenacre Cres. (Udd.) G71 57 GG16
Glenacre Dr. G45 64 W18
Glenacre Quad. G45 64 W18
Glenacre Rd. (Cumb.) G67 70 NN4
Glenacre St. G45 64 W18
Glenacre Ter. G45 64 W18
Glenallan Way, Pais. PA2 45 G16
Glenalmond Rd. (Ruther.) 65 Z18
G73
Glenalmond St. G32 54 BB14
Glenapp Av., Pais. PA2 47 L15
Glenapp Pl. (Mood.) G69 15 GG6
Whithorn Cres.
Glenapp Rd., Pais. PA2 47 L15
Glenapp St. G41 51 U14
Glenarklet Dr., Pais. PA2 47 L15
Glenartney Row (Chry.) 14 FF7
G69
Glenashdale Way, Pais. 47 L15
PA2
Glenbrittle Dr.
Glenavon Av. (Ruther.) G73 65 Z18
Glenavon Rd. G20 20 T8
Thornton St.
Glenavon Ter. G11 34 S11
Crow Rd.
Glenbank Av. (Lenzie) G66 13 CC6
Glenbank Dr. (Thorn.) G46 61 R19
Glenbank Rd. (Lenzie) G66 13 CC6
Glenbarr St. G21 36 X11
Glenbervie Cres. (Cumb.) 70 NN2
G68
Glenbervie Pl. G23 8 T7
Glenbrittle Dr., Pais. PA2 47 L15
Glenbrittle Way, Pais. PA2 47 L15
Glenbuck Av. G33 24 AA9
Glenbuck Dr. G33 24 AA9
Glenburn Av. (Bail.) G69 40 FF13
Glenburn Av. (Chry.) G69 15 GG7
Glenburn Av. (Camb.) G72 65 Z17
Glenburn Cres., Pais. PA2 46 J16
Glenburn Gdns. (Bishop.) 10 X7
G64
Glenburn La. G20 21 U8
Thornton St.
Glenburn Rd. (Giff.) G46 62 S19
Glenburn Rd. (Bears.) G61 7 Q5
Glenburn Rd., Pais. PA2 45 H16
Glenburn St. G20 21 U8
Glenburnie Pl. G34 40 EE12
Glencairn Dr. G41 50 T15
Glencairn Dr. (Chry.) G69 15 GG7
Glencairn Dr. (Ruther.) G73 52 X16
Glencairn Gdns. G41 51 U15
Glencairn Dr.
Glencairn La. G41 51 U15
Shields Rd.
Glencairn Rd. (Cumb.) G67 71 QQ3

Glencairn Rd., Pais. PA3 31 L12
Glencally Av., Pais. PA2 47 L15
Glencart Gro. (Mill.Pk.), 43 C15
John. PA10
Milliken Pk. Rd.
Glenclora Dr., Pais. PA2 47 L15
Glencloy St. G20 20 T8
Glencoats Cres., Pais. PA3 29 H13
Glencoats Dr., Pais. PA3 29 H13
Glencoe Pl. G13 19 R8
Glencoe Rd. (Ruther.) G73 65 Z18
Glencoe St. G13 19 R8
Glencorse Rd., Pais. PA2 46 J15
Glencorse St. G32 38 AA12
Glencroft Av. (Udd.) G71 57 GG16
Glencroft Rd. G44 64 W17
Glencryan Rd. (Cumb.) G67 71 PP4
Glendale Cres. (Bishop.) 23 Z8
G64
Glendale Dr. (Bishop.) G64 23 Z8
Glendale Pl. G31 37 Y13
Glendale St.
Glendale Pl. (Bishop.) G64 23 Z8
Glendale St. G31 37 Y13
Glendaruel Av. (Bears.) G61 8 S6
Glendaruel Rd. (Ruther.) 66 AA19
G73
Glendarvel Gdns. G22 22 W10
Glendee Gdns., Renf. PA4 31 M11
Glendee Rd., Renf. PA4 31 M11
Glendenning Rd. G13 7 R7
Glendevon Pl., Clyde. G81 4 K6
Glendevon Sq. G33 38 BB11
Glendore St. G14 33 R11
Glendower Way, Pais. PA2 45 G16
Spencer Dr.
Glenduffhill Rd. (Bail.) G69 39 DD13
Gleneagles Av. (Cumb.) 71 PP1
G67
Gleneagles Cotts. G14 19 Q10
Dumbarton Rd.
Gleneagles Dr. (Bishop.) 11 Y6
G64
Gleneagles Gdns. (Bishop.) 11 Y6
G64
Gleneagles La. N. G14 19 Q10
Dunglass Av.
Gleneagles La. S. G14 19 Q10
Harland St.
Gleneagles Pk. (Both.) G71 69 GG19
Gleneagles Ter. G14 19 Q10
Dumbarton Rd.
Glenelg Quad. G34 40 FF11
Glenfarg Cres. (Bears.) G61 8 S6
Glenfarg Rd. (Ruther.) G73 65 Y18
Glenfarg St. G20 35 V11
Glenfield Cres., Pais. PA2 58 J17
Glenfield Rd., Pais. PA2 46 J16
Glenfinnan Dr. G20 20 T9
Glenfinnan Dr. (Bears.) G61 8 T6
Glenfinnan Pl. G20 20 T9
Glenfinnan Rd. G20 20 T9
Glenfruin Dr., Pais. PA2 47 L15
Glengarry Dr. G52 33 Q13
Glengavel Cres. G33 24 AA9
Glengyre St. G34 40 FF11
Glenhead Cres. G22 22 W9
Glenhead Rd. (Lenzie) G66 13 CC6
Glenhead Rd., Clyde. G81 5 L5
Glenhead St. G22 22 W9
Glenholme, Pais. PA2 45 H15
Glenhove Rd. (Cumb.) G67 71 PP3
Gleniffer Av. G13 18 P9
Gleniffer Cres. (Elder.), 44 F15
John. PA5
Gleniffer Dr. (Barr.) G78 59 L17
Gleniffer Rd., Pais. PA2 45 H16
Gleniffer Rd., Renf. PA4 31 L11
Gleniffer Vw., Clyde. G81 5 M6
Kirkoswald Dr.
Glenisa Av. (Chry.) G69 15 HH6
Glenisla St. G31 53 Z14
Glenkirk Dr. G15 6 P7
Glenlee Cres. G52 48 N14
Glenlora Dr. G53 48 P16
Glenlora Ter. G53 48 P16
Glenluce Dr. G32 55 CC14
Glenluce Gdns. (Mood.) G69 15 HH6
Brady Cres.

116

Heathcliffe Av. (Blan.) G72 68 FF19
Heathcot Av. G15 6 N7
Heathcot Pl. G15 6 N7
Heathcot Av.
Heather Av. (Barr.) G78 59 L17
Heather Dr. (Kirk.) G66 12 BB6
Heather Gdns. (Kirk.) G66 12 BB6
Heather Pl. (Kirk.) G66 12 BB5
Heather Pl., John. PA5 44 E15
Heather St. G41 35 U13
Scotland St.
Heatherbrae (Bishop.) G64 10 X7
Heatheryknowe Rd. (Bail.) 41 GG12
G69
Heathfield Av. (Mood.) G69 15 GG7
Heathfield St. G33 39 CC12
Heathfield Ter. G21 22 X9
Broomfield Rd.
Heathside Rd. (Giff.) G46 62 T18
Heathwood Dr. (Thorn.) 62 S18
G46
Hecla Av. G15 6 N6
Hecla Pl. G15 6 N6
Hecla Sq. G15 6 N7
Hector Rd. G41 50 T16
Heddle Pl. G2 35 V12
Cadogan St.
Heggie Ter. G14 19 Q10
Dumbarton Rd.
Helen St. G51 34 S12
Helen St. G52 33 R13
Helensburgh Dr. G13 19 Q9
Helenslea (Camb.) G72 67 CC18
Helenvale Ct. G31 37 Z13
Helenvale St.
Helenvale St. G31 53 Z14
Helmsdale Av. (Blan.) G72 68 FF18
Helmsdale Ct. (Camb.) G72 67 CC17
Hemlock St. G13 19 R8
Henderson Rd. (Bears.) 7 R7
G61
Henderson Av. (Camb.) 67 CC17
G72
Henderson St. G20 21 U10
Henderson St., Clyde. G81 18 N8
Henderson St., Pais. PA1 30 J13
Henrietta St. G14 19 Q10
Henry St. (Barr.) G78 59 L18
Hepburn Rd. G52 32 P12
Herald Av. G13 7 Q7
Herald Way, Renf. PA4 31 M11
Viscount Av.
Herbert St. G20 21 U10
Herbertson St. G5 35 V13
Eglinton St.
Hercla Av. G15 6 N6
Hercla Pl. G15 6 N6
Hercla Sq. G15 6 N7
Hercules Way, Renf. PA4 31 M11
Friendship Way
Heriot Av., Pais. PA2 45 G16
Heriot Cres. (Bishop.) G64 11 Y6
Heriot Rd. (Lenzie) G66 13 CC6
Herma St. G23 21 U8
Hermiston Av. G32 39 CC13
Hermiston Pl. G32 39 CC13
Hermiston Rd. G32 38 BB12
Hermitage Av. G13 19 Q9
Heron Ct., Clyde. G81 5 L5
Heron Pl., John. PA5 43 C16
Heron Way, Renf. PA4 31 M11
Britannia Way
Herries Rd. G41 50 T15
Herriet St. G41 51 U14
Herschell St. G13 19 R9
Hertford Av. G12 20 S9
Hexham Gdns. G41 50 T15
Heys St. (Barr.) G78 59 M19
Hickman St. G42 51 V15
Hickory St. G22 22 X9
High Barholm (Kilb.), John. 42 B14
PA10
High Calside, Pais. PA2 46 J14
High Craighall Rd. G4 35 V11
High Parksail, Ersk. PA8 16 J8
High Rd. (Castlehead), 46 J14
Pais. PA2
High St. G1 36 W13
High St. G4 36 W13

High St. (Ruther.) G73 53 Y16
High St., John. PA5 43 D14
High St., Pais. PA1 46 J14
High St., Renf. PA4 17 M10
Highburgh Dr. (Ruther.) 65 Y17
G73
Highburgh Rd. G12 34 T11
Highburgh Ter. G12 34 T11
Highburgh Rd.
Highcraig Av., John. PA5 43 C15
Highcroft Av. G44 64 W17
Highfield Av., Pais. PA2 46 J16
Highfield Cres., Pais. PA2 46 J16
Highfield Dr. G12 20 S9
Highfield Dr. (Ruther.) G73 65 Z18
Highfield Pl. G12 20 S9
Highkirk Vw., John. PA5 43 D15
Highland La. G51 34 T12
Hilary Av. (Ruther.) G73 65 Z17
Hilary Dr. (Bail.) G69 39 DD13
Hilda Cres. G33 24 AA10
Hill Pk., Clyde. G81 5 L5
Hill Path G52 32 P13
Hill Pl. G52 32 P13
Hill Rd. (Cumb.) G67 70 NN3
Hill St. G3 35 V11
Hillcrest (Chry.) G69 26 FF8
Hillcrest Av. G32 54 BB16
Hillcrest Av. G44 63 U18
Hillcrest Av. (Cumb.) G67 70 NN3
Hillcrest Av., Pais. PA2 58 J17
Hillcrest Ct. (Cumb.) G67 70 NN3
Hillcrest Rd. G32 55 CC16
Hillcrest Rd. (Bears.) G61 7 R6
Hillcrest Rd. (Udd.) G71 57 HH16
Hillcrest Ter. (Both.) G71 69 HH18
Churchill Cres.
Hillcroft Ter. (Bishop.) G64 22 X8
Hillend Cres., Clyde. G81 4 K5
Hillend Rd. G22 21 V8
Hillend Rd. (Ruther.) G73 65 Y17
Hillfoot Av. (Bears.) G61 7 R5
Hillfoot Av. (Ruther.) G73 53 Y16
Hillfoot Dr. (Bears.) G61 7 R5
Hillfoot Gdns. (Udd.) G71 57 GG16
Hillfoot St. G31 37 Y12
Hillfoot Ter. (Bears.) G61 8 S5
Milngavie Rd.
Hillhead Av. (Chry.) G69 15 GG7
Hillhead Av. (Ruther.) G73 65 Y18
Hillhead Gdns. G12 34 T11
Hillhead St.
Hillhead Pl. G12 35 U11
Bank St.
Hillhead Rd. G21 23 Z8
Hillhead St. G12 34 T11
Hillhouse St. G21 23 Y10
Hillington Gdns. G52 49 Q14
Hillington Ind. Est. G52 32 N12
Hillington Pk. Cres. G52 33 Q13
Hillington Quad. G52 32 P13
Hillington Rd. G52 32 N11
Hillington Rd. S. G52 32 P13
Hillington Ter. G52 32 P13
Hillkirk Pl. G21 22 X10
Hillkirk St. G21 22 X10
Hillkirk St. La. G21 22 X10
Hillkirk St.
Hillneuk Av. (Bears.) G61 7 R5
Hillneuk Dr. (Bears.) G61 8 S5
Hillpark Av., Pais. PA2 46 J15
Hillpark Dr. G43 62 T17
Hillsborough Rd. (Bail.) G69 39 DD13
Hillsborough Sq. G12 34 T11
Hillhead St.
Hillsborough Ter. G12 21 U10
Bower St.
Hillside Av. (Bears.) G61 7 R5
Hillside Ct. (Thorn.) G46 61 R18
Hillside Dr. (Bears.) G61 8 S5
Hillside Dr. (Bishop.) G64 11 Y7
Hillside Dr. (Barr.) G78 59 L18
Hillside Gdns. G11 20 S10
Turnberry Rd.
Hillside Gdns. La. G11 20 S10
North Gardner St.
Hillside Gro. (Bishop.) G64 23 Z8
Hillside Gro. (Barr.) G78 59 L19
Hillside Quad. G43 62 S17

Hillside Rd. G43 62 S17
Hillside Rd. (Barr.) G78 59 L18
Hillside Rd., Pais. PA2 47 L15
Hillswick Cres. G22 21 V8
Hilltop Rd. (Chry.) G69 15 GG7
Eastwood Rd.
Hillview Cres. (Udd.) G71 57 GG16
Hillview Dr. (Blan.) G72 68 FF19
Hillview Rd. (Elder.), John. 44 F15
PA5
Hillview St. G32 38 AA13
Hilton Gdns. G13 19 R8
Hilton Gdns. La. G13 19 R8
Fulton St.
Hilton Pk. (Bishop.) G64 10 X6
Hilton Rd. (Bishop.) G64 10 X6
Hilton Ter. G13 19 R8
Hilton Ter. (Bishop.) G64 10 X6
Hilton Ter. (Camb.) G72 66 AA18
Hinshaw St. G20 21 V10
Hinshelwood Dr. G51 34 S13
Hinshelwood Pl. G51 34 S13
Edmiston Dr.
Hirsel Pl. (Both.) G71 69 HH18
Lomond Dr.
Hobart Cres., Clyde. G81 4 J5
Hobart St. G22 21 V10
Hobden St. G21 23 Y10
Hoddam Av. G45 64 X18
Hoddam Ter. G45 65 Y18
Hoey St. G51 34 T12
Hogan Ct., Clyde. G81 4 K5
Dalgleish Av.
Hogarth Av. G32 37 Z12
Hogarth Cres. G32 37 Z12
Hogarth Dr. G32 37 Z12
Hogarth Gdns. G32 37 Z12
Hogg Av., John. PA5 43 D15
Hogganfield St. G33 37 Z11
Hole Brae (Cumb.) G67 71 PP2
Holeburn Rd. G43 62 T17
Holehouse Dr. G13 18 P9
Holland St. G2 35 V12
Hollinwell Rd. G23 21 U8
Hollowglen Rd. G32 38 BB13
Hollows Av., Pais. PA2 45 G16
Hollows Cres., Pais. PA2 45 G16
Holly Dr. G21 23 Y10
Holly Pl., John. PA5 44 E16
Holly St., Clyde. G81 5 L6
Hollybank Pl. (Camb.) G72 66 BB18
Hollybank St. G21 37 Y11
Hollybrook St. G42 51 V15
Hollybush Av., Pais. PA2 45 H16
Hollybush Rd. G52 32 N13
Hollymount (Bears.) G61 7 R7
Holm Av. (Udd.) G71 57 GG16
Holm Av., Pais. PA2 46 K15
Holm Pl. (Linw.), Pais. PA3 28 E12
Holm St. G2 35 V12
Holmbank Av. G41 50 T16
Holmbrae Av. (Udd.) G71 57 GG16
Holmbrae Rd. (Udd.) G71 57 GG16
Holmbyre Rd. G45 64 W19
Holmbyre Ter. G45 64 W19
Holmes Av., Renf. PA4 31 M11
Holmfauld Rd. G51 33 R11
Holmfauldhead Dr. G51 33 R12
Holmfauldhead Pl. G51 33 R12
Govan Rd.
Holmhead Cres. G44 63 V17
Holmhead Pl. G44 63 V17
Holmhead Rd. G44 63 V17
Holmhill Av. (Camb.) G72 66 BB18
Holmhills Dr. (Camb.) G72 66 AA18
Holmhills Gdns. (Camb.) 66 AA18
G72
Holmhills Gro. (Camb.) 66 AA18
G72
Holmhills Pl. (Camb.) G72 66 AA18
Holmhills Rd. (Camb.) G72 66 AA18
Holmhills Ter. (Camb.) G72 66 AA18
Holmlea Rd. G44 51 V16
Holms Pl. (Gart.) G69 27 GG8
Holmswood Av. (Blan.) 68 FF19
G72
Holmwood Av. (Udd.) G71 57 GG16
Holmwood Gdns. (Udd.) 69 GG17
G71

117

Street	Page	Grid
Holyrood Cres. G20	35	U11
Holyrood Quad. G20	35	U11
Holywell St. G31	37	Y13
Homeston Av. (Both.) G71	69	HH18
Honeybog Rd. G52	32	N13
Hood St., Clyde. G81	5	M7
Hope St. G2	35	V12
Hopefield Av. G12	20	T9
Hopehill Pl. G20	21	V10
Hopehill Rd.		
Hopehill Rd. G20	21	V10
Hopeman Av. (Thorn.) G46	61	R18
Hopeman Dr. (Thorn.) G46	61	R18
Hopeman Path (Thorn.) G46	61	R18
Kennishead Pl.		
Hopeman Rd. (Thorn.) G46	61	R18
Hopeman St. (Thorn.) G46	61	R18
Hopetoun Pl. G23	9	U7
Hopetoun Ter. G21	23	Y10
Foresthall Dr.		
Hornal Rd. (Udd.) G71	69	HH18
Hornbeam Dr., Clyde. G81	5	L6
Hornbeam Rd. (Udd.) G71	57	HH16
Horndean Ct. (Bishop.) G64	11	Y6
Horndean Cres. G33	39	CC11
Horne St. G22	22	X9
Hawthorn St.		
Hornshill Rd. (Stepps) G33	25	DD8
Hornshill St. G21	23	Y10
Horsburgh St. G33	39	CC11
Horse Shoe La. (Bears.) G61	7	R6
Horse Shoe Rd. (Bears.) G61	7	R5
Horselethill Rd. G12	20	T10
Hospital St. G5	51	V14
Hotspur St. G20	21	U10
Houldsworth La. G3	35	U12
Finnieston St.		
Houldsworth St. G3	35	U12
Househillmuir Cres. G53	49	Q16
Househillmuir La. G53	49	Q16
Househillmuir Pl. G53	49	Q16
Househillmuir Rd. G53	60	P17
Househillwood Cres. G53	48	P16
Househillwood Rd. G53	60	P17
Housel Av. G13	18	P8
Houston Pl. G5	35	U13
Houston Pl. (Elder.), John. PA5	44	F15
Houston Sq., John. PA5	43	D14
Houston St. G5	35	U13
Houston St., Renf. PA4	17	M10
Howard St. G1	35	V13
Howard St., Pais. PA1	47	L14
Howat St. G51	34	S12
Howden Dr. (Linw.), Pais. PA3	28	E13
Howford Rd. G52	48	P14
Howgate Av. G15	6	N6
Howieshill Av. (Camb.) G72	66	BB17
Howieshill Rd. (Camb.) G72	66	BB18
Howth Dr. G13	19	R8
Howth Ter. G13	19	R8
Howwood St. G41	35	U13
Hoylake Pk. (Both.) G71	69	GG19
Hoylake Pl. G23	9	U7
Hozier Cres. (Udd.) G71	57	GG16
Hozier St. G40	52	X14
Hubbard Dr. G11	33	R11
Hugh Murray Gro. (Camb.) G72	67	CC17
Hughenden Dr. G12	20	S10
Hughenden Gdns. G12	20	S10
Hughenden La. G12	20	S10
Hughenden Rd. G12	20	S10
Hughenden Ter. G12	20	S10
Hughenden Rd.		
Hugo St. G20	21	U9
Hume Dr. (Both.) G71	69	HH18
Hume Dr. (Udd.) G71	57	GG16
Hume Rd. (Cumb.) G67	71	PP2
Hume St., Clyde. G81	5	L7
Hunter Pl. (Kilb.), John. PA10	42	B15
Hunter Rd. (Ruther.) G73	53	Z15
Hunter St. G4	36	X13
Hunter St., Pais. PA1	30	K13
Hunterfield Dr. (Camb.) G72	66	AA17
Hunterhill Av., Pais. PA2	46	K14
Hunterhill Rd.		
Hunterhill Rd., Pais. PA2	46	K14
Hunters Hill Ct. G21	22	X9
Belmont Rd.		
Huntersfield Rd., John. PA5	43	C15
Huntershill Rd. (Bishop.) G64	22	X8
Huntershill St. G21	22	X9
Huntershill Way (Bishop.) G64	22	X8
Crowhill Rd.		
Huntingdon Rd. G21	36	X11
Huntingdon Sq. G21	36	X11
Huntingdon Rd.		
Huntingtower Rd. (Bail.) G69	56	EE14
Huntley Rd. G52	32	N12
Huntly Av. (Giff.) G46	62	T19
Huntly Dr. (Camb.) G72	66	BB18
Huntly Gdns. G12	20	T10
Huntly Path (Chry.) G69	15	HH7
Burnbrae Av.		
Huntly Rd. G12	20	T10
Huntly Ter., Pais. PA2	47	L15
Hurlet Rd. G53	48	N16
Hurlet Rd., Pais. PA2	47	M16
Hurley Hawkin (Bishop.) G64	23	Z8
Hurlford Av. G13	18	N8
Hutcheson Rd. (Thorn.) G46	62	S19
Hutcheson St. G1	36	W12
Hutchinson Ct. G2	35	V12
Hope St.		
Hutchinson Pl. (Camb.) G72	67	DD18
Hutchison Ct. (Giff.) G46	62	S19
Berryhill Rd.		
Hutchison Dr. (Bears.) G61	8	S7
Hutton Dr. G51	33	R12
Huxley St. G20	21	U9
Hydepark Pl. G21	22	X9
Springburn Rd.		
Hydepark St. G3	35	U12
Hyndal Av. G53	49	Q15
Hyndland Av. G11	34	S11
Hyndland Rd. G12	20	S10
Hyndland St. G11	34	T11
Hyndlee Dr. G52	33	Q13
Hyslop Pl., Clyde. G81	5	L6
Albert Rd.		

I

Street	Page	Grid
Iain Dr. (Bears.) G61	7	Q5
Iain Rd. (Bears.) G61	7	Q5
Ibrox St. G51	34	T13
Ibrox Ter. G51	34	S13
Ibrox Ter. La. G51	34	S13
Ibroxholm Av. G51	34	S13
Edmiston Dr.		
Ibroxholm La. G51	34	T13
Paisley Rd. W.		
Ibroxholm Oval G51	34	S13
Ibroxholm Pl. G51	34	S13
Paisley Rd. W.		
Ilay Av. (Bears.) G61	19	R8
Ilay Ct. (Bears.) G61	20	S8
Ilay Rd. (Bears.) G61	20	S8
Inchbrae Rd. G52	49	Q14
Inchcruin Pl. G15	6	N6
Inchfad Dr. G15	6	N6
Inchfad Pl. G15	6	N6
Inchinnan Rd., Pais. PA3	30	K12
Inchinnan Rd., Renf. PA4	17	L10
Inchkeith Pl. G32	38	BB12
Inchlaggan Pl. G15	6	N6
Inchlee St. G14	33	R11
Inchmoan Pl. G15	6	N6
Inchmurrin Dr. (Ruther.) G73	65	Z19
Inchmurrin Gdns. (Ruther.) G73	65	Z19
Inchmurrin Pl. (Ruther.) G73	65	Z19
Inchoch St. G33	39	DD11
Incholm La. G11	33	R11
Byron St.		
Incholm St. G11	33	R11
Byron St.		
Inchrory Pl. G15	6	N6
Incle St., Pais. PA1	30	K13
India Dr. (Inch.), Renf. PA4	16	J9
India St. G2	35	V12
Inga St. G20	21	U8
Ingerbreck Av. (Ruther.) G73	65	Z18
Ingleby Dr. G31	37	Y12
Inglefield St. G42	51	V15
Ingleneuk Av. G33	24	BB9
Ingleside (Lenzie) G66	13	CC5
Inglestone Av. (Thorn.) G46	62	S19
Inglis St. G31	37	Y13
Ingram St. G1	36	W12
Inishail Rd. G33	39	CC11
Inkerman Rd. G52	32	N13
Innerwick Dr. G52	32	P13
Inver Rd. G33	39	DD12
Inveraray Dr. (Bishop.) G64	11	Y6
Invercanny Dr. G15	6	N6
Invercanny Pl. G15	6	P6
Inverclyde Gdns. G11	19	R10
Broomhill Dr.		
Inverclyde Gdns. (Ruther.) G73	66	AA18
Inveresk Cres. G32	38	BB13
Inveresk St. G32	38	BB13
Inverewe Av. (Thorn.) G46	61	Q18
Inverewe Dr. (Thorn.) G46	61	Q19
Inverewe Gdns. (Thorn.) G46	61	Q19
Inverewe Pl. (Thorn.) G46	61	Q18
Invergarry Av. (Thorn.) G40	61	Q19
Invergarry Ct. (Thorn.) G46	61	Q19
Invergarry Dr. (Thorn.) G46	61	Q19
Invergarry Gdns. (Thorn.) G46	61	Q19
Invergarry Gro. (Thorn.) G46	61	Q19
Invergarry Pl. (Thorn.) G46	61	Q19
Invergarry Quad. (Thorn.) G46	61	R19
Invergarry Vw. (Thorn.) G46	61	R19
Inverglas Av., Renf. PA4	32	N11
Morriston Cres.		
Invergordon Av. G43	51	U16
Invergyle Dr. G52	32	P13
Inverkar Dr., Pais. PA2	45	H15
Inverkip St. G5	36	W13
Inverlair Av. G43	63	U17
Inverlair Av. G44	63	U17
Inverleith St. G32	37	Z13
Inverlochy St. G33	39	CC11
Inverness St. G51	33	Q13
Inveroran Dr. (Bears.) G61	8	S6
Invershiel Rd. G23	8	T7
Invershin Dr. G20	20	T9
Wyndford Rd.		
Inverurie St. G21	22	W10
Inzievar Ter. G32	54	BB15
Iona Cres. (Old Kil.) G60	4	J5
Iona Dr. (Old Kil.) G60	4	J5
Iona Dr., Pais. PA2	46	J16
Iona Gdns. (Old Kil.) G60	4	J5
Iona La. (Chry.) G69	15	HH7
Heathfield Av.		
Iona Pl. (Old Kil.) G60	4	J5
Iona Rd. (Ruther.) G73	66	AA18
Iona Rd., Renf. PA4	31	M11
Iona St. G51	34	S12
Iona Way (Stepps) G33	25	CC10
Iris Av. G45	65	Y18
Irongray St. G31	37	Z12
Irvine Dr. (Linw.), Pais. PA3	28	E13
Irvine St. G40	53	Y14
Irving Av., Clyde. G81	5	L5
Stewart Dr.		
Irving Quad., Clyde. G81	5	L5
Stewart Dr.		
Iser La. G41	51	U16
Island Rd. (Cumb.) G67	70	MM4
Islay Av. (Ruther.) G73	66	AA18
Islay Cres. (Old Kil.) G60	4	J5
Islay Cres., Pais. PA2	46	J16
Islay Dr. (Old Kil.) G60	4	J5

Ivanhoe Rd. G13   19   Q8
Ivanhoe Rd. (Cumb.) G67   70   NN4
Ivanhoe Rd., Pais. PA2   45   G15
Ivanhoe Way, Pais. PA2   45   G15
  Ivanhoe Rd.
Ivybank Av. (Camb.) G72   67   CC18

J

Jacks Rd. (Udd.) G71   69   HH17
Jagger Gdns. (Bail.) G69   55   DD14
Jamaica St. G1   35   V13
James Dunlop Gdns.   23   Y8
  (Bishop.) G64
  Graham Ter.
James Gray St. G41   51   U16
James Morrison St. G1   36   W13
  St. Andrews Sq.
James Nisbet St. G21   36   X11
James St. G40   52   X14
James Watt La. G2   35   V12
  James Watt St.
James Watt St. G2   35   V12
Jamieson Ct. G42   51   V15
Jamieson Path G42   51   V15
  Jamieson St.
Jamieson St. G42   51   V15
Janebank Av. (Camb.) G72   67   CC18
Janefield Av., John. PA5   43   D15
Janefield St. G31   37   Y13
Janes Brae (Cumb.) G67   70   NN4
Janetta St., Clyde. G81   5   L6
Jardine St. G20   21   U10
Jardine Ter. (Gart.) G69   27   GG9
Jasgray St. G42   51   U15
Jean Armour Dr., Clyde.   5   M6
  G81
Jean Maclean Pl. (Bishop.)   11   Y5
  G64
Jedburgh Av. (Ruther.)   53   Y16
  G73
Jedburgh Dr., Pais. PA2   45   H15
Jedburgh Gdns. G20   21   U10
Jedworth Av. G15   6   P6
Jedworth Rd. G15   6   P6
Jellicoe St., Clyde. G81   4   K6
Jenny's Well Ct., Pais. PA2   47   L15
  Jenny's Well Rd.
Jenny's Well Rd., Pais. PA2   47   L15
Jerviston Rd. G33   39   CC11
Jessie St. G42   52   W15
Jessiman Sq., Renf. PA4   31   L11
Jocelyn Sq. G1   36   W13
John Brown Pl. (Chry.) G69   26   FF8
John Knox La. G4   36   X12
  Drygate
John Knox St. G4   36   X12
John Knox St., Clyde. G81   17   M8
John Lang St., John. PA5   44   E14
John St. G1   36   W12
John St. (Barr.) G78   59   L18
John St., Pais. PA1   46   J14
Johnsburn Dr. G53   60   P17
Johnsburn Rd. G53   60   P17
Johnshaven St. G43   50   T16
  Shawbridge St.
Johnston Rd. (Gart.) G69   27   HH9
Johnston St., Pais. PA1   46   K14
  Gordon St.
Johnstone Av. G52   32   P13
Johnstone Av., Clyde. G81   17   M8
Johnstone Dr. (Camb.) G72   66   BB17
Johnstone Dr. (Ruther.)   53   Y16
  G73
Joppa St. G33   38   AA12
Jordan St. G14   33   Q11
Jordanhill Cres. G13   19   Q9
Jordanhill Dr. G13   19   Q9
Jordanhill La. G13   19   R9
  Austen Rd.
Jordanvale Av. G14   33   Q11
Jowitt Av., Clyde. G81   5   M7
Jubilee Bk. (Kirk.) G66   13   CC6
  Heriot Rd.
Jubilee Path (Bears.) G61   7   R6
Jubilee Ter., John. PA5   43   C15
Julian Av. G12   20   T10
Julian La. G12   20   T10
  Julian Av.

Juniper Ct. (Kirk.) G66   12   BB5
Juniper Pl. G32   55   DD14
Juniper Pl., John. PA5   44   E16
Juniper Ter. G32   55   DD14
Jura Av., Renf. PA4   31   M11
Jura Ct. G52   33   R13
Jura Dr. (Old Kil.) G60   4   J5
  Jura Rd.
Jura Dr. (Blan.) G72   68   FF18
Jura Gdns. (Old Kil.) G60   4   J5
  Jura Rd.
Jura Pl. (Old Kil.) G60   4   J5
  Jura Rd.
Jura Rd. (Old Kil.) G60   4   J5
Jura Rd., Pais. PA2   46   J16
Jura St. G52   33   R13

K

Kaim Dr. G53   61   Q17
Kames St. G5   51   V14
Karol Path G4   35   V11
  St. Peters St.
Katewell Av. G15   6   N6
Katrine Av. (Bishop.) G64   11   Y7
Katrine Dr., Pais. PA2   45   G15
Katrine Pl. (Camb.) G72   66   BB17
Kay St. G21   22   X10
Kaystone Rd. G15   6   P7
Keal Av. G15   18   P8
Keal Cres. G15   18   P8
Keal Dr. G15   18   P8
Keal Pl. G15   18   P8
Kearn Av. G15   6   P7
Kearn Pl. G15   6   P7
Keats Pk. (Both.) G71   69   HH18
Keir Dr. (Bishop.) G64   10   X7
Keir St. G41   51   U14
Keirhill Rd. (Cumb.) G68   70   MM3
  Woodburn Way
Keirs Wk. (Camb.) G72   66   BB17
Keith Av. (Giff.) G46   62   T18
Keith Ct. G11   34   T11
  Keith St.
Keith St. G11   34   T11
Kelbourne St. G20   21   U10
Kelburn St. (Barr.) G78   59   L19
Kelburne Dr., Pais. PA1   31   L13
Kelburne Gdns. (Bail.) G69   56   EE14
Kelburne Gdns., Pais. PA1   31   L13
Kelburne Oval, Pais. PA1   31   L13
Kelhead Av. G52   32   N13
Kelhead Dr. G52   32   N13
Kelhead Path G52   32   P13
Kelhead Pl. G52   32   N13
Kellas St. G51   34   S13
Kells Pl. G15   6   N6
Kelso Av. (Ruther.) G73   53   Y16
Kelso Av., Pais. PA2   45   H15
Kelso Gdns. (Mood.) G69   15   GG6
  Whithorn Cres.
Kelso Pl. G14   18   N9
Kelso St. G13   18   N9
Kelso St. G14   18   N9
Kelton St. G32   54   BB14
Kelty Pl. G5   35   V13
  Bedford St.
Kelty St. G5   51   V14
  Eglinton St.
Kelvin Av. G52   32   N11
Kelvin Ct. G12   19   R9
Kelvin Cres. (Bears.) G61   7   R7
Kelvin Dr. G20   20   T10
Kelvin Dr. (Bishop.) G64   11   Y7
Kelvin Dr. (Chry.) G69   15   GG7
Kelvin Dr. (Barr.) G78   59   M19
Kelvin Rd. (Cumb.) G67   71   PP4
Kelvin Rd. (Udd.) G71   57   GG16
Kelvin Way G3   34   T11
Kelvin Way (Both.) G71   69   HH18
  Bracken Ter.
Kelvindale Bldgs. G12   20   T9
  Kelvindale Rd.
Kelvindale Cotts. G12   20   T9
  Kelvindale Rd.
Kelvindale Gdns. G20   20   T9
Kelvindale Glen G12   20   T9
  Kelvindale Rd.
Kelvindale Pl. G20   20   T9

Kelvindale Rd. G12   20   T9
Kelvindale Rd. G20   20   T9
Kelvingrove St. G3   35   U12
Kelvingrove Ter. G3   35   U12
  Kelvingrove St.
Kelvinhaugh Pl. G3   34   T12
  Kelvinhaugh St.
Kelvinhaugh St. G3   34   T12
Kelvinside Av. G20   21   U10
  Queen Margaret Dr.
Kelvinside Dr. G20   21   U10
Kelvinside Gdns. G20   21   U10
Kelvinside Gdns. E. G20   21   U10
Kelvinside Gdns. La. G20   21   U10
  Kelvinside Gdns.
Kelvinside Ter. S. G20   21   U10
Kelvinside Ter. W. G20   21   U10
Kemp Av., Pais. PA3   31   L11
Kemp St. G21   22   X10
Kempock St. G31   53   Z14
Kempsthorn Cres. G53   48   P15
Kempsthorn Path G53   48   P15
Kempsthorn Rd. G53   48   P15
Kendal Av. G12   20   S9
Kendal Av. (Giff.) G46   62   T18
Kendal Dr. G12   20   S9
Kendal Ter. G12   20   S9
Kendoon Av. G15   6   N6
Kenilworth Av. G41   50   T16
Kenilworth Cres. (Bears.)   7   Q5
  G61
Kenilworth Way, Pais. PA2   45   G16
Kenmar Gdns. (Udd.) G71   56   FF16
Kenmore Gdns. (Bears.)   8   S5
  G61
Kenmore Rd. (Cumb.) G67   71   PP3
Kenmore St. G32   38   BB13
Kenmuir Av. G32   55   DD14
Kenmuir Rd. G32   55   CC16
Kenmuirhill Rd. G32   55   CC15
Kenmure Av. (Bishop.) G64   10   X7
Kenmure Cres. (Bishop.)   10   X7
  G64
Kenmure Dr. (Bishop.) G64   10   X7
Kenmure Gdns. (Bishop.)   10   X7
  G64
Kenmure Row G22   9   V7
Kenmure St. G41   51   U14
Kenmure Way (Ruther.)   65   Y18
  G73
Kennedar Dr. G51   33   R12
Kennedy Ct. (Giff.) G46   62   T18
  Braidholm Cres.
Kennedy St. G4   36   W12
Kennet St. G21   37   Y11
Kennishead Av. (Thorn.)   61   R17
  G46
Kennishead Path (Thorn.)   61   R17
  G46
  Kennishead Pl.
Kennishead Pl. (Thorn.)   61   R17
  G46
Kennishead Rd. G43   61   R17
Kennishead Rd. (Thorn.)   61   R17
  G46
Kennishead Rd. G53   61   Q18
Kennisholm Av. (Thorn.)   61   R17
  G46
Kennisholm Path (Thorn.)   61   R18
  G46
  Kennisholm Av.
Kennisholm Pl. (Thorn.)   61   R17
  G46
Kennoway Dr. G11   33   R11
Kennoway La. G11   33   R11
  Thornwood Dr.
Kennyhill Sq. G31   37   Y12
Kensington Dr. (Giff.) G46   62   T19
Kensington Gate G12   20   T10
Kensington Rd. G12   20   T10
Kent Dr. (Ruther.) G73   65   Z17
Kent Rd. G3   35   U12
Kent St. G40   36   X13
Kentallen Rd. G33   39   DD13
Kentigern Ter. (Bishop.)   23   Y8
  G64
Keppel Dr. G44   52   X16
Keppoch St. G21   22   W10
Keppochhill Rd. G21   22   X10

Keppochhill Rd. G22 22 W10
Kerfield La. G15 6 N6
Kerfield Pl. G15 6 N6
Kerr Dr. G40 36 X13
Kerr Gdns. (Udd.) G71 57 HH16
Kerr Pl. G40 36 X13
Kerr St. G40 36 X13
Kerr St. (Barr.) G78 59 L19
Kerr St., Pais. PA3 30 J13
Kerrera Pl. G33 39 CC13
Kerrera Rd. G33 39 CC13
Kerry Pl. G15 6 N6
Kerrycroy Av. G42 52 W16
Kerrycroy Pl. G42 52 W16
Kerrycroy Av.
Kerrycroy St. G42 52 W16
Kerrydale St. G40 53 Y14
Kerrylamont Av. G42 52 X16
Kersland La. G12 20 T10
Kersland St.
Kersland St. G12 20 T10
Kessington Dr. (Bears.) G61 8 S6
Kessington Rd. (Bears.) G61 8 S6
Kessock Dr. G22 21 V10
Kessock Pl. G22 21 V10
Kestral Ct., Clyde. G81 5 L5
Kestrel Pl., John. PA5 43 C16
Kestrel Rd. G13 19 Q9
Kew Gdns. G12 20 T10
Ruthven St.
Kew Gdns. (Udd.) G71 57 HH16
Kew La. G12 20 T10
Saltoun St.
Kew Ter. G12 20 T10
Keyden St. G41 35 U13
Kibbleston Rd. (Kilb.), 42 B14
John. PA10
Kidston Dr. G5 52 W14
Kierhill Rd. (Cumb.) G68 70 MM3
Kilbarchan Rd., John. PA5 43 C15
Kilbarchan Rd. (Mill.Pk.), 43 C15
John. PA10
Kilbarchan St. G5 35 V13
Bedford St.
Kilbeg Ter. (Thorn.) G46 61 Q18
Kilberry St. G21 37 Y11
Kilbirnie St. G5 51 V14
Kilbowie Ct., Clyde. G81 5 L6
Crown Av.
Kilbowie Rd. (Cumb.) G67 71 PP3
Kilbowie Rd., Clyde. G81 5 L5
Kilbrennan Rd. (Linw.), 28 E13
Pais. PA3
Kilbride St. G5 52 W15
Kilbride Vw. (Udd.) G71 57 HH16
Hamilton Vw.
Kilburn Gro. (Blan.) G72 68 FF19
Kilburn Pl. G13 18 P9
Kilchattan Dr. G44 52 W16
Kilchoan Rd. G33 39 CC11
Kilcloy Av. G15 6 P6
Kildale St. (Ruther.) G73 52 X16
Kildale Way (Ruther.) G73 52 X16
Kildary Av. G44 63 V17
Kildary Rd. G44 63 V17
Kildermorie Rd. G34 40 EE12
Kildonan Dr. G11 34 S11
Kildonan Ter. G51 34 S13
Copland Rd.
Kildrostan St. G41 51 U15
Terregles Av.
Kildrum Rd. (Cumb.) G67 71 PP2
Kilearn Rd., Pais. PA3 31 L12
Kilearn Way, Pais. PA3 31 L12
Clyde Rd.
Kilfinan St. G22 21 V8
Kilkerran Dr. G33 24 AA9
Killarn Way, Pais. PA3 31 L12
Killearn Dr., Pais. PA1 48 N14
Killearn St. G22 21 V10
Killermont Av. (Bears.) G61 8 S7
Killermont Ct. (Bears.) G61 8 S6
Killermont Meadows 69 GG19
(Both.) G71
Killermont Rd. (Bears.) G61 8 S6
Killermont St. G2 36 W12
Killermont Vw. G20 8 S7
Killiegrew Rd. G41 50 T15
Killin St. G32 54 BB14

Killoch Av., Pais. PA3 29 H13
Killoch Dr. G13 18 P8
Killoch Dr. (Barr.) G78 59 M19
Killoch Rd., Pais. PA3 29 H13
Kilmailing Rd. G44 63 V17
Kilmair Pl. G20 20 T9
Wyndford Rd.
Kilmaluag Ter. (Thorn.) 61 Q18
G46
Kilmany Dr. G32 38 AA13
Kilmany Gdns. G32 38 AA13
St. Mark St.
Kilmardinny Av. (Bears.) 7 R5
G61
Kilmardinny Cres. (Bears.) 7 R5
G61
Kilmardinny Dr. (Bears.) 7 R5
G61
Kilmardinny Gate (Bears.) 7 R5
G61
Kilmardinny Av.
Kilmardinny Gro. (Bears.) 7 R5
G61
Kilmarnock Rd. G41 62 T17
Kilmarnock Rd. G43 62 T17
Kilmartin Pl. (Thorn.) G46 61 R18
Kilmaurs Dr. (Giff.) G46 63 U18
Kilmaurs St. G51 33 R13
Kilmorie Dr. (Ruther.) G73 52 X16
Kilmory Av. (Udd.) G71 57 HH16
Spindlehowe Rd.
Kilmuir Cres. (Thorn.) G46 61 Q18
Kilmuir Dr. (Thorn.) G46 61 R18
Kilmuir Rd. (Thorn.) G46 61 R18
Kilmuir Rd. (Udd.) G71 57 GG15
Kilmun La. G20 20 T8
Kilmun St.
Kilmun Pl. G20 20 T8
Kilmun St.
Kilmun St. G20 20 T8
Kilnside Rd., Pais. PA1 30 K13
Kiloran St. (Thorn.) G46 61 R18
Kilpatrick Av., Pais. PA2 45 H15
Kilpatrick Cres., Pais. PA2 46 J15
Kilpatrick Dr., Renf. PA4 31 L12
Campsie Dr.
Kilpatrick Way (Udd.) G71 57 HH16
Kiltearn Rd. G33 39 DD12
Kilvaxter Dr. (Thorn.) G46 61 R18
Kilwynet Way, Pais. PA3 31 L12
Kimberley St., Clyde. G81 4 J5
Kinalty Rd. G44 63 V17
Kinarvie Cres. G53 48 N16
Kinarvie Gdns. G53 48 N16
Kinarvie Rd.
Kinarvie Pl. G53 48 N16
Kinarvie Rd. G53 48 N16
Kinarvie Ter. G53 48 N16
Kinbuck St. G22 22 W10
Kincaid Gdns. (Camb.) G72 66 BB17
Kincardine Cres. (Bishop.) 23 Y8
G64
Graham Ter.
Kincardine Dr. (Bishop.) 23 Y8
G64
Kincardine Pl. (Bishop.) 23 Z8
G64
Kincardine Sq. G33 39 CC11
Kincath Av. (Ruther.) G73 65 Z18
Kinclaven Av. G15 6 P6
Kincraig St. G51 33 Q13
Kinellan Rd. (Bears.) G61 7 R7
Kinellar Dr. G14 18 P9
Kinfauns Dr. G15 6 N6
Kinfauns Ter. G51 34 S13
Copland Rd.
King Edward La. G13 19 R9
King Edward Rd.
King Edward Rd. G13 19 R9
King George V Bri. G1 35 V13
King George V Bri. G5 35 V13
King George V Dock G51 32 P11
King Pl. (Bail.) G69 41 HH13
King St. G1 36 W13
King St. (Ruther.) G73 53 Y16
King St., Clyde. G81 17 M8
King St., Pais. PA1 30 J13
Kingarth La. G42 51 V15
Kingarth St.

Kingarth St. G42 51 V15
Kingfisher Dr. G13 18 N8
Kinghorn Dr. G44 52 W16
Kinglas Rd. (Bears.) G61 7 Q7
King's Bri. G5 52 W14
King's Bri. G40 52 W14
Kings Cres. (Camb.) G72 66 BB17
Kings Cres. (Elder.), John. 44 F14
PA5
Kings Cross G31 36 X12
King's Dr. G40 52 X14
Kings Dr. (Cumb.) G68 70 NN1
Kings Inch Rd., Renf. PA4 17 M9
Kings La. W., Renf. PA4 17 M10
Bell St.
King's Pk. Av. G44 63 V17
King's Pk. Av. (Ruther.) 63 V17
G73
Kings Pk. Rd. G44 51 V16
Kings Pl. G22 21 V8
Kings Rd., John. PA5 44 E15
King's Vw. (Cumb.) G68 70 NN1
Kingsacre Rd. G44 51 V16
Kingsacre Rd. (Ruther.) G73 52 W16
Kingsbarns Dr. G44 51 V16
Kingsborough Gdns. G12 20 S10
Kingsborough Gate G12 20 S10
Prince Albert Rd.
Kingsborough La. G12 20 S10
Prince Albert Rd.
Kingsborough La. E. G12 20 S10
Kingsborough Gdns.
Kingsborough Ter. G12 20 S10
Hyndland Rd.
Kingsbrae Av. G44 52 W16
Kingsbridge Cres. G44 64 W17
Kingsbridge Dr. G44 64 W17
Kingsbridge Dr. (Ruther.) 64 W17
G73
Kingsburgh Dr., Pais. PA1 31 L13
Kingsburn Dr. (Ruther.) G73 65 Y17
Kingsburn Gro. (Ruther.) 65 Y17
G73
Kingscliffe Av. G44 64 W17
Kingscourt Av. G44 64 W17
Kingsdale Av. G44 52 W16
Kingsdyke Av. G44 52 W16
Kingsford Av. G44 63 U18
Kingsheath Av. (Ruther.) 64 X17
G73
Kingshill Dr. G44 64 W17
Kingshouse Av. G44 64 W17
Kingshurst Av. G44 52 W16
Kingsknowe Dr. (Ruther.) 64 X17
G73
Kingsland Cres. G52 32 P13
Kingsland Dr. G52 32 P13
Kingsland La. G52 33 Q13
Berryknowes Rd.
Kingsley Av. G42 51 V15
Kingsley Ct. (Udd.) G71 57 HH16
Kingslynn Dr. G44 64 W17
Kingslynn La. G44 64 W17
Kingslynn Dr.
Kingsmuir Dr. (Ruther.) 64 X17
G73
Kingston Av. (Udd.) G71 57 HH16
Kingston Bri. G3 35 U13
Kingston Bri. G5 35 U13
Kingston Pl., Clyde. G81 4 J6
Kingston St. G5 35 V13
Kingsway G14 18 P9
Kingsway Ct. G14 18 P9
Kingswood Dr. G44 64 W17
Kingussie Dr. G44 64 W17
Kiniver Dr. G15 6 P7
Kinloch Av. (Camb.) G72 66 BB18
Kinloch Av. (Linw.), Pais. 28 E13
PA3
Pentland Av.
Kinloch Rd., Renf. PA4 31 L11
Kinloch St. G40 53 Z14
Kinmount Av. G44 51 V16
Kinmount La. G44 51 V16
Kinmount Av.
Kinnaird Cres. (Bears.) G61 8 S6
Kinnaird Dr. (Linw.), Pais. 28 E13
PA3
Kinnaird Pl. (Bishop.) G64 23 Y8

Kinnear Rd. G40 53 Y14
Kinnell Av. G52 49 Q14
Kinnell Cres. G52 49 Q14
Kinnell Path G52 49 Q14
  Kinnell Cres.
Kinnell Pl. G52 49 R15
  Mosspark Dr.
Kinnell Sq. G52 49 Q14
Kinning St. G5 35 U13
Kinnoul La. G12 20 T10
  Dowanhill St.
Kinpurnie Rd., Pais. PA1 31 M13
Kinross Av. G52 48 P14
Kinsail Dr. G52 32 N13
Kinstone Av. G14 18 P9
Kintessack Pl. (Bishop.) G64 11 Z7
Kintillo Dr. G13 18 P9
Kintore Rd. G43 63 U17
Kintra St. G51 34 S13
Kintyre Av. (Linw.), Pais. PA3 28 E13
Kintyre St. G21 37 Y11
Kippen St. G22 22 W9
Kippford St. G32 55 CC14
Kirk La. G43 50 T16
  Riverbank St.
Kirk Pl. (Udd.) G71 69 GG17
Kirk Rd. (Bears.) G61 7 R5
Kirkaig Av., Renf. PA4 32 N11
Kirkbean Av. (Ruther.) G73 65 Y18
Kirkburn Av. (Camb.) G72 66 BB18
Kirkcaldy Rd. G41 50 T15
Kirkconnel Av. G13 18 N9
Kirkconnel Dr. (Ruther.) G73 64 X17
Kirkdale Dr. G52 49 R14
Kirkfield Rd. (Both.) G71 69 HH18
Kirkford Rd. (Chry.) G69 15 GG7
  Bridgeburn Dr.
Kirkhill Av. (Camb.) G72 66 BB18
Kirkhill Dr. G20 20 T9
Kirkhill Gdns. (Camb.) G72 66 BB18
Kirkhill Gro. (Camb.) G72 66 BB18
Kirkhill Pl. G20 20 T9
Kirkhill Rd. (Gart.) G69 27 GG9
Kirkhill Rd. (Udd.) G71 57 GG16
Kirkhill Ter. (Camb.) G72 66 BB18
Kirkhope Dr. G15 6 P7
Kirkinner Rd. G32 55 CC14
Kirkintilloch Rd. (Bishop.) G64 22 X8
Kirkintilloch Rd. (Kirk.) G66 13 CC5
Kirkland Gro., John. PA5 43 D14
Kirkland St. G20 21 U10
Kirklandneuk Cres., Renf. PA4 17 L10
  Kirklandneuk Rd.
Kirklandneuk Rd., Renf. PA4 17 L10
Kirklands Cres. (Both.) G71 69 HH18
Kirklea Av., Pais. PA3 29 H13
Kirklee Circ. G12 20 T10
Kirklee Gdns. G12 20 T9
  Bellshaugh Rd.
Kirklee Gdns. La. G12 20 T9
  Bellshaugh Rd.
Kirklee Pl. G12 20 T10
Kirklee Quad. G12 20 T10
Kirklee Quad. La. G12 20 T10
  Kirklee Quad.
Kirklee Rd. G12 20 T10
Kirklee Ter. G12 20 T10
Kirklee Ter. La. G12 20 T10
  Kirklee Ter.
Kirkliston St. G32 38 AA13
Kirkmuir Av., Renf. PA4 31 L11
Kirkmuir Dr. (Ruther.) G73 65 Y18
Kirknewton St. G32 38 BB13
Kirkoswald Dr., Clyde. G81 5 M6
Kirkoswald Rd. G43 62 T17
Kirkpatrick St. G40 37 Y13
Kirkriggs Av. (Ruther.) G73 65 Y17
Kirkriggs Gdns. (Ruther.) G73 65 Y17
Kirkriggs Way (Ruther.) G73 65 Y17
Kirkstall Gdns. (Bishop.) G64 11 Y6
Kirkton Av. G13 18 P9
Kirkton Cres. G13 18 P9

Kirkton Rd. (Camb.) G72 66 BB17
Kirktonside (Barr.) G78 59 L19
Kirkview Gdns. (Udd.) G71 57 GG16
  Glencroft Av.
Kirkville Pl. G15 6 P7
Kirkwall (Cumb.) G67 71 PP1
Kirkwall Av. (Blan.) G72 68 FF18
Kirkwell Rd. G44 63 V17
Kirkwood Av., Clyde. G81 5 M7
Kirkwood Quad., Clyde. G81 5 M7
  Kirkwood Av.
Kirkwood Rd. (Udd.) G71 57 GG15
  Newlands Rd.
Kirkwood St. G51 34 T13
Kirkwood St. (Ruther.) G73 53 Y16
Kirn St. G20 20 T8
  Kilmun St.
Kirriemuir Av. G52 49 Q14
Kirriemuir Gdns. (Bishop.) G64 11 Z7
Kirriemuir Pl. G52 49 Q14
  Kirriemuir Av.
Kirriemuir Rd. (Bishop.) G64 11 Z7
Kirtle Dr., Renf. PA4 32 N11
Kirton Av. (Barr.) G78 59 L19
Kishorn Pl. G33 39 CC11
Knapdale St. G22 21 V8
Knights Gate (Both.) G71 69 GG17
Knightsbridge Rd. G13 19 Q9
Knightsbridge St. G13 19 Q9
Knightscliffe Av. G13 19 Q8
Knightswood Cross G13 19 Q8
Knightswood Rd. G13 7 Q7
Knightswood Ter. (Blan.) G72 69 GG19
Knock Way, Pais. PA3 31 L12
Knockburnie Rd. (Both.) G71 69 HH18
Knockhall St. G33 39 CC11
Knockhill Dr. G44 51 V16
Knockhill La. G44 51 V16
  Mount Annan Dr.
Knockhill Rd., Renf. PA4 31 L11
Knockside Av., Pais. PA2 46 J16
Knowe Rd. (Chry.) G69 26 FF8
Knowe Rd., Pais. PA3 31 L12
Knowe Ter. G22 21 V8
  Hillend Rd.
Knowehead Dr. (Udd.) G71 69 GG17
Knowehead Gdns. G41 51 U14
  Knowehead Ter.
Knowehead Gdns. (Udd.) G71 69 GG17
Knowehead Ter. G41 51 U14
Knowetap St. G20 21 U8
Knox St., Pais. PA1 45 H14
Kyle Dr. (Giff.) G46 62 T18
Kyle Rd. (Cumb.) G67 71 PP2
Kyle Sq. (Ruther.) G73 65 Y17
Kyle St. G4 36 W11
Kyleakin Gdns. (Blan.) G72 68 EE19
Kyleakin Rd. (Thorn.) G46 61 Q18
Kyleakin Ter. (Thorn.) G46 61 Q18
Kylepark Av. (Udd.) G71 68 FF17
Kylepark Cres. (Udd.) G71 56 FF16
Kylepark Dr. (Udd.) G71 56 FF16
Kylerhea Rd. (Thorn.) G46 61 Q18

L

La Belle Pl. G3 35 U11
La Crosse Ter. G12 21 U10
Laburnum Gdns. (Kirk.) G66 12 BB5
  Laburnum Gro.
Laburnum Gro. (Kirk.) G66 12 BB5
Laburnum Pl., John. PA5 44 E16
Laburnum Rd. G41 50 T14
  Gower St.
Laburnum Rd. (Cumb.) G67 71 QQ3
Lacy St., Pais. PA1 31 L13
Lade Ter. G52 48 P14
Ladeside Dr., John. PA5 43 C15
Ladhope Pl. G13 18 N8
Lady Anne St. G14 18 N9
Lady Isle Cres. (Udd.) G71 69 GG17
Lady Jane Gate (Both.) G71 69 GG18

Lady La., Pais. PA1 46 J14
Ladyacres (Inch.), Renf. PA4 16 J9
Ladyacres Way (Inch.), Renf. PA4 16 J9
Ladybank Dr. G52 49 R14
Ladyburn St., Pais. PA1 47 L14
Ladyhill Dr. (Bail.) G69 56 EE14
Ladykirk Cres. G52 32 P13
Ladykirk Cres., Pais. PA2 46 K14
Ladykirk Dr. G52 32 P13
Ladyloan Av. G15 6 N6
Ladyloan Ct. G15 6 N6
Ladyloan Pl. G15 6 N6
Ladymuir Cres. G53 49 Q15
Ladysmith Av. (Mill.Pk.), John. PA10 42 B15
Ladywell St. G4 36 X12
Laggan Rd. G43 63 U17
Laggan Rd. (Bishop.) G64 11 Y7
Laggan Ter., Renf. PA4 17 L10
Laidlaw Gdns. (Udd.) G71 57 GG15
Laidlaw St. G5 35 V13
Laigh Kirk La., Pais. PA1 46 K14
  Causeyside St.
Laigh Possil Rd. G23 21 V8
  Balmore Rd.
Laighcartside St., John. PA5 44 E14
Laighlands Rd. (Both.) G71 69 HH19
Laighmuir St. (Udd.) G71 69 GG17
Laighpark Harbour, Pais. PA3 30 K12
Laighpark Vw., Pais. PA3 30 K12
Lainshaw Dr. G45 63 V19
Laird Gro. (Udd.) G71 57 HH16
Laird Pl. G40 52 X14
Lairds Gate (Udd.) G71 69 GG17
Lairds Hill (Cumb.) G67 70 NN3
Lairg Dr. (Blan.) G72 68 FF19
Lamb St. G22 21 V9
Lambhill St. G41 34 T13
Lamerton Dr. G52 32 P13
Lamerton Rd. (Cumb.) G67 71 QQ3
Lamington Rd. G52 48 P14
Lamlash Cres. G33 38 BB12
Lammermoor Av. G52 49 Q14
Lammermoor Dr. (Cumb.) G67 70 NN4
Lammermoor Ct., Pais. PA2 46 K16
Lammermuir Dr., Pais. PA2 46 J15
Lamont Rd. G21 23 Y9
Lanark St. G1 36 W13
Lancaster Cres. G12 20 T10
Lancaster Cres. La. G12 20 S9
  Cleveden Rd.
Lancaster Rd. (Bishop.) G64 11 Y6
Lancaster Ter. G12 20 T10
  Westbourne Gdns. W.
Lancaster Ter. La. G12 20 T10
  Westbourne Gdns. W.
Lancefield Quay G3 35 U12
Lancefield St. G3 35 U12
Landemer Dr. (Ruther.) G73 64 X17
Landressy Pl. G40 52 X14
Landressy St. G40 52 X14
Lane Gdns. G11 20 S10
  North Gardner St.
Lanfine Rd., Pais. PA1 47 L14
Lang Av., Renf. PA4 31 M11
Lang St., Pais. PA1 47 L14
Langa St. G20 21 U8
Langbank St. G5 51 V14
  Eglinton St.
Langbar Cres. G33 39 DD12
Langbar Path G33 39 CC12
Langcraigs Dr., Pais. PA2 58 J17
Langcraigs Ter., Pais. PA2 58 J17
Langcroft Dr. (Camb.) G72 67 CC18
Langcroft Pl. G51 33 Q12
Langcroft Rd. G51 33 Q12
Langcroft Ter. G51 33 Q12
Langdale Av. G33 24 AA10
Langdale St. G33 24 AA10
Langdale's Av. (Cumb.) G68 70 MM3
Langford Av. G53 60 P18
Langford Dr. G53 60 P18

Street	Page	Grid
Liddel Rd. (Cumb.) G67	70	NN3
Liddell St. G32	55	CC15
Liddesdale Av., Pais. PA2	44	F16
Liddesdale Pl. G22	22	W8
Liddesdale Sq.		
Liddesdale Rd. G22	22	W8
Liddesdale Sq. G22	22	W8
Liddesdale Ter. G22	22	X8
Liff Gdns. (Bishop.) G64	23	Z8
Liff Pl. G34	40	FF11
Lightburn Pl. G32	38	BB12
Lightburn Rd. G31	37	Z13
Duke St.		
Lightburn Rd. (Camb.) G72	67	CC18
Lilac Av., Clyde. G81	4	J6
Lilac Cres. (Udd.) G71	57	HH16
Lilac Gdns. (Bishop.) G64	23	Y8
Lillyburn Pl. G15	6	N5
Lily St. G40	53	Y14
Lilybank Av. (Muir.) G69	26	FF8
Lilybank Av. (Camb.) G72	67	CC18
Lilybank Gdns. G12	34	T11
Lilybank Gdns. La. G12	20	T10
Great George St.		
Lilybank La. G12	34	T11
Lilybank Gdns.		
Lilybank Ter. G12	20	T10
Great George St.		
Lilybank Ter. La. G12	20	T10
Great George St.		
Lime Gro. (Lenzie) G66	13	CC5
Lime Gro. (Blan.) G72	68	FF19
Lime La. G14	19	Q10
Lime St.		
Lime St. G14	19	Q10
Limecraigs Cres., Pais. PA2	46	J16
Limecraigs Rd., Pais. PA2	45	H16
Limeside Av. (Ruther.) G73	53	Y16
Limeside Gdns. (Ruther.) G73	53	Z16
Calderwood Rd.		
Limetree Av. (Udd.) G71	57	HH16
Limetree Dr., Clyde. G81	5	L6
Limeview Av., Pais. PA2	45	H16
Limeview Cres., Pais. PA2	45	H16
Limeview Rd., Pais. PA2	45	H16
Limeview Av.		
Limeview Way, Pais. PA2	45	H16
Limeview Av.		
Linacre Dr. G32	39	CC13
Linacre Gdns. G32	39	CC13
Linbank Av. G53	49	Q16
Linburn Pl. G52	32	P13
Linburn Rd. G52	32	N12
Linclive Link Rd. (Linw.), Pais. PA3	28	F13
Linclive Ter. (Linw.), Pais. PA3	28	F13
Lincoln Av. G13	18	P9
Lincoln Av. (Udd.) G71	57	GG15
Lindams (Udd.) G71	69	GG17
Linden Dr., Clyde. G81	5	L5
Linden Pl. G13	19	R8
Linden St. G13	19	R8
Lindores Av. (Ruther.) G73	53	Y16
Lindores St. G42	51	V16
Somerville Dr.		
Lindrick Dr. G23	9	U7
Lindsay Dr. G12	20	S9
Lindsay Pl. G12	20	S9
Lindsay Pl. (Lenzie) G66	13	CC6
Lindsay Pl., John. PA5	44	E14
Thorn Brae		
Lindsaybeg Rd. (Lenzie) G66	13	DD6
Lindsaybeg Rd. (Chry.) G69	14	EE7
Linfern Rd. G12	20	T10
Links Rd. G32	55	CC14
Links Rd. G44	64	W18
Linkwood Av. G15	6	N6
Kinfauns Dr.		
Linkwood Cres. G15	6	N6
Linkwood Dr. G15	6	N6
Linkwood Pl. G15	6	N6
Kinfauns Dr.		
Linlithgow Gdns. G32	39	CC13
Linn Brae, John. PA5	43	D15
Linn Cres., Pais. PA2	46	J16
Linn Dr. G44	63	U18
Linn Pk. G44	63	V18
Linn Pk. Gdns., John. PA5	44	E15
Linnet Av., John. PA5	43	C16
Linnet Pl. G13	18	N8
Linnhe Av. G44	63	V18
Linnhe Av. (Bishop.) G64	11	Y7
Linnhe Dr. (Barr.) G78	59	L17
Linnhe Pl. (Blan.) G72	68	FF19
Linnhead Dr. G53	60	P17
Linnhead Pl. G14	18	P10
Linnpark Av. G44	63	U19
Linnpark Ct. G44	63	U19
Linnwood Ct. G44	63	V17
Bowling Grn. Rd.		
Linside Av., Pais. PA1	47	L14
Lintfield Ln. (Udd.) G71	69	HH17
Myers Cres.		
Linthaugh Rd. G53	48	P15
Linthaugh Ter. G53	49	Q15
Linthaugh Rd.		
Linthouse Bldgs. G51	33	R12
Holmfauld Rd.		
Linthouse Rd. G51	33	R11
Lintlaw (Blan.) G72	68	FF19
Lintlaw Dr. G52	33	Q13
Linton St. G33	38	AA12
Linwell Cres., Pais. PA2	46	J16
Linwood Moss Rd. (Linw.), Pais. PA3	28	F13
Linwood Rd., Pais. PA1	28	F13
Linwood Rd. (Linw.), Pais. PA3	28	F13
Linwood Ter. G12	21	U10
Glasgow St.		
Lismore Av., Renf. PA4	31	M11
Lismore Dr., Pais. PA2	46	J16
Lismore Gdns. (Mill.Pk.), John. PA10	43	C15
Tandlehill Rd.		
Lismore Pl. (Chry.) G69	15	HH6
Altnacreag Gdns.		
Lismore Rd. G12	20	S10
Lister Rd. G52	32	P12
Lister St. G4	36	W11
Lithgow Cres., Pais. PA2	47	L15
Little Dovehill G1	36	W13
Little Holm, Clyde. G81	4	K6
Little St. G3	35	U12
Littlehill St. G21	22	X10
Edgefauld Rd.		
Littleton Dr. G23	8	T7
Rothes Dr.		
Littleton St. G23	8	T7
Rothes Dr.		
Livingstone Av. G52	32	P12
Livingstone Cres. (Blan.) G72	68	FF19
Livingstone St. G21	22	W10
Keppochhill Rd.		
Livingstone St., Clyde. G81	5	M7
Lloyd Av. G32	54	BB15
Lloyd St. G31	37	Y12
Lloyd St. (Ruther.) G73	53	Y15
Loanbank Quad. G51	34	S12
Loancroft Av. (Bail.) G69	56	FF14
Loancroft Gdns. (Udd.) G71	69	GG17
Loancroft Pl. (Bail.) G69	56	EE14
Loanend Cotts. (Camb.) G72	67	DD19
Loanfoot Av. G13	18	P8
Loanhead Av. (Linw.), Pais. PA3	28	E13
Loanhead Av., Renf. PA4	17	M10
Loanhead La. (Linw.), Pais. PA3	28	E13
Loanhead Rd.		
Loanhead Rd. (Linw.), Pais. PA3	28	E13
Loanhead St. G32	38	AA12
Lobnitz Av., Renf. PA4	17	M10
Loch Achray St. G32	55	CC14
Loch Katrine St. G32	55	CC14
Loch Laidon St. G32	55	CC14
Loch Rd. (Stepps) G33	25	CC9
Loch Voil St. G32	55	CC14
Lochaber Dr. (Ruther.) G73	65	Z18
Lochaber Rd. (Bears.) G61	8	S7
Lochaline Av., Pais. PA2	45	H15
Lochaline Dr. G44	63	V18
Lochalsh Dr., Pais. PA2	45	G15
Lochalsh Pl. (Blan.) G72	68	EE19
Lochar Cres. G53	49	Q15
Lochard Dr., Pais. PA2	45	H15
Lochay St. G32	55	CC14
Lochbrae Dr. (Ruther.) G73	65	Z18
Lochbridge Rd. G34	40	EE12
Lochbroom Dr., Pais. PA2	45	H15
Lochburn Cres. G20	21	U8
Lochburn Gro. G20	21	U8
Cadder Rd.		
Lochburn Pas. G20	21	U8
Lochburn Rd. G20	20	T9
Lochdochart Path G34	40	FF12
Lochdochart Rd.		
Lochdochart Rd. G34	40	FF12
Lochearn Cres., Pais. PA2	45	H15
Lochearnhead Rd. G33	25	CC9
Lochend Av. (Gart.) G69	27	GG8
Lochend Cres. (Bears.) G61	7	Q6
Lochend Dr. (Bears.) G61	7	Q6
Lochend Rd. G34	40	EE11
Lochend Rd. (Bears.) G61	7	R6
Lochend Rd. (Gart.) G69	27	GG8
Locher Rd. (Kilb.), John. PA10	42	A14
Lochfauld Rd. G23	9	V7
Lochfield Cres., Pais. PA2	46	K15
Lochfield Dr., Pais. PA2	47	L15
Lochfield Gdns. G34	40	FF11
Lochfield Rd., Pais. PA2	46	K15
Lochgilp St. G20	20	T8
Lochgoin Av. G15	6	N6
Lochgreen St. G33	24	AA10
Lochhead Av. (Linw.), Pais. PA3	28	E13
Lochiel La. (Ruther.) G73	65	Z18
Lochiel Rd. (Thorn.) G46	61	R18
Lochinver Cres., Pais. PA2	45	H15
Lochinver Dr. G44	63	V18
Lochinver Gro. (Camb.) G72	67	CC17
Andrew Sillars Av.		
Lochlea Av., Clyde. G81	5	M6
Lochlea Rd. G43	62	T17
Lochlea Rd. (Cumb.) G67	71	QQ2
Lochlea Rd. (Ruther.) G73	64	X17
Lochleven La. G42	51	V16
Battlefield Rd.		
Lochleven Rd. G42	51	V16
Lochlibo Av. G13	18	N9
Lochlibo Cres. (Barr.) G78	59	L19
Lochlibo Rd. (Barr.) G78	59	L19
Lochlibo Ter. (Barr.) G78	59	L19
Lochmaben Rd. G52	48	N14
Lochmaddy Av. G44	63	V18
Lochside (Bears.) G61	7	R6
Drymen Rd.		
Lochside (Gart.) G69	27	GG9
Lochside Rd. G41	51	U15
Minard Rd.		
Lochview Cotts. (Gart.) G69	27	GG10
Lochview Cres. G33	24	AA10
Lochview Dr. G33	24	AA10
Lochview Gdns. G33	24	AA10
Lochview Pl. G33	24	AA10
Lochview (Bears.) G61	7	R6
Lochview Ter. (Gart.) G69	27	GG9
Lochwood Ln. (Mood.) G69	15	HH6
Lochwood St. G33	38	AA11
Lochy Av., Renf. PA4	32	N11
Lochy Gdns. (Bishop.) G64	11	Y7
Lockerbie Av. G43	63	U17
Lockhart Av. (Camb.) G72	67	CC17
Lockhart Dr. (Camb.) G72	67	CC17
Lockhart St. G21	37	Y11
Locksley Av. G13	19	Q8
Locksley Rd., Pais. PA2	45	G15
Logan Dr. (Cumb.) G68	70	MM2
Logan Dr., Pais. PA3	30	J13
Logan St. G5	52	W15
Logan Twr. (Camb.) G72	67	DD18
Claude Av.		
Loganswell Dr. (Thorn.) G46	61	Q19
Loganswell Gdns. (Thorn.) G46	61	R19
Loganswell Pl. (Thorn.) G46	61	R19
Loganswell Rd. (Thorn.) G46	61	R19
Logie St. G51	34	S12
Lomax St. G33	37	Z12
Lomond Av., Renf. PA4	31	L11

Name	Page	Grid
Lomond Ct. (Barr.) G78	59	M19
Lomond Cres., Pais. PA2	46	J16
Lomond Dr. (Both.) G71	69	HH18
Lomond Dr. (Barr.) G78	59	L18
Lomond Gdns. (Elder.), John. PA5	44	F15
Lomond Pl. (Stepps) G33	25	CC10
Lomond Rd. (Bears.) G61	7	R7
Lomond Rd. (Bishop.) G64	10	X6
Lomond Rd. (Lenzie) G66	13	CC5
Lomond Rd. (Udd.) G71	57	GG15
Lomond St. G22	21	V9
Lomond Vw., Clyde. G81	5	L6
Granville St.		
London Arc. G1	36	W13
London Rd.		
London La. G1	36	W13
London Rd.		
London Rd. G1	36	W13
London Rd. G31	53	Z14
London Rd. G32	54	BB15
London Rd. G40	52	X14
London St., Renf. PA4	17	M9
Lonend, Pais. PA1	46	K14
Long Row (Bail.) G69	40	FF13
Longay Pl. G22	22	W8
Longay St. G22	22	W8
Longcroft Dr., Renf. PA4	17	M10
Longdale Rd. (Chry.) G69	15	GG7
Longden St., Clyde. G81	17	M8
Longford St. G33	37	Z12
Longlee (Bail.) G69	56	EE14
Longmeadow, John. PA5	43	C15
Longstone Rd. G33	38	BB12
Longwill Ter. (Cumb.) G67	71	PP2
Lonmay Rd. G33	39	CC12
Lonsdale Av. (Giff.) G46	62	T18
Loom St. G40	36	X13
Stevenson St.		
Loom Wk. (Kilb.), John. PA10	42	B14
Shuttle St.		
Lora Dr. G52	49	R14
Lord Way (Bail.) G69	41	GG13
Dukes Rd.		
Loretto Pl. G33	38	AA12
Loretto St. G33	38	AA12
Lorne Av. (Chry.) G69	26	FF8
Lorne Cres. (Bishop.) G64	11	Z7
Lorne Dr. (Linw.), Pais. PA3	28	E13
Lorne Rd. G52	32	N12
Lorne St. G51	34	T13
Lorne Ter. (Camb.) G72	66	AA18
Lorraine Gdns. G12	20	T10
Kensington Rd.		
Lorraine Rd. G12	20	T10
Loskin Dr. G22	21	V8
Lossie Cres., Renf. PA4	32	N11
Lossie St. G33	37	Z11
Lothian Cres., Pais. PA2	46	J15
Lothian Gdns. G20	21	U10
Lothian St. G52	32	N12
Loudon Gdns., John. PA5	44	E14
Loudon Rd. G33	24	BB9
Loudon Ter. G12	20	T10
Observatory Rd.		
Lounsdale Av., Pais. PA2	45	H14
Lounsdale Cres., Pais. PA2	45	H15
Lounsdale Dr., Pais. PA2	45	H15
Lounsdale Gro., Pais. PA2	45	H15
Lounsdale Ho., Pais. PA2	45	H15
Gallacher Av.		
Lounsdale Pl. G14	18	P10
Lounsdale Rd., Pais. PA2	45	H15
Lounsdale Way, Pais. PA2	45	H14
Lourdes Av. G52	49	Q14
Lourdes Ct. G52	49	Q14
Lourdes Av.		
Lovat Pl. (Ruther.) G73	65	Z18
Lovat St. G4	36	W11
Love St., Pais. PA3	30	K13
Low Barholm (Kilb.), John. PA10	42	B15
Low Cres., Clyde. G81	18	N8
Low Parksail, Ersk. PA8	16	J8
Low Rd. (Castlehead), Pais. PA2	46	J14
Lower Bourtree Dr. (Ruther.) G73	65	Z18
Lower English Bldgs. G42	51	V14
Lower Millgate (Udd.) G71	57	GG16
Lowndes La., Pais. PA3	30	K13
New Sneddon St.		
Lowndes St. (Barr.) G78	59	M19
Lowther Ter. G12	20	T10
Loyne Dr., Renf. PA4	32	N11
Morriston Cres.		
Luath St. G51	34	S12
Lubas Av. G42	52	W16
Lubas Pl. G42	52	W16
Lubnaig Rd. G43	63	U17
Luckingsford Av. (Inch.), Renf. PA4	16	J8
Luckingsford Dr. (Inch.), Renf. PA4	16	J8
Luckingsford Rd. (Inch.), Renf. PA4	16	J8
Lucy Brae (Udd.) G71	57	GG16
Ludovic Sq., John. PA5	43	D14
Luffness Gdns. G32	54	BB15
Lugar Dr. G52	49	R14
Lugar Pl. G44	64	X17
Luggiebank Pl. (Bail.) G69	57	HH14
Luing Rd. G52	33	R13
Luma Gdns. G51	33	Q12
Lumloch St. G21	23	Y10
Lumsden La. G3	34	T12
Lumsden St.		
Lumsden St. G3	34	T12
Lunan Dr. (Bishop.) G64	23	Z8
Lunan Pl. G51	33	R12
Luncarty Pl. G32	54	BB14
Luncarty St. G32	54	BB14
Lunderston Dr. G53	48	P16
Lundie Gdns. (Bishop.) G64	23	Z8
Lundie St. G32	54	AA14
Luss Rd. G51	33	R12
Lusset Vw., Clyde. G81	5	L6
Radnor St.		
Lusshill Ter. (Udd.) G71	56	EE15
Lyall Pl. G21	22	W10
Keppochhill Rd.		
Lyall St. G21	22	W10
Lybster Cres. (Ruther.) G73	65	Z18
Lye Brae (Cumb.) G67	71	PP3
Lyle Ter., Pais. PA2	46	K15
Lylesland Ct., Pais. PA2	46	K15
Lymburn St. G3	34	T12
Lyndale Pl. G20	20	T8
Lyndale Rd. G20	20	T8
Lyndhurst Gdns. G20	21	U10
Lyndhurst Gdns. La. G20	21	U10
Melrose Gdns.		
Lyne Cft. (Bishop.) G64	11	Y6
Lyne Dr. G23	9	U7
Lynedoch Cres. G3	35	U11
Lynedoch Cres. La. G3	35	U11
Woodlands Rd.		
Lynedoch Pl. G3	35	U11
Lynedoch St. G3	35	U11
Lynedoch Ter. G3	35	U11
Lynn Gdns. G12	20	T10
Great George St.		
Lynn Wk. (Udd.) G71	69	HH17
Flax Rd.		
Lynnhurst (Udd.) G71	57	GG16
Lynton Av. (Giff.) G46	62	S19
Lyon Rd., Pais. PA2	45	G15
Lyon Rd. (Linw.), Pais. PA3	44	E14
Lyoncross Av. (Barr.) G78	59	M19
Lyoncross Cres. (Barr.) G78	59	M18
Lyoncross Rd. G53	48	P15
Lytham Dr. G23	9	U7
Lytham Meadows (Both.) G71	69	GG19

M

Name	Page	Grid
Macbeth Pl. G31	53	Z14
Macbeth St.		
Macbeth St. G31	53	Z14
Macdonald St. (Ruther.) G73	53	Y16
Greenhill Rd.		
Macdougal St. G43	50	T16
Macdowall St., John. PA5	43	D14
Macdowall St., Pais. PA3	30	J13
Macduff Pl. G31	53	Z14
Macduff St. G31	53	Z14
Mace Rd. G13	7	Q7
Macfarlane Rd. (Bears.) G61	7	R6
Machrie Dr. G45	64	X18
Machrie Rd. G45	64	X18
Machrie St. G45	64	X18
Mackean St., Pais. PA3	30	J13
Mackechnie St. G51	34	S12
Mackeith St. G40	52	X14
Mackenzie Dr. (Mill.Pk.), John. PA10	42	B15
Mackie St. G4	22	W10
Borron St.		
Mackiesmill Rd. (Elder.), John. PA5	44	F16
Mackinlay St. G5	51	V14
Maclay Av. (Kilb.), John. PA10	42	B15
Maclean St. G51	34	T13
Maclean St., Clyde. G81	18	N8
Wood Quad.		
Maclehose Rd. (Cumb.) G67	71	QQ2
Maclellan St. G41	34	T13
Macmillan Gdns. (Udd.) G71	57	HH16
Madison Av. G44	63	V17
Madison La. G44	63	V17
Carmunnock Rd.		
Madras Pl. G40	52	X14
Madras St.		
Madras St. G40	52	X14
Mafeking St. G51	34	S13
Magdalen Way, Pais. PA2	44	F16
Magnus Cres. G44	63	V18
Mahon Ct. (Mood.) G69	15	GG7
Maida St. G43	50	S16
Maidland Rd. G53	49	Q16
Mailerbeg Gdns. (Chry.) G69	15	GG6
Mailing Av. (Bishop.) G64	11	Y7
Main Rd. (Elder.), John. PA5	44	F14
Main Rd. (Millarston), Pais. PA1	44	F14
Main Rd. (Castlehead), Pais. PA2	46	J14
Main St. G40	52	X14
Main St. (Thorn.) G46	61	R18
Main St. (Cumb.) G67	71	PP1
Main St. (Bail.) G69	56	EE14
Main St. (Chry.) G69	26	FF8
Main St. (Both.) G71	69	HH19
Main St. (Udd.) G71	69	GG17
Main St. (Camb.) G72	66	BB17
Main St. (Ruther.) G73	53	Y16
Main St. (Barr.) G78	59	L19
Mainhead Ter. (Cumb.) G67	71	PP1
Roadside		
Mainhill Av. (Bail.) G69	40	FF13
Mainhill Dr. (Bail.) G69	40	FF13
Mainhill Pl. (Bail.) G69	40	FF13
Mainhill Rd. (Bail.) G69	41	GG13
Mains Av. (Giff.) G46	62	S19
Mains Dr., Ersk. PA8	4	J7
Mains Hill, Ersk. PA8	4	J7
Mains River, Ersk. PA8	4	J7
Mains Wd., Ersk. PA8	4	J7
Mainscroft, Ersk. PA8	4	J7
Mair St. G51	35	U13
Maitland Pl., Renf. PA4	31	L11
Maitland St. G4	35	V11
Malcolm St. G31	37	Z13
Malin Pl. G33	38	AA12
Mallaig Path G51	33	Q12
Mallaig Pl. G51	33	Q12
Mallaig Rd. G51	33	Q12
Mallard Rd., Clyde. G81	5	L5
Malloch Cres. (Elder.), John. PA5	44	E15
Malloch St. G20	21	U9
Malta St., Clyde. G81	17	M8
Maltbarns St. G20	21	V10
Malvern Ct. G31	37	Y13
Malvern Way, Pais. PA3	30	J12
Mambeg Dr. G51	33	R12
Mamore Pl. G43	62	T17
Mamore St. G43	62	T17
Manchester Dr. G12	20	S9
Manitoba Pl. G31	37	Y13
Janefield St.		
Mannering Ct. G41	50	T16
Pollokshaws Rd.		

Liddel Rd. (Cumb.) G67 70 NN3
Liddell St. G32 55 CC15
Liddesdale Av., Pais. PA2 44 F16
Liddesdale Pl. G22 22 W8
Liddesdale Sq.
Liddesdale Rd. G22 22 W8
Liddesdale Sq. G22 22 W8
Liddesdale Ter. G22 22 X8
Liff Gdns. (Bishop.) G64 23 Z8
Liff Pl. G34 40 FF11
Lightburn Pl. G32 38 BB12
Lightburn Rd. G31 37 Z13
Duke St.
Lightburn Rd. (Camb.) G72 67 CC18
Lilac Av., Clyde. G81 4 J6
Lilac Cres. (Udd.) G71 57 HH16
Lilac Gdns. (Bishop.) G64 23 Y8
Lillyburn Pl. G15 6 N5
Lily St. G40 53 Y14
Lilybank Av. (Muir.) G69 26 FF8
Lilybank Av. (Camb.) G72 67 CC18
Lilybank Gdns. G12 34 T11
Lilybank Gdns. La. G12 20 T10
Great George St.
Lilybank La. G12 34 T11
Lilybank Gdns.
Lilybank Ter. G12 20 T10
Great George St.
Lilybank Ter. La. G12 20 T10
Great George St.
Lime Gro. (Lenzie) G66 13 CC5
Lime Gro. (Blan.) G72 68 FF19
Lime La. G14 19 Q10
Lime St.
Lime St. G14 19 Q10
Limecraigs Cres., Pais. PA2 46 J16
Limecraigs Rd., Pais. PA2 45 H16
Limeside Av. (Ruther.) G73 53 Y16
Limeside Gdns. (Ruther.) 53 Z16
G73
Calderwood Rd.
Limetree Av. (Udd.) G71 57 HH16
Limetree Dr., Clyde. G81 5 L6
Limeview Av., Pais. PA2 45 H16
Limeview Cres., Pais. PA2 45 H16
Limeview Rd., Pais. PA2 45 H16
Limeview Av.
Limeview Way, Pais. PA2 45 H16
Limeview Av.
Linacre Dr. G32 39 CC13
Linacre Gdns. G32 39 CC13
Linbank Av. G53 49 Q16
Linburn Pl. G52 32 P13
Linburn Rd. G52 32 N12
Linclive Link Rd. (Linw.), 28 F13
Pais. PA3
Linclive Ter. (Linw.), Pais. 28 F13
PA3
Lincoln Av. G13 18 P9
Lincoln Av. (Udd.) G71 57 GG15
Lindams (Udd.) G71 69 GG17
Linden Dr., Clyde. G81 5 L5
Linden Pl. G13 19 R8
Linden St. G13 19 R8
Lindores Av. (Ruther.) G73 53 Y16
Lindores St. G42 51 V16
Somerville Dr.
Lindrick Dr. G23 9 U7
Lindsay Dr. G12 20 S9
Lindsay Pl. G12 20 S9
Lindsay Pl. (Lenzie) G66 13 CC6
Lindsay Pl., John. PA5 44 E14
Thorn Brae
Lindsaybeg Rd. (Lenzie) G66 13 DD6
Lindsaybeg Rd. (Chry.) G69 14 EE7
Linfern Rd. G12 20 T10
Links Rd. G32 55 CC14
Links Rd. G44 64 W18
Linkwood Av. G15 6 N6
Kinfauns Dr.
Linkwood Cres. G15 6 N6
Linkwood Dr. G15 6 N6
Linkwood Pl. G15 6 N6
Kinfauns Dr.
Linlithgow Gdns. G32 39 CC13
Linn Brae, John. PA5 43 D15
Linn Cres., Pais. PA2 46 J16
Linn Dr. G44 63 U18
Linn Pk. G44 63 V18

Linn Pk. Gdns., John. PA5 44 E15
Linnet Av., John. PA5 43 C16
Linnet Pl. G13 18 N8
Linnhe Av. G44 63 V18
Linnhe Av. (Bishop.) G64 11 Y7
Linnhe Dr. (Barr.) G78 59 L17
Linnhe Pl. (Blan.) G72 68 FF19
Linnhead Dr. G53 60 P17
Linnhead Pl. G14 18 P10
Linnpark Av. G44 63 U19
Linnpark Ct. G44 63 U19
Linnwood Ct. G44 63 V17
Bowling Grn. Rd.
Linside Av., Pais. PA1 47 L14
Lintfield Ln. (Udd.) G71 69 HH17
Myers Cres.
Linthaugh Rd. G53 48 P15
Linthaugh Ter. G53 49 Q15
Linthaugh Rd.
Linthouse Bldgs. G51 33 R12
Holmfauld Rd.
Linthouse Rd. G51 33 R11
Lintlaw (Blan.) G72 68 FF19
Lintlaw Dr. G52 33 Q13
Linton St. G33 38 AA12
Linwell Cres., Pais. PA2 46 J16
Linwood Moss Rd. (Linw.), 28 F13
Pais. PA3
Linwood Rd., Pais. PA1 28 F13
Linwood Rd. (Linw.), Pais. 28 F13
PA3
Linwood Ter. G12 21 U10
Glasgow St.
Lismore Av., Renf. PA4 31 M11
Lismore Dr., Pais. PA2 46 J16
Lismore Gdns. (Mill.Pk.), 43 C15
John. PA10
Tandlehill Rd.
Lismore Pl. (Chry.) G69 15 HH6
Altnacreag Gdns.
Lismore Rd. G12 20 S10
Lister Rd. G52 32 P12
Lister St. G4 36 W11
Lithgow Cres., Pais. PA2 47 L15
Little Dovehill G1 36 W13
Little Holm, Clyde. G81 4 K6
Little St. G3 35 U12
Littlehill St. G21 22 X10
Edgefauld Rd.
Littleton Dr. G23 8 T7
Rothes Dr.
Littleton St. G23 8 T7
Rothes Dr.
Livingstone Av. G52 32 P12
Livingstone Cres. (Blan.) 68 FF19
G72
Livingstone St. G21 22 W10
Keppochhill Rd.
Livingstone St., Clyde. G81 5 M7
Lloyd Av. G32 54 BB15
Lloyd St. G31 37 Y12
Lloyd St. (Ruther.) G73 53 Y15
Loanbank Quad. G51 34 S12
Loancroft Av. (Bail.) G69 56 FF14
Loancroft Gdns. (Udd.) G71 69 GG17
Loancroft Pl. (Bail.) G69 56 EE14
Loanend Cotts. (Camb.) G72 67 DD19
Loanfoot Av. G13 18 P8
Loanhead Av. (Linw.), Pais. 28 E13
PA3
Loanhead Av., Renf. PA4 17 M10
Loanhead La. (Linw.), Pais. 28 E13
PA3
Loanhead Rd.
Loanhead Rd. (Linw.), Pais. 28 E13
PA3
Loanhead St. G32 38 AA12
Lobnitz Av., Renf. PA4 17 M10
Loch Achray St. G32 55 CC14
Loch Katrine St. G32 55 CC14
Loch Laidon St. G32 55 CC14
Loch Rd. (Stepps) G33 25 CC9
Loch Voil St. G32 55 CC14
Lochaber Dr. (Ruther.) G73 65 Z18
Lochaber Rd. (Bears.) G61 8 S7
Lochaline Av., Pais. PA2 45 H15
Lochaline Dr. G44 63 V18
Lochalsh Dr., Pais. PA2 45 G15
Lochalsh Pl. (Blan.) G72 68 EE19

Lochar Cres. G53 49 Q15
Lochard Dr., Pais. PA2 45 H15
Lochay St. G32 55 CC14
Lochbrae Dr. (Ruther.) G73 65 Z18
Lochbridge Rd. G34 40 EE12
Lochbroom Dr., Pais. PA2 45 H15
Lochburn Cres. G20 21 U8
Lochburn Gro. G20 21 U8
Cadder Rd.
Lochburn Pas. G20 21 U8
Lochburn Rd. G20 20 T9
Lochdochart Path G34 40 FF12
Lochdochart Rd.
Lochdochart Rd. G34 40 FF12
Lochearn Cres., Pais. PA2 45 H15
Lochearnhead Rd. G33 25 CC9
Lochend Av. (Gart.) G69 27 GG8
Lochend Cres. (Bears.) G61 7 Q6
Lochend Dr. (Bears.) G61 7 Q6
Lochend Rd. G34 40 EE11
Lochend Rd. (Bears.) G61 7 R6
Lochend Rd. (Gart.) G69 27 GG8
Locher Rd. (Kilb.), John. 42 A14
PA10
Lochfauld Rd. G23 9 V7
Lochfield Cres., Pais. PA2 46 K15
Lochfield Dr., Pais. PA2 47 L15
Lochfield Gdns. G34 40 FF11
Lochfield Rd., Pais. PA2 46 K15
Lochgilp St. G20 20 T8
Lochgoin Av. G15 6 N6
Lochgreen St. G33 24 AA10
Lochhead Av. (Linw.), Pais. 28 E13
PA3
Lochiel La. (Ruther.) G73 65 Z18
Lochiel Rd. (Thorn.) G46 61 R18
Lochinver Cres., Pais. PA2 45 H15
Lochinver Dr. G44 63 V18
Lochinver Gro. (Camb.) G72 67 CC17
Andrew Sillars Av.
Lochlea Av., Clyde. G81 5 M6
Lochlea Rd. G43 62 T17
Lochlea Rd. (Cumb.) G67 71 QQ2
Lochlea Rd. (Ruther.) G73 64 X17
Lochleven La. G42 51 V16
Battlefield Rd.
Lochleven Rd. G42 51 V16
Lochlibo Av. G13 18 N9
Lochlibo Cres. (Barr.) G78 59 L19
Lochlibo Rd. (Barr.) G78 59 L19
Lochlibo Ter. (Barr.) G78 59 L19
Lochmaben Rd. G52 48 N14
Lochmaddy Av. G44 63 V18
Lochside (Bears.) G61 7 R6
Drymen Rd.
Lochside (Gart.) G69 27 GG9
Lochside St. G41 51 U15
Minard Rd.
Lochview Cotts. (Gart.) G69 27 GG10
Lochview Cres. G33 24 AA10
Lochview Dr. G33 24 AA10
Lochview Gdns. G33 24 AA10
Lochview Pl. G33 24 AA10
Lochview Rd. (Bears.) G61 7 R6
Lochview Ter. (Gart.) G69 27 GG9
Lochwood Ln. (Mood.) G69 15 HH6
Lochwood St. G33 38 AA11
Lochy Av., Renf. PA4 32 N11
Lochy Gdns. (Bishop.) G64 11 Y7
Lockerbie Av. G43 63 U17
Lockhart Av. (Camb.) G72 67 CC17
Lockhart Dr. (Camb.) G72 67 CC17
Lockhart St. G21 37 Y11
Locksley Av. G13 19 Q8
Locksley Rd., Pais. PA2 45 G15
Logan Dr. (Cumb.) G68 70 MM2
Logan Dr., Pais. PA3 30 J13
Logan St. G5 52 W15
Logan Twr. (Camb.) G72 67 DD18
Claude Av.
Loganswell Dr. (Thorn.) G46 61 Q19
Loganswell Gdns. (Thorn.) 61 R19
G46
Loganswell Pl. (Thorn.) G46 61 R19
Loganswell Rd. (Thorn.) 61 R19
G46
Logie St. G51 34 S12
Lomax St. G33 37 Z12
Lomond Av., Renf. PA4 31 L11

Lomond Ct. (Barr.) G78 59 M19
Lomond Cres., Pais. PA2 46 J16
Lomond Dr. (Both.) G71 69 HH18
Lomond Dr. (Barr.) G78 59 L18
Lomond Gdns. (Elder.), 44 F15
John. PA5
Lomond Pl. (Stepps) G33 25 CC10
Lomond Rd. (Bears.) G61 7 R7
Lomond Rd. (Bishop.) G64 10 X6
Lomond Rd. (Lenzie) G66 13 CC5
Lomond Rd. (Udd.) G71 57 GG15
Lomond St. G22 21 V9
Lomond Vw., Clyde. G81 5 L6
Granville St.
London Arc. G1 36 W13
London Rd.
London La. G1 36 W13
London Rd.
London Rd. G1 36 W13
London Rd. G31 53 Z14
London Rd. G32 54 BB15
London Rd. G40 52 X14
London St., Renf. PA4 17 M9
Lonend, Pais. PA1 46 K14
Long Row (Bail.) G69 40 FF13
Longay Gdns. G22 22 W8
Longay St. G22 22 W8
Longcroft Dr., Renf. PA4 17 M10
Longdale Rd. (Chry.) G69 15 GG7
Longden St., Clyde. G81 17 M8
Longford St. G33 37 Z12
Longlee (Bail.) G69 56 EE14
Longmeadow, John. PA5 43 C15
Longstone Rd. G33 38 BB12
Longwill Ter. (Cumb.) G67 71 PP2
Lonmay Rd. G33 39 CC12
Lonsdale Av. (Giff.) G46 62 T18
Loom St. G40 36 X13
Stevenson St.
Loom Wk. (Kilb.), John. 42 B14
PA10
Shuttle St.
Lora Dr. G52 49 R14
Lord Way (Bail.) G69 41 GG13
Dukes Rd.
Loretto Pl. G33 38 AA12
Loretto St. G33 38 AA12
Lorne Av. (Chry.) G69 26 FF8
Lorne Cres. (Bishop.) G64 11 Z7
Lorne Dr. (Linw.), Pais. PA3 28 E13
Lorne Rd. G52 32 N12
Lorne St. G51 34 T13
Lorne Ter. (Camb.) G72 66 AA18
Lorraine Gdns. G12 20 T10
Kensington Rd.
Lorraine Rd. G12 20 T10
Loskin Dr. G22 21 V8
Lossie Cres., Renf. PA4 32 N11
Lossie St. G33 37 Z11
Lothian Cres., Pais. PA2 46 J15
Lothian Gdns. G20 21 U10
Lothian St. G52 32 N12
Loudon Gdns., John. PA5 44 E14
Loudon Rd. G33 24 BB9
Loudon Ter. G12 20 T10
Observatory Rd.
Lounsdale Av., Pais. PA2 45 H14
Lounsdale Cres., Pais. PA2 45 H15
Lounsdale Dr., Pais. PA2 45 H15
Lounsdale Gro., Pais. PA2 45 H15
Lounsdale Ho., Pais. PA2 45 H15
Gallacher Av.
Lounsdale Pl. G14 18 P10
Lounsdale Rd., Pais. PA2 45 H15
Lounsdale Way, Pais. PA2 45 H14
Lourdes Av. G52 49 Q14
Lourdes Ct. G52 49 Q14
Lourdes Av.
Lovat Pl. (Ruther.) G73 65 Z18
Lovat St. G4 36 W11
Love St., Pais. PA3 30 K13
Low Barholm (Kilb.), John. 42 B15
PA10
Low Cres., Clyde. G81 18 N8
Low Parksail, Ersk. PA8 16 J8
Low Rd. (Castlehead), Pais. 46 J14
PA2
Lower Bourtree Dr. 65 Z18
(Ruther.) G73

Lower English Bldgs. G42 51 V14
Lower Millgate (Udd.) G71 57 GG16
Lowndes La., Pais. PA3 30 K13
New Sneddon St.
Lowndes St. (Barr.) G78 59 M19
Lowther Ter. G12 20 T10
Loyne Dr., Renf. PA4 32 N11
Morriston Cres.
Luath St. G51 34 S12
Lubas Av. G42 52 W16
Lubas Pl. G42 52 W16
Lubnaig Rd. G43 63 U17
Luckingsford Av. (Inch.), 16 J8
Renf. PA4
Luckingsford Dr. (Inch.), 16 J8
Renf. PA4
Luckingsford Rd. (Inch.), 16 J8
Renf. PA4
Lucy Brae (Udd.) G71 57 GG16
Ludovic Sq., John. PA5 43 D14
Luffness Gdns. G32 54 BB15
Lugar Dr. G52 49 R14
Lugar Pl. G44 64 X17
Luggiebank Pl. (Bail.) G69 57 HH14
Luing Rd. G52 33 R13
Luma Gdns. G51 33 Q12
Lumloch St. G21 23 Y10
Lumsden La. G3 34 T12
Lumsden St.
Lumsden St. G3 34 T12
Lunan Dr. (Bishop.) G64 23 Z8
Lunan Pl. G51 33 R12
Luncarty Pl. G32 54 BB14
Luncarty St. G32 54 BB14
Lunderston Dr. G53 48 P16
Lundie Gdns. (Bishop.) G64 23 Z8
Lundie St. G32 54 AA14
Luss Rd. G51 33 R12
Lusset Vw., Clyde. G81 5 L6
Radnor St.
Lusshill Ter. (Udd.) G71 56 EE15
Lyall Pl. G21 22 W10
Keppochhill Rd.
Lyall St. G21 22 W10
Lybster Cres. (Ruther.) G73 65 Z18
Lye Brae (Cumb.) G67 71 PP3
Lyle Ter., Pais. PA2 46 K15
Lylesland Ct., Pais. PA2 46 K15
Lymburn St. G3 34 T12
Lyndale Pl. G20 20 T8
Lyndale Rd. G20 20 T8
Lyndhurst Gdns. G20 21 U10
Lyndhurst Gdns. La. G20 21 U10
Melrose Gdns.
Lyne Cft. (Bishop.) G64 11 Y6
Lyne Dr. G23 9 U7
Lynedoch Cres. G3 35 U11
Lynedoch Cres. La. G3 35 U11
Woodlands Rd.
Lynedoch Pl. G3 35 U11
Lynedoch St. G3 35 U11
Lynedoch Ter. G3 35 U11
Lynn Gdns. G12 20 T10
Great George St.
Lynn Wk. (Udd.) G71 69 HH17
Flax Rd.
Lynnhurst (Udd.) G71 57 GG16
Lynton Av. (Giff.) G46 62 S19
Lyon Rd., Pais. PA2 45 G15
Lyon Rd. (Linw.), Pais. PA3 44 E14
Lyoncross Av. (Barr.) G78 59 M19
Lyoncross Cres. (Barr.) G78 59 M18
Lyoncross Rd. G53 48 P15
Lytham Dr. G23 9 U7
Lytham Meadows (Both.) 69 GG19
G71

M

Macbeth Pl. G31 53 Z14
Macbeth St.
Macbeth St. G31 53 Z14
Macdonald St. (Ruther.) G73 53 Y16
Greenhill Rd.
Macdougal St. G43 50 T16
Macdowall St., John. PA5 43 D14
Macdowall St., Pais. PA3 30 J13
Macduff Pl. G31 53 Z14
Macduff St. G31 53 Z14

Mace Rd. G13 7 Q7
Macfarlane Rd. (Bears.) G61 7 R6
Machrie Dr. G45 64 X18
Machrie Rd. G45 64 X18
Machrie St. G45 64 X18
Mackean St., Pais. PA3 30 J13
Mackechnie St. G51 34 S12
Mackeith St. G40 52 X14
Mackenzie Dr. (Mill.Pk.), 42 B15
John. PA10
Mackie St. G4 22 W10
Borron St.
Mackiesmill Rd. (Elder.), 44 F16
John. PA5
Mackinlay St. G5 51 V14
Maclay Av. (Kilb.), John. 42 B15
PA10
Maclean St. G51 34 T13
Maclean St., Clyde. G81 18 N8
Wood Quad.
Maclehose Rd. (Cumb.) G67 71 QQ2
Maclellan St. G41 34 T13
Macmillan Gdns. (Udd.) G71 57 HH16
Madison Av. G44 63 V17
Madison La. G44 63 V17
Carmunnock Rd.
Madras Pl. G40 52 X14
Madras St.
Madras St. G40 52 X14
Mafeking St. G51 34 S13
Magdalen Way, Pais. PA2 44 F16
Magnus Cres. G44 63 V18
Mahon Ct. (Mood.) G69 15 GG7
Maida St. G43 50 S16
Maidland Rd. G53 49 Q16
Mailerbeg Gdns. (Chry.) 15 GG6
G69
Mailing Av. (Bishop.) G64 11 Y7
Main Rd. (Elder.), John. PA5 44 F14
Main Rd. (Millarston), Pais. 44 F14
PA1
Main Rd. (Castlehead), 46 J14
Pais. PA2
Main St. G40 52 X14
Main St. (Thorn.) G46 61 R18
Main St. (Cumb.) G67 71 PP1
Main St. (Bail.) G69 56 EE14
Main St. (Chry.) G69 26 FF8
Main St. (Both.) G71 69 HH19
Main St. (Udd.) G71 69 GG17
Main St. (Camb.) G72 66 BB17
Main St. (Ruther.) G73 53 Y16
Main St. (Barr.) G78 59 L19
Mainhead Ter. (Cumb.) G67 71 PP1
Roadside
Mainhill Av. (Bail.) G69 40 FF13
Mainhill Dr. (Bail.) G69 40 FF13
Mainhill Pl. (Bail.) G69 40 FF13
Mainhill Rd. (Bail.) G69 41 GG13
Mains Av. (Giff.) G46 62 S19
Mains Dr., Ersk. PA8 4 J7
Mains Hill, Ersk. PA8 4 J7
Mains River, Ersk. PA8 4 J7
Mains Wd., Ersk. PA8 4 J7
Mainscroft, Ersk. PA8 4 J7
Mair St. G51 35 U13
Maitland Pl., Renf. PA4 31 L11
Maitland St. G4 35 V11
Malcolm St. G31 37 Z13
Malin Pl. G33 38 AA12
Mallaig Path G51 33 Q12
Mallaig Pl. G51 33 Q12
Mallaig Rd. G51 33 Q12
Mallard Rd., Clyde. G81 5 L5
Malloch Cres. (Elder.), 44 E15
John. PA5
Malloch St. G20 21 U9
Malta St., Clyde. G81 17 M8
Maltbarns St. G20 21 V10
Malvern Ct. G31 37 Y13
Malvern Way, Pais. PA3 30 J12
Mambeg Dr. G51 33 R12
Mamore Pl. G43 62 T17
Mamore St. G43 62 T17
Manchester Dr. G12 20 S9
Manitoba Pl. G31 37 Y13
Janefield St.
Mannering Ct. G41 50 T16
Pollokshaws Rd.

Mannering Rd. G41	50	T16
Mannering Rd., Pais. PA2	45	G16
Mannofield (Bears.) G61	7	Q6
Chesters Rd.		
Manor Rd. G14	19	R10
Manor Rd. G15	6	N7
Manor Rd. (Gart.) G69	27	GG9
Manor Rd., Pais. PA2	45	G15
Manor Way (Ruther.) G73	65	Y18
Manresa Pl. G4	35	V11
Braid Sq.		
Manse Av. (Bears.) G61	7	R5
Manse Av. (Both.) G71	69	HH19
Manse Brae G44	63	V17
Manse Ct. (Barr.) G78	59	M18
Manse Rd. G32	55	CC14
Manse Rd. (Bears.) G61	7	R5
Manse Rd. (Bail.) G69	41	GG13
Manse St., Renf. PA4	17	M10
Mansefield Av. (Camb.) G72	66	BB18
Mansefield Dr. (Udd.) G71	69	GG17
Mansel St. G21	22	X9
Mansewood Rd. G43	62	S17
Mansfield Rd. G52	32	N12
Mansfield St. G11	34	T11
Mansion Ct. (Camb.) G72	66	BB17
Mansion St. G22	22	W9
Mansion St. (Camb.) G72	66	BB17
Mansionhouse Av. G32	55	CC16
Mansionhouse Dr. G32	39	CC13
Mansionhouse Gdns. G41	51	U16
Mansionhouse Rd.		
Mansionhouse Gro. G32	55	DD14
Mansionhouse Rd. G32	55	DD14
Mansionhouse Rd. G41	51	U16
Mansionhouse Rd. G42	51	U16
Mansionhouse Rd., Pais. PA1	31	L13
Maple Dr. (Kirk.) G66	12	BB5
Maple Dr., Clyde. G81	4	K5
Maple Dr., John. PA5	44	E16
Maple Rd. G41	50	S14
Mar Gdns. (Ruther.) G73	65	Z18
March La. G41	51	U15
Nithsdale Dr.		
March St. G41	51	U15
Marchbank Gdns., Pais. PA1	47	M14
Marchfield (Bishop.) G64	10	X6
Marchfield Av., Pais. PA3	30	J12
Marchglen Pl. G51	33	Q12
Mallaig Rd.		
Marchmont Gdns. (Bishop.) G64	10	X6
Marchmont Ter. G12	20	T10
Observatory Rd.		
Maree Dr. G52	49	R14
Maree Gdns. (Bishop.) G64	11	Y7
Maree Rd., Pais. PA2	45	H15
Marfield St. G32	38	AA13
Margaret St. G1	36	W12
Martha St.		
Margaretta Bldgs. G44	63	V17
Clarkston Rd.		
Marguerite Av. (Lenzie) G66	13	CC5
Marguerite Dr. (Kirk.) G66	13	CC5
Marguerite Gdns. (Kirk.) G66	13	CC5
Marguerite Gdns. (Both.) G71	69	HH18
Marguerite Gro. (Kirk.) G66	13	CC5
Marine Cres. G51	35	U13
Marine Gdns. G51	35	U13
Mavisbank Gdns.		
Mariscat Rd. G41	51	U15
Marjory Dr., Pais. PA3	31	L12
Marjory Rd., Renf. PA4	31	L11
Market St. G40	36	X13
Markinch St. G5	35	V13
West St.		
Marlborough Av. G11	19	R10
Marlborough La. N. G11	19	R10
Marlborough Av.		
Marlborough La. S. G11	19	R10
Marlborough Av.		
Marldon La. G11	19	R10
Marlborough Av.		
Marlow St. G41	51	U14
Marlow Ter. G41	35	U13
Seaward St.		
Marmion Pl. (Cumb.) G67	70	NN4
Marmion Rd. (Cumb.) G67	70	NN4
Marmion Rd., Pais. PA2	45	G16
Marmion St. G20	21	U10
Marne St. G31	37	Y12
Marnock Ter., Pais. PA2	47	L15
Marnock Way (Chry.) G69	15	GG7
Braeside Av.		
Marshall's La., Pais. PA1	46	K14
Mart St. G1	36	W13
Martha St. G1	36	W12
Martin Cres. (Bail.) G69	40	FF13
Martin St. G40	52	X14
Martlet Dr., John. PA5	43	C16
Martyr St. G4	36	X12
Martyrs Pl. (Bishop.) G64	23	Y8
Marwick St. G31	37	Y12
Mary Sq. (Bail.) G69	41	GG13
Mary St., John. PA5	44	E14
Mary St., Pais. PA2	46	K15
Marywood Sq. G41	51	U15
Masonfield Av. (Cumb.) G68	70	MM3
Masterton St. G21	22	W10
Mathieson La. G5	52	W14
Mathieson St.		
Mathieson Rd. (Ruther.) G73	53	Z15
Mathieson St. G5	52	W14
Mathieson St., Pais. PA1	31	L13
Matilda Rd. G41	51	U14
Mauchline St. G5	51	V14
Maukinfauld Ct. G32	54	AA14
Maukinfauld Rd. G32	54	AA14
Mauldslie St. G40	53	Y14
Maule Dr. G11	34	S11
Mavis Bk. (Bishop.) G64	22	X8
Mavisbank Gdns. G51	35	U13
Mavisbank Rd. G51	34	S12
Govan Rd.		
Mavisbank Ter., Pais. PA1	46	K14
Maxton Av. (Barr.) G78	59	L18
Maxton Gro. (Barr.) G78	59	L18
Maxton Ter. (Camb.) G72	66	AA18
Maxwell Av. G41	51	U14
Maxwell Av. (Bears.) G61	7	R7
Maxwell Av. (Bail.) G69	56	EE14
Maxwell Dr. G41	50	T14
Maxwell Dr. (Bail.) G69	40	EE13
Maxwell Gdns. G41	50	T14
Maxwell Gro. G41	50	T14
Maxwell Oval G41	51	U14
Maxwell Pl. G41	51	V14
Maxwell Rd. G41	51	U14
Maxwell Sq. G41	51	U14
Maxwell St. G1	36	W13
Maxwell St. (Bail.) G69	56	EE14
Maxwell St., Clyde. G81	4	K6
Maxwell St., Pais. PA3	30	K13
Old Sneddon St.		
Maxwellton Rd., Pais. PA1	45	H14
Maxwellton St., Pais. PA1	46	J14
Maxwellton Trd. Est., Pais. PA1	45	H14
Maxwelton Rd. G33	37	Z11
May Rd., Pais. PA2	46	K16
May Ter. G42	51	V16
Prospecthill Rd.		
May Ter. (Giff.) G46	62	T18
Maybank La. G42	51	V15
Victoria Rd.		
Maybank St. G42	51	V15
Mayberry Cres. G32	39	CC13
Mayberry Gdns. G32	39	CC13
Mayberry Gro. G32	39	CC13
Maybole St. G53	60	N17
Mayfield St. G20	21	U9
McAlpine St. G2	35	V13
McArthur St. G43	50	T16
Pleasance St.		
McArthur St., Clyde. G81	17	M8
McAslin Ct. G4	36	W12
McAslin St. G4	36	X12
McCallum Av. (Ruther.) G73	53	Y16
McClue Av., Renf. PA4	17	L10
McClue Rd., Renf. PA4	17	L10
McCracken Av., Renf. PA4	31	L11
McCreery St., Clyde. G81	17	M8
McCulloch St. G41	51	U14
McDonald Av., John. PA5	43	D15
McDonald Cres., Clyde. G81	17	M8
McEwan St. G31	37	Z13
McFarlane St. G4	36	X13
McFarlane St., Pais. PA3	30	J12
McGhee St., Clyde. G81	5	L6
McGown St., Pais. PA3	30	J13
McGregor Av., Renf. PA4	31	L11
Porterfield Rd.		
McGregor Rd. (Cumb.) G67	70	NN3
McGregor St. G51	33	R13
McGregor St., Clyde. G81	17	M8
McIntosh Ct. G31	36	X12
McIntosh St.		
McIntosh St. G31	36	X12
McIntyre Pl., Pais. PA2	46	K15
McIntyre St. G3	35	U12
McIntyre Ter. (Camb.) G72	66	BB17
McIver St. (Camb.) G72	67	CC17
McKay Cres., John. PA5	44	E15
McKenzie Av., Clyde. G81	5	L6
McKenzie St., Pais. PA3	29	H13
McKerrel St., Pais. PA1	31	L13
McLaren Av., Renf. PA4	31	M11
Newmains Rd.		
McLaren Cres. G20	21	U8
McLaren Gdns. G20	21	U8
McLaurin Cres., John. PA5	43	C15
McLean Pl., Pais. PA3	30	J12
McLean Sq. G51	34	T13
McLennan St. G42	51	V16
McLeod St. G4	36	X12
McNair St. G32	38	BB13
McNeil St. G5	52	W14
McNeill Av., Clyde. G81	6	N7
McPhail St. G40	52	X14
McPhater St. G4	35	V11
Dunblane St.		
McPherson Dr. (Both.) G71	69	HH18
Wordsworth Way		
McPherson St. G1	36	W13
High St.		
McTaggart Rd. (Cumb.) G67	70	NN4
Meadow La., Renf. PA4	17	M9
Meadow Rd. G11	34	S11
Meadow Vw. (Cumb.) G67	71	QQ2
Meadowbank La. (Udd.) G71	68	FF17
Meadowburn (Bishop.) G64	11	Y6
Meadowburn Av. (Lenzie) G66	13	DD5
Meadowhead Av. (Chry.) G69	15	GG7
Meadowpark St. G31	37	Y12
Meadowside (Elder.), John. PA5	44	F15
Meadowside Quay G11	33	R11
Meadowside St. G11	34	S11
Meadowside St., Renf. PA4	17	M9
Meadowwell St. G32	38	BB13
Meadside Av. (Kilb.), John. PA10	42	B14
Meadside Rd. (Kilb.), John. PA10	42	B14
Mears Way (Bishop.) G64	11	Z7
Medlar Rd. (Cumb.) G67	71	QQ3
Medwin St. (Camb.) G72	67	DD17
Mill Rd.		
Medwyn St. G14	19	Q10
Meek Pl. (Camb.) G72	66	BB17
Meetinghouse La., Pais. PA1	30	K13
Moss St.		
Megan Gate G40	52	X14
Megan St.		
Megan St. G40	52	X14
Meikle Av., Renf. PA4	31	M11
Meikle Rd. G53	49	Q16
Meiklerig Cres. G53	49	Q15
Meikleriggs Dr., Pais. PA2	45	H15

Meiklewood Rd. G51 33 Q13
Melbourne Av., Clyde. G81 4 J5
Melbourne Ct. (Giff.) G46 62 T18
Melbourne St. G31 36 X13
Meldon Pl. G51 33 R12
Meldrum Gdns. G41 50 T15
Meldrum St., Clyde. G81 18 N8
Melford Av. (Giff.) G46 62 T19
Melford Way, Pais. PA3 31 L12
  Knock Way
Melfort Av. G41 50 S14
Melfort Av., Clyde. G81 5 L6
Melfort Gdns. (Mill.Pk.), 43 C15
  John. PA10
  Milliken Pk. Rd.
Mellerstain Dr. G14 18 N9
Melness Pl. G51 33 Q12
  Mallaig Rd.
Melrose Av. (Bail.) G69 41 GG13
Melrose Av. (Ruther.) G73 53 Y16
Melrose Av., Pais. PA2 45 H15
Melrose Av. (Linw.), Pais. 28 E13
  PA3
Melrose Ct. (Ruther.) G73 53 Y16
  Dunard Rd.
Melrose Gdns. G20 21 U10
Melrose Gdns. (Udd.) G71 57 GG15
  Lincoln Av.
Melrose Pl. (Blan.) G72 68 FF19
Melrose St. G4 35 V11
  Queens Cres.
Melvaig Pl. G20 20 T9
Melvick Pl. G51 33 Q12
  Mallaig Rd.
Melville Ct. G1 36 W12
  Brunswick St.
Melville Gdns. (Bishop.) 11 Y7
  G64
Melville St. G41 51 U14
Memel St. G21 22 X9
Memus Av. G52 49 Q14
Mennock Dr. (Bishop.) G64 11 Y6
Menock Rd. G44 63 V17
Menteith Av. (Bishop.) G64 11 Y7
Menteith Dr. (Ruther.) G73 65 Z19
Menteith Pl. (Ruther.) G73 65 Z19
Menzies Dr. G21 23 Y9
Menzies Pl. G21 23 Y9
Menzies Rd. G21 23 Y9
Merchant La. G1 36 W13
  Clyde St.
Merchants Clo. (Kilb.), 42 B14
  John. PA10
  Church St.
Merchiston St. G32 38 AA12
Merkland Ct. G11 34 S11
  Vine St.
Merkland St. G11 34 S11
Merksworth Way, Pais. PA3 30 J12
  Mosslands Rd.
Merlewood Av. (Both.) G71 69 HH18
Merlin Way, Pais. PA3 31 L12
Merlinford Av., Renf. PA4 18 N10
Merlinford Cres., Renf. PA4 18 N10
Merlinford Dr., Renf. PA4 18 N10
Merlinford Way, Renf. PA4 18 N10
Merrick Gdns. G51 34 S13
Merrick Ter. (Udd.) G71 57 HH16
Merrick Way (Ruther.) G73 65 Y18
Merryburn Av. (Giff.) G46 62 T17
Merrycrest Av. (Giff.) G46 62 T18
Merrycroft Av. (Giff.) G46 62 T18
Merryland Pl. G51 34 T12
Merryland St. G51 34 S12
Merrylee Cres. (Giff.) G46 62 T17
Merrylee Pk. Av. (Giff.) G46 62 T18
Merrylee Pk. La. (Giff.) G46 62 T18
Merrylee Pk. Ms. (Giff.) G46 62 T18
Merrylee Rd. G43 62 T17
Merrylee Rd. G44 62 T17
Merryton Av. G15 6 P6
Merryton Av. (Giff.) G46 62 T18
Merryton Pl. G15 6 P6
Merryvale Av. (Giff.) G46 62 T18
Merryvale Pl. (Giff.) G46 62 T17
Merton Dr. G52 32 P13
Meryon Gdns. G32 55 CC15
Meryon Rd. G32 55 CC15
Methil St. G14 19 Q10

Methuen Rd., Pais. PA3 31 L11
Methven Av. (Bears.) G61 8 S5
Methven St. G31 53 Z14
Methven St., Clyde. G81 4 K6
Metropole La. G1 35 V13
  Howard St.
Mews La., Pais. PA3 30 K12
  Renfrew Rd.
Micklehouse Oval (Bail.) 40 EE13
  G69
  Micklehouse Rd.
Micklehouse Pl. (Bail.) G69 40 EE13
  Micklehouse Rd.
Micklehouse Rd. (Bail.) G69 40 EE13
Micklehouse Wynd (Bail.) 40 EE13
  G69
  Micklehouse Rd.
Mid Cotts. (Gart.) G69 26 FF10
Midcroft (Bishop.) G64 10 X6
Midcroft Av. G44 64 W17
Middle Pk., Pais. PA2 46 J15
Middlemuir Av. (Kirk.) G66 13 CC5
Middlemuir Rd. (Lenzie) 13 CC5
  G66
Middlerigg Rd. (Cumb.) G68 70 MM3
Middlesex Gdns. G41 35 U13
Middlesex St. G41 35 U13
Middleton Cres., Pais. PA3 30 J13
Middleton Rd., Pais. PA3 28 F13
Middleton St. G51 34 T13
Midland St. G1 35 V13
Midlem Dr. G52 33 Q13
Midlem Oval G52 33 Q13
Midlock St. G51 34 T13
Midlothian Dr. G41 50 T15
Midton Cotts. (Mood.) G69 15 HH7
Midton St. G21 22 X10
Midwharf St. G4 36 W11
Migvie Pl. G20 20 T9
  Wyndford Rd.
Milan St. G41 51 V14
Milford St. G33 38 BB12
Mill Ct. (Ruther.) G73 53 Y16
Mill Cres. G40 52 X14
Mill Pl. (Linw.), Pais. PA3 28 E13
Mill Ri. (Lenzie) G66 13 CC6
Mill Rd. (Both.) G71 69 HH19
Mill Rd. (Camb.) G72 67 CC18
Mill Rd., Clyde. G81 17 M8
Mill St. G40 52 X14
Mill St. (Ruther.) G73 53 Y16
Mill St., Pais. PA1 46 K14
Mill Vennel, Renf. PA4 18 N10
  High St.
Millands Av. (Blan.) G72 68 FF19
Millar St., Pais. PA1 30 K13
Millar Ter. (Ruther.) G73 53 Y15
Millarbank St. G21 22 X10
Millarston Av., Pais. PA1 45 H14
Millarston Dr., Pais. PA1 45 H14
Millbeg Cres. G33 39 DD13
Millbeg Pl. G33 39 DD13
Millbrae Ct. G42 51 U16
  Millbrae Rd.
Millbrae Cres. G42 51 U16
Millbrae Cres., Clyde. G81 17 M8
Millbrae Rd. G42 51 U16
Millbrix Av. G14 18 P9
Millburn Av. (Ruther.) G73 65 Y17
Millburn Av., Clyde. G81 18 N8
Millburn Av., Renf. PA4 18 N10
Millburn Dr., Renf. PA4 17 M10
Millburn Rd., Renf. PA4 17 M10
Millburn St. G21 37 Y11
Millburn Way, Renf. PA4 18 N10
Millcroft Rd. (Cumb.) G67 71 PP3
Millcroft Rd. (Ruther.) G73 52 X15
Miller St. G1 36 W12
Miller St. (Bail.) G69 56 EE14
Miller St., Clyde. G81 5 L7
Miller St., John. PA5 . 44 E14
Millerfield Pl. G40 53 Y14
Millerfield Rd. G40 53 Y14
Millers Pl. (Lenzie) G66 13 CC6
Millersneuk Av. (Lenzie) 13 CC6
  G66
Millersneuk Cres. G33 24 BB9
Millersneuk Dr. (Lenzie) G66 13 CC6
Millerston St. G31 37 Y13

Millford Dr. (Linw.), Pais. 28 E13
  PA3
Millgate (Udd.) G71 57 GG16
Millgate Av. (Udd.) G71 57 GG16
Millholm Rd. G44 63 V18
Millhouse Cres. G20 20 T8
Millhouse Dr. G20 20 T8
Millichen Rd. G23 8 T5
Milliken Dr. (Mill.Pk.), 43 C15
  John. PA10
Milliken Pk. Rd. (Mill.Pk.), 43 C15
  John. PA10
Milliken Rd. (Mill.Pk.), 43 C15
  John. PA10
Millpond Dr. G40 36 X13
Millport Av. G44 52 W16
Millroad Dr. G40 36 X13
Millroad Gdns. G40 36 X13
  Millroad St.
Millroad St. G40 36 X13
Millview (Barr.) G78 59 M18
Millview Pl. G53 60 P18
Millwood St. G41 51 U16
Milnbank St. G31 37 Y12
Milncroft Rd. G33 38 BB11
Milner La. G13 19 R9
  Southbrae Dr.
Milner Rd. G13 19 R9
Milngavie Rd. (Bears.) G61 7 R6
Milnpark Gdns. G41 35 U13
Milnpark St. G41 35 U13
Milovaig St. G23 8 T7
Milrig Rd. (Ruther.) G73 52 X16
Milton Av. (Camb.) G72 66 AA17
Milton Douglas Rd., Clyde. 5 L5
  G81
Milton Dr. (Bishop.) G64 22 X8
Milton Gdns. (Udd.) G71 57 GG16
Milton Mains Rd., Clyde. 5 L5
  G81
Milton St. G4 35 V11
Milverton Av. (Bears.) G61 7 Q5
Milverton Rd. (Giff.) G46 62 S19
Minard Rd. G41 51 U15
Minard Way (Udd.) G71 57 HH16
  Newton Dr.
Minerva St. G3 35 U12
Minerva Way G3 35 U12
Mingarry La. G20 20 T10
  Clouston St.
Mingarry St. G20 21 U10
Mingulay Cres. G22 22 W8
Mingulay Pl. G22 22 X8
Mingulay St. G22 22 W8
Minister Wk. (Bail.) G69 41 GG13
  Dukes Rd.
Minmoir Rd. G53 48 N16
Minstrel Rd. G13 7 Q7
Minto Av. (Ruther.) G73 65 Z18
Minto Cres. G52 33 R13
Minto St. G52 33 R13
Mireton St. G22 21 V9
Mirrlees Dr. G12 20 T10
Mirrlees La. G12 20 T10
  Redlands Rd.
Mitchell Av. (Camb.) G72 67 DD17
Mitchell Av., Renf. PA4 31 L11
Mitchell Dr. (Ruther.) G73 65 Y17
Mitchell La. G1 35 V12
  Buchanan St.
Mitchell Rd. (Cumb.) G67 71 PP3
Mitchell St. G1 35 V12
Mitchell St., Coat. ML5 57 HH14
Mitchellhill Rd. G45 64 X19
Mitchison Rd. (Cumb.) G67 71 PP2
Mitre Ct. G11 19 R10
  Mitre Rd.
Mitre La. G14 19 R10
Mitre La. W. G14 19 R10
  Mitre La.
Mitre Rd. G11 19 R10
Mitre Rd. G14 19 R10
Moat Av. G13 19 Q8
Mochrum Rd. G43 63 U17
Moffat Pl. (Blan.) G72 68 FF19
Moffat St. G5 52 W14
Mogarth Av., Pais. PA2 45 H16
  Amochrie Rd.
Moidart Av., Renf. PA4 17 L10
Moidart Ct. (Barr.) G78 59 L18

Moidart Cres. G52 33 R13
  Moidart Rd.
Moidart Pl. G52 33 R13
  Moidart Rd.
Moidart Rd. G52 33 R13
Moir La. G1 36 W13
  Moir St.
Moir St. G1 36 W13
Molendinar St. G1 36 W13
Mollinsburn St. G21 22 X10
Monach Rd. G33 39 CC12
Monachie Gdns. (Bishop.) 11 Z7
  G64
  Muirhead Way
Monar Dr. G22 21 V10
Monar Pl. G22 21 V10
Monar St. G22 21 V10
Monart Pl. G20 21 U10
  Caithness St.
Moncrieff Av. (Lenzie) G66 13 CC5
Moncrieff Gdns. (Kirk.) G66 13 CC5
  Moncrieff Av.
Moncrieff Pl. G20 35 V11
  North Woodside Rd.
Moncrieff St. G4 35 V11
  Braid Sq.
Moncur St. G40 36 X13
Moness Dr. G52 49 R14
Monifieth Av. G52 49 Q14
Monikie Gdns. (Bishop.) 11 Z7
  G64
  Muirhead Way
Monkcastle Dr. (Camb.) G72 66 BB17
Monkland Av. (Kirk.) G66 13 CC5
Monkland Vw. (Udd.) G71 57 HH15
  Lincoln Av.
Monkland Vw. Cres. (Bail.) 41 HH13
  G69
Monksbridge Av. G13 7 Q7
Monkscroft Av. G11 20 S10
Monkscroft Ct. G11 34 S11
Monkscroft Gdns. G11 20 S10
  Monkscroft Av.
Monkton Dr. G15 6 P7
Monmouth Av. G12 20 S9
Monreith Av. (Bears.) G61 7 Q7
Monreith Rd. G43 62 T17
Monreith Rd. E. G44 63 V17
Monroe Dr. (Udd.) G71 57 GG15
Monroe Pl. (Udd.) G71 57 GG15
Montague La. G12 20 S10
Montague St. G4 35 U11
Montague Ter. G12 20 S10
  Hyndland Rd.
Montclair Pl. (Linw.), Pais. 28 E13
  PA3
Monteith Dr. (Clark.) G76 63 V19
Monteith Pl. G40 36 X13
Monteith Row G40 36 X13
Monteith Row La. G40 36 X13
  Monteith Pl.
Montford Av. G44 52 W16
Montford Av. (Ruther.) G73 52 W16
Montgomerie Gdns. G14 19 Q10
  Lennox Av.
Montgomery Av. Pais. PA3 31 L12
Montgomery Dr. (Giff.) G46 62 T19
Montgomery Dr. (Kilb.), 42 B14
  John. PA10
  Meadside Av.
Montgomery La. G42 51 V16
  Somerville Dr.
Montgomery Rd., Pais. PA3 31 L12
Montgomery St. G40 52 X14
  London Rd.
Montgomery St. (Camb.) 67 DD17
  G72
  Mill Rd.
Montrave St. G52 49 Q14
Montrave St. (Ruther.) G73 53 Z15
Montreal Ho., Clyde. G81 4 J5
  Perth Cres.
Montron Dr. G15 6 P7
  Moraine Av.
Montrose Av. G32 54 BB15
Montrose Av. G52 32 N12
Montrose Gdns. (Blan.) G72 68 FF19
Montrose Pl. (Linw.), Pais. 28 E13
  PA3

Montrose Rd., Pais. PA2 45 G16
Montrose St. G1 36 W12
Montrose St. G4 36 W12
Montrose St., Clyde. G81 5 L7
Montrose Ter. (Bishop.) G64 23 Z8
Monymusk Gdns. (Bishop.) 11 Z7
  G64
Monymusk Pl. G15 6 N5
Moodies Ct. G1 36 W13
  Osborne St.
Moodiesburn St. G33 37 Z11
Moorburn Av. (Giff.) G46 62 S18
Moore Dr. (Bears.) G61 7 R6
Moore St. G31 37 Y13
  Gallowgate
Moorehouse Av., Pais. PA2 45 H15
Moorfoot (Bishop.) G64 11 Z7
Moorfoot Av. (Thorn.) G46 62 S18
Moorfoot Av., Pais. PA2 46 J15
Moorfoot St. G32 38 AA13
Moorhouse Av. G13 18 N9
Moorhouse St. (Barr.) G78 59 M19
Moorings, The, Pais. PA2 45 H14
Moorpark Av. (Muir.) G69 26 FF8
  Cumbernauld Rd.
Moorpark Dr. G52 32 P13
Moorpark Pl. G52 32 N13
Moorpark Sq., Renf. PA4 31 L11
Morag Av. (Blan.) G72 68 FF19
Moraine Av. G15 6 P7
Moraine Circ. G15 6 P7
Moraine Dr. G15 6 P7
Moraine Pl. G15 6 P7
  Moraine Dr.
Morar Av., Clyde. G81 5 L6
Morar Ct. (Cumb.) G67 70 LL4
Morar Ct., Clyde. G81 5 L6
Morar Cres. (Bishop.) G64 10 X7
Morar Cres., Clyde. G81 5 L6
Morar Dr. (Bears.) G61 8 S6
Morar Dr. (Cumb.) G67 70 LL4
Morar Dr. (Ruther.) G73 65 Y18
Morar Dr., Clyde. G81 5 L6
Morar Dr., Pais. PA2 45 G15
Morar Dr. (Linw.), Pais. PA3 28 E13
Morar Pl., Clyde. G81 5 L6
Morar Pl., Renf. PA4 17 L10
Morar Rd. G52 33 R13
Morar Rd., Clyde. G81 5 L6
Morar Ter. (Udd.) G71 57 HH16
Morar Ter. (Ruther.) G73 65 Z18
Moravia Av. (Both.) G71 69 HH18
Moray Gdns. (Cumb.) G68 71 PP1
Moray Gdns. (Udd.) G71 57 GG16
Moray Gate (Both.) G71 69 GG18
Moray Pl. G41 51 U15
Moray Pl. (Bishop.) G64 11 Z7
Moray Pl. (Linw.), Pais. PA3 28 E13
Mordaunt St. G40 53 Y14
Moredun Cres. G32 39 CC12
Moredun Dr., Pais. PA2 45 H15
Moredun Rd., Pais. PA2 45 H15
Moredun St. G32 39 CC12
Morefield Rd. G51 33 Q12
Morgan Ms. G42 51 V14
Morina Gdns. G53 61 Q19
Morion Rd. G13 19 Q8
Morley St. G42 51 V16
Morna Pl. G14 33 R11
  Victoria Pk. Dr. S.
Morningside St. G33 37 Z12
Morrin Path G21 22 X10
  Crichton St.
Morrin Sq. G4 36 X12
  Collins St.
Morrin St. G21 22 X10
Morris Pl. G40 36 X13
Morrison Quad., Clyde. G81 6 N7
Morrison St. G5 35 V13
Morrison St., Clyde. G81 4 K5
Morrisons Ct. G2 35 V12
  Argyle St.
Morriston Cres., Renf. PA4 32 N11
Morriston Pk. Dr. (Camb.) 54 BB16
  G72
Morriston St. (Camb.) G72 66 BB17
Mortimer St. G20 21 U10
  Hotspur St.

Morton Gdns. G41 50 T15
Morven Av. (Bishop.) G64 11 Z7
Morven Av. (Blan.) G72 68 FF19
Morven Av., Pais. PA2 46 J16
Morven Dr. (Linw.), Pais. 28 E13
  PA3
Morven Gdns. (Udd.) G71 57 GG16
Morven Rd. (Bears.) G61 7 R5
Morven Rd. (Camb.) G72 66 AA18
Morven St. G52 33 R13
Mosesfield St. G21 22 X9
Mosesfield Ter. G21 22 X9
  Balgrayhill Rd.
Moss Av. (Linw.), Pais. PA3 28 E13
Moss Dr. (Barr.) G78 59 L17
Moss Heights Av. G52 33 Q13
Moss Knowe (Cumb.) G67 71 QQ3
Moss Path (Bail.) G69 55 DD14
  Castle St.
Moss Rd. G51 33 Q12
Moss Rd. (Kirk.) G66 13 CC5
Moss Rd. (Cumb.) G67 71 QQ2
Moss Rd. (Muir.) G69 26 FF8
Moss St., Pais. PA1 30 K13
Moss-side Rd. G41 50 T15
Mossbank Av. G33 24 AA10
Mossbank Dr. G33 24 AA10
Mosscastle Rd. G33 39 CC11
Mossend La. G33 39 CC12
Mossend Rd., Pais. PA3 30 J12
  Mosslands Rd.
Mossend St. G33 39 CC12
Mossgiel Av. (Ruther.) G73 65 Y17
Mossgiel Dr., Clyde. G81 5 M6
Mossgiel Gdns. (Udd.) G71 57 GG16
Mossgiel Pl. (Ruther.) G73 65 Y17
Mossgiel Rd. G43 62 T17
Mossgiel Rd. (Cumb.) G67 71 PP3
Mossgiel Ter. (Blan.) G72 68 FF19
Mossland Rd. G52 32 N12
Mosslands Rd., Pais. PA3 30 J12
Mossneuk Dr., Pais. PA2 46 J16
Mosspark Av. G52 49 R14
Mosspark Boul. G52 49 R14
Mosspark Dr. G52 49 Q14
Mosspark La. G52 49 R15
  Mosspark Dr.
Mosspark Oval G52 49 R14
Mosspark Sq. G52 49 R14
Mossvale Cres. G33 39 CC11
Mossvale La., Pais. PA3 30 J13
Mossvale Path G33 25 CC10
Mossvale Rd. G33 24 BB10
Mossvale Sq. G33 39 CC11
Mossvale St., Pais. PA3 30 J12
Mossvale Ter. (Chry.) G69 15 HH6
Mossvale Wk. G33 39 CC11
Mossvale Way G33 39 CC11
Mossview Cotts. (Muir.) 26 FF9
  G69
Mossview Quad. G52 33 Q13
Mossview Rd. G33 25 DD9
Mote Hill Rd., Pais. PA3 31 L13
Moulin Circ. G52 48 P14
Moulin Pl. G52 48 P14
Moulin Rd. G52 48 P14
Moulin Ter. G52 48 P14
Mount Annan Dr. G44 51 V16
Mount Harriet Av. (Stepps) 25 DD9
  G33
Mount Harriet Dr. (Stepps) 25 CC9
  G33
Mount St. G20 21 U10
Mount Stuart St. G41 51 U16
Mount Vernon Av. G32 55 DD14
Mountainblue St. G31 37 Y13
Mountblow Ho., Clyde. G81 4 J5
  Melbourne Av.
Mountblow Rd., Clyde. G81 4 K5
Mountgarrie Path G51 33 Q12
  Mountgarrie Rd.
Mountgarrie Rd. G51 33 Q12
Mowbray Av. (Gart.) G69 27 GG9
Mowcraigs Ct., Clyde. G81 17 M8
  Yokerburn Ter.
Moy St. G11 34 T11
  Church St.
Moyne Rd. G53 48 P15
Muckcroft Rd. (Chry.) G69 14 EE6

Muir Pk. Ter. (Bishop.) G64	22	X8	Murray St., Pais. PA3	30	J13	Ness Dr. (Blan.) G72	69	GG19
Muir St. G21	22	X10	Murray St., Renf. PA4	17	M10	Ness Gdns. (Bishop.) G64	11	Y7
Muir St. (Bishop.) G64	11	Y7	Murrayfield (Bishop.) G64	11	Y6	Ness Rd., Renf. PA4	17	L10
Muir St., Renf. PA4	17	M10	*Ashfield*			Ness St. G33	38	AA11
Muir Ter., Pais. PA3	31	L12	Murrayfield Dr. (Bears.) G61	7	R7	Nether Auldhouse Rd. G43	62	S17
Muirbank Av. (Ruther.) G73	52	X16	Murrayfield St. G32	38	AA12	Netherburn Av. G44	63	U19
Muirbank Gdns. (Ruther.)	52	X16	Murrin Av. (Bishop.) G64	11	Z7	Netherby Dr. G41	50	T14
G73			Murroes Rd. G51	33	Q12	Nethercairn Rd. G43	62	T18
Muirbrae Rd. (Ruther.) G73	65	Y18	Muslin St. G40	52	X14	Nethercliffe Av. G44	63	U19
Muirbrae Way (Ruther.) G73	65	Y18	Mybster Pl. G51	33	Q12	Nethercommon Harbour,	30	K12
Muirburn Av. G44	63	U18	Mybster Rd. G51	33	Q12	Pais. PA3		
Muirdrum Av. G52	49	Q14	Myers Cres. (Udd.) G71	69	HH17	Nethercraig Cotts., Pais.	58	J17
Muirdykes Av. G52	32	P13	Myres Rd. G53	49	Q16	PA2		
Muirdykes Cres., Pais. PA3	29	H13	Myreside Pl. G32	37	Z13	*Glenfield Rd.*		
Muirdykes Rd. G52	32	P13	Myreside St. G32	37	Z13	Nethercraigs Dr., Pais. PA2	46	J16
Muirdykes Rd., Pais. PA3	29	H13	Myrie Gdns. (Bishop.) G64	11	Y7	Nethercraigs Rd., Pais. PA2	45	H16
Muiredge Ct. (Udd.) G71	69	GG17	Myroch Pl. G34	40	FF11	Netherdale Dr., Pais. PA1	48	N14
Watson St.			Myrtle Av. (Lenzie) G66	13	CC5	Netherfield St. G31	37	Z13
Muiredge Ter. (Bail.) G69	56	EE14	Myrtle Hill La. G42	52	W16	Netherhill Av. G44	63	U19
Muirend Av. G44	63	U18	Myrtle Hill Vw. G42	52	W16	Netherhill Cotts., Pais. PA3	31	L12
Muirend Rd. G44	63	U18	Myrtle Pk. G42	52	W15	*Netherhill Rd.*		
Muirfield Ct. G44	63	U18	Myrtle Pl. G42	52	W16	Netherhill Cres., Pais. PA3	31	L13
Muirend Rd.			Myrtle Rd. (Udd.) G71	57	HH16	Netherhill Rd. (Chry.) G69	15	GG7
Muirfield Cres. G23	9	U7	Myrtle Rd., Clyde. G81	4	J6	Netherhill Rd., Pais. PA3	30	K13
Muirfield Meadows (Both.)	69	GG19	Myrtle Sq. (Bishop.) G64	23	Y8	Netherhouse Av. (Lenzie)	13	DD6
G71			Myrtle St. (Blan.) G72	68	FF19	G66		
Muirfield Rd. (Cumb.) G68	71	PP1	Myrtle Wk. (Camb.) G72	66	AA17	Netherhouse Pl. G34	41	GG12
Muirhead Ct. (Bail.) G69	56	FF14				Netherhouse Rd. (Bail.) G69	40	FF12
Muirhead Dr. (Linw.), Pais.	28	E13				Netherlee Rd. G44	63	U18
PA3			**N**			Netherpark Av. G44	63	U19
Muirhead Gdns. (Bail.) G69	56	FF14	Naburn St. G5	52	W14	Netherplace Cres. G53	48	P16
Muirhead Gate (Udd.) G71	57	HH16	Nairn Av. (Blan.) G72	68	FF19	*Netherplace Rd.*		
Muirhead Gro. (Bail.) G69	56	FF14	Nairn Gdns. (Bears.) G61	7	Q6	Netherplace Rd. G53	48	P16
Muirhead Rd. (Bail.) G69	56	FF14	Nairn Pl., Clyde. G81	4	K6	Netherton Ct. G45	64	X19
Muirhead Rd. (Udd.) G71	56	EE14	*Dumbarton Rd.*			Netherton Dr. (Barr.) G78	60	N19
Muirhead St. G11	34	S11	Nairn St. G3	34	T11	Netherton Rd. G13	19	R8
Purdon St.			Nairn St., Clyde. G81	4	K6	Netherton St. G13	19	R8
Muirhead Way (Bishop.)	11	Z7	Nairn Way (Cumb.) G68	71	PP1	*Crow Rd.*		
G64			Nairnside Rd. G21	23	Z8	Nethervale Av. G44	63	U19
Muirhill Av. G44	63	U18	Naismith St. G32	55	CC16	Netherview Rd. G44	63	V19
Muirhill Cres. G13	18	P8	Nansen St. G20	21	V10	Netherway G44	63	U19
Muirhouse St. G41	51	U15	Napier Ct. (Old Kil.) G60	4	J5	Nethy Way, Renf. PA4	32	N11
Pollokshaws Rd.			*Freelands Rd.*			*Teith Av.*		
Muirkirk Dr. G13	19	R8	Napier Dr. G51	34	S12	Neuk Way G32	55	CC16
Muirpark Av., Renf. PA4	31	M11	Napier Gdns. (Linw.), Pais.	28	F13	Nevis Rd. G43	62	S17
Muirpark Dr. (Bishop.) G64	23	Y8	PA3			Nevis Rd. (Bears.) G61	6	P5
Muirpark St. G11	34	S11	Napier Pl. G51	34	S12	Nevis Rd. (Abbots.), Pais.	30	K11
Muirpark Ter. (Bishop.) G64	22	X8	Napier Pl. (Old Kil.) G60	4	J5	PA3		
Crowhill Rd.			*Old Dalnottar Rd.*			Nevis Rd., Renf. PA4	31	L11
Muirshiel Av. G53	61	Q17	Napier Rd. G51	34	S12	New City Rd. G4	35	V11
Muirshiel Cres. G53	61	Q17	Napier Rd. G52	32	N11	New Edinburgh Rd. (Udd.)	57	GG16
Muirside Av. G32	55	DD14	Napier St. G51	34	T12	G71		
Muirside Rd. (Bail.) G69	56	EE14	Napier St., Clyde. G81	17	M8	New Inchinnan Rd., Pais.	30	K12
Muirside Rd., Pais. PA3	29	H12	Napier St., John. PA5	43	D14	PA3		
Muirside St. (Bail.) G69	56	EE14	*Barrochan Rd.*			New Kirk Pl. (Bears.) G61	7	R5
Muirskeith Cres. G43	63	U17	Napier St. (Linw.), Pais. PA3	28	F13	*New Kirk Rd.*		
Muirskeith Pl. G43	63	U17	Napier Ter. G51	34	S12	New Kirk Rd. (Bears.) G61	7	R5
Muirskeith Rd. G43	63	U17	Napiershall La. G20	35	U11	New Loop Av. (Barr.) G78	59	M18
Muirton Dr. (Bishop.) G64	10	X6	*Napiershall St.*			New Rd. (Camb.) G72	67	DD18
Muirton Gdns. (Bishop.)	10	X6	Napiershall Pl. G20	35	U11	New Sneddon St., Pais. PA3	30	K13
G64			*Napiershall St.*			New St., Clyde. G81	4	K5
Muiryfauld Dr. G31	54	AA14	Napiershall St. G20	35	U11	New St. (Kilb.), John. PA10	42	B14
Mulben Cres. G53	48	N16	Naseby Av. G11	19	R10	New St., Pais. PA1	46	K14
Mulben Pl. G53	48	N16	Nasmyth Pl. G52	32	P12	New Wynd G1	36	W13
Mulben Ter. G53	48	N16	Nasmyth Rd. G52	32	P12	Newall Rd., Pais. PA3	30	K12
Mulberry Rd. G43	62	T17	Nasmyth Rd. N. G52	32	P12	Newark Dr. G41	50	T14
Mull Av., Pais. PA2	46	J16	Nasmyth Rd. S. G52	32	P12	Newark Dr., Pais. PA2	46	J16
Mull Av., Renf. PA4	31	M11	National Bk. La. G2	35	V12	Newbattle Ct. G32	54	BB15
Mull St. G21	37	Y11	*St. Vincent St.*			Newbattle Gdns. G32	54	BB15
Mullardoch St. G23	8	T7	Navar Pl., Pais. PA2	47	L15	Newbattle Pl. G32	54	BB15
Rothes Dr.			Naver St. G33	38	AA11	Newbattle Rd. G32	54	BB15
Mungo Pl. (Udd.) G71	57	HH15	Neil St., Pais. PA1	46	J14	Newbold Av. G21	22	X8
Lincoln Av.			Neil St., Renf. PA4	17	M9	Newburgh St. G43	50	T16
Munlochy Rd. G51	33	Q12	Neilsland Oval G53	49	Q16	Newcastleton Dr. G23	9	U7
Munro Ct., Clyde. G81	4	K5	Neilsland Sq. G53	49	Q15	Newcroft Dr. G44	64	W17
Gentle Row			Neilston Av. G53	61	Q17	Newfield Pl. (Thorn.) G46	61	R19
Munro La. G13	19	R9	Neilston Rd. (Barr.) G78	59	L19	*Rouken Glen Rd.*		
Munro Pl. G13	19	R9	Neilston Rd., Pais. PA2	46	K14	Newfield Pl. (Ruther.) G73	52	X16
Munro Pl. (Udd.) G71	57	HH15	Neilvaig Dr. (Ruther.) G73	65	Z18	Newfield Sq. G53	60	P17
Newlands Rd.			Nelson Mandela Pl. G2	36	W12	Newhall St. G40	52	X14
Munro Rd. G13	19	R9	*Buchanan St.*			Newhaven Rd. G33	38	BB12
Munro Vw. (Udd.) G71	57	HH15	Nelson Pl. (Bail.) G69	56	EE14	Newhaven St. G32	38	BB12
Newlands Rd.			Nelson St. G5	35	V13	Newhills Rd. G33	39	DD12
Murano St. G20	21	U10	Nelson St. (Bail.) G69	56	EE14	Newington St. G32	38	AA13
Murdoch St. G21	22	X9	Nelson Ter. G12	21	U10	Newlands Gdns. (Elder.),	44	F15
Lenzie St.			*Glasgow St.*			John. PA5		
Muriel St. (Barr.) G78	59	M18	Neptune St. G51	34	S12	*Renshaw Rd.*		
Murray Pl. (Barr.) G78	59	M18	Nerston Av. G53	49	Q16	Newlands Rd. G43	63	U17
Murray Rd. (Both.) G71	69	HH18	Ness Av., John. PA5	43	C16	Newlands Rd. G44	63	V17

Newlands Rd. (Udd.) G71 57 GG16
Newlandsfield Rd. G43 50 T16
Newluce Dr. G32 55 CC14
Newmains Rd., Renf. PA4 31 L11
Newmill Rd. G21 23 Z9
Newnham Rd., Pais. PA1 48 N14
Newpark Cres. (Camb.) G72 54 BB16
Newshot Ct., Clyde. G81 17 M8
  Clydeholm Ter.
Newshot Dr., Ersk. PA8 4 J7
Newstead Gdns. G23 9 U7
Newton Av. (Camb.) G72 67 CC17
Newton Av. (Barr.) G78 59 M19
Newton Av. (Elder.), John. 45 G14
  PA5
Newton Brae (Camb.) G72 67 DD17
Newton Dr. (Udd.) G71 57 HH16
Newton Dr. (Elder.), John. 45 G14
  PA5
Newton Fm. Rd. (Camb.) 55 DD16
  G72
Newton Pl. G3 35 U11
Newton Rd. (Lenzie) G66 13 DD6
Newton Sta. Rd. (Camb.) 67 DD17
  G72
Newton St. G2 35 V12
Newton St., Pais. PA1 46 J14
Newton Ter. G3 35 U12
  Sauchiehall St.
Newton Ter. La. G3 35 U11
  Elderslie St.
Newtongrange Av. G32 54 BB15
Newtongrange Gdns. G32 54 BB15
Newtyle Pl. (Bishop.) G64 11 Z7
Newtyle Rd., Pais. PA1 47 L14
Nicholas St. G1 36 W12
Nicholson Ct. (Stepps) G33 25 CC9
Nicholson La. G5 35 V13
  Nicholson St.
Nicholson St. G5 35 V13
Niddrie Rd. G42 51 U15
Niddrie Sq. G42 51 U15
Niddry St., Pais. PA3 30 K13
Nigel Gdns. G41 50 T15
Nigg Pl. G34 40 EE12
Nightingale Pl., John. PA5 43 C16
Nimmo Dr. G51 33 R12
Nisbet St. G31 37 Z13
Nith Av., Pais. PA2 45 G15
Nith Dr., Renf. PA4 32 N11
Nith Pl., John. PA5 43 C16
Nith St. G33 37 Z11
Nithsdale Cres. (Bears.) G61 7 Q5
Nithsdale Dr. G41 51 U15
Nithsdale Pl. G41 51 U14
  Nithsdale Rd.
Nithsdale Rd. G41 50 S14
Nithsdale St. G41 51 U15
Nitshill Rd. (Thorn.) G46 61 Q18
Nitshill Rd. G53 60 N17
Niven St. G20 20 T9
Noldrum Av. G32 55 CC16
Noldrum Gdns. G32 55 CC16
Norbreck Dr. (Giff.) G46 62 T18
Norby Rd. G11 19 R10
Norfield Dr. G44 51 V16
Norfolk Ct. G5 35 V13
Norfolk Cres. (Bishop.) G64 10 X6
Norfolk La. G5 35 V13
  Norfolk St.
Norfolk St. G5 35 V13
Norham St. G41 51 U15
Norman St. G40 52 X14
Norse La. N. G14 19 Q10
  Ormiston Av.
Norse La. S. G14 19 Q10
  Verona Av.
Norse Rd. G14 19 Q10
North Av. (Camb.) G72 66 AA17
North Av., Clyde. G81 5 L7
North Bk. Pl., Clyde. G81 17 M8
  North Bk. St.
North Bk. St., Clyde. G81 17 M8
North Berwick Av. (Cumb.) 70 NN1
  G68
North Berwick Gdns. 70 NN1
  (Cumb.) G68
  North Berwick Av.
North Brae Pl. G13 18 P8

North British Rd. (Udd.) G71 69 GG17
North Canal Bk. G4 36 W11
North Canal Bk. St. G4 36 W11
North Carbrain Rd. 70 NN4
  (Cumb.) G67
North Claremont St. G3 35 U11
North Corsebar Av., Pais. 46 J15
  PA2
North Ct. La. G1 36 W12
  Buchanan St.
North Cft. St., Pais. PA3 30 K13
North Deanpark Av. (Both.) 69 HH18
  G71
North Douglas St., Clyde. 17 M8
  G81
North Dr. G1 36 W13
North Dr. (Linw.), Pais. 28 E13
  PA3
North Elgin St., Clyde. G81 17 M8
North Erskine Pk. (Bears.) 7 Q5
  G61
North Frederick St. G1 36 W12
North Gardner St. G11 20 S10
North Gower Ter. G51 34 T13
North Gra. Rd. (Bears.) G61 7 R5
North Greenhill Rd., Pais. 30 J12
  PA3
North Hanover Pl. G4 36 W11
North Hanover St. G1 36 W12
North Iverton Pk. Rd., 44 E14
  John. PA5
North La. (Linw.), Pais. PA3 28 F13
  Napier St.
North Lo. Rd., Renf. PA4 17 M10
North Moraine La. G15 7 Q7
  Moraine Av.
North Pk. Av. (Thorn.) G46 61 R18
North Pk. Av. (Barr.) G78 59 L18
North Pl. G3 35 U12
  North St.
North Portland St. G1 36 W12
North Queen St. G2 36 W12
  George Sq.
North Rd., John. PA5 43 D15
North Spiers Wf. G4 35 V11
North St. G3 35 U12
North St., Clyde. G81 5 L7
  Dumbarton Rd.
North St., Pais. PA3 30 K13
North Wallace St. G4 36 W11
North Way (Blan.) G72 68 FF19
North Woodside Rd. G20 21 U10
Northampton Dr. G12 20 S9
Northampton La. G12 20 S9
  Northampton Dr.
Northbank Av. (Camb.) G72 67 CC17
Northbank St. (Camb.) G72 67 CC17
Northcroft Rd. G21 22 X10
Northcroft Rd. (Chry.) G69 15 GG7
Northgate Quad. G21 23 Z8
Northgate Rd. G21 23 Z8
Northinch St. G14 33 Q11
Northland Av. G14 19 Q9
Northland Dr. G14 19 Q9
Northland Gdns. G14 19 Q9
Northland La. G14 19 Q10
  Upland Rd.
Northmuir Rd. G15 6 P6
Northpark St. G20 21 U10
Northpark Ter. G12 21 U10
  Hamilton Dr.
Northumberland St. G20 21 U10
Norval St. G11 34 S11
Norwich Dr. G12 20 S9
Norwood (Bears.) G61 7 R6
Norwood Dr. (Giff.) G46 62 S19
Norwood Ter. G12 35 U11
  Southpark Av.
Norwood Ter. (Udd.) G71 57 HH16
Nottingham Av. G12 20 S9
Nottingham La. G12 20 S9
  Northampton Dr.
Novar Dr. G12 20 S10
Novar Gdns. (Bishop.) G64 10 X7
Numrow Ct., Clyde. G81 4 K5
Nuneaton St. G40 53 Y14
Nurseries Rd. (Bail.) G69 39 DD13
Nursery La. G41 51 U15

Nursery St. G41 51 U15
  Pollokshaws Rd.
Nursery St. La. G41 51 U15
  Nithsdale Dr.
Nutberry Ct. G42 51 V15

O

Oak Cres. (Bail.) G69 56 EE14
Oak Dr. (Kirk.) G66 12 BB5
Oak Dr. (Camb.) G72 67 CC18
Oak Pk. (Bishop.) G64 11 Y7
Oak Rd., Clyde. G81 4 K5
Oak Rd., Pais. PA2 47 L15
Oak St. G2 35 V12
  Cadogan St.
Oakbank Dr. (Barr.) G78 60 N19
Oakbank La. G20 21 V10
Oakbank Ter. G20 21 V10
Oakdene Av. (Udd.) G71 57 HH16
Oakfield Av. G12 35 U11
Oakfield La. G12 35 U11
  Gibson St.
Oakfield Ter. G12 35 U11
  Oakfield Av.
Oakhill Av. (Bail.) G69 55 DD14
Oakley Dr. G44 63 U18
Oakley Ter. G31 36 X12
Oaks, The, John. PA5 43 D15
Oakshaw Sch. Brae, Pais. 30 J13
  PA1
Oakshaw St. E., Pais. PA1 30 K13
Oakshaw St. W., Pais. PA1 30 J13
Oakshawhead, Pais. PA1 30 J13
Oakwood Av., Pais. PA2 45 H15
Oatfield St. G21 23 Y10
Oban Ct. G20 21 U10
Oban Dr. G20 21 U10
Oban La. G20 21 U10
  Oban Dr.
Observatory La. G12 20 T10
  Observatory Rd.
Observatory Rd. G12 20 T10
Ochil Dr. (Barr.) G78 59 M19
Ochil Dr., Pais. PA2 46 K16
Ochil Pl. G32 54 BB14
Ochil Rd. (Bishop.) G64 11 Z7
Ochil Rd., Renf. PA4 31 L11
Ochil St. G32 54 BB14
Ochil Vw. (Udd.) G71 57 HH16
Ochiltree Av. G13 19 R8
Ogilvie Pl. G31 54 AA14
Ogilvie St. G31 53 Z14
Old Bothwell Rd. (Both.) 69 HH19
  G71
Old Castle Rd. G44 63 V17
Old Cotts., Pais. PA2 47 M16
  Grahamston Rd.
Old Dalmarnock Rd. G40 52 X14
Old Dalnottar Rd. (Old Kil.) 4 J5
  G60
Old Dumbarton Rd. G3 34 T11
Old Edinburgh Rd. (Udd.) 57 GG15
  G71
Old Gartcosh Rd. (Gart.) 27 GG9
  G69
Old Glasgow Rd. (Udd.) G71 56 FF16
Old Govan Rd., Renf. PA4 18 N10
Old Greenock Rd. (Inch.), 16 J8
  Renf. PA4
Old Manse Rd. G32 39 CC13
Old Mill Rd. (Both.) G71 69 HH19
Old Mill Rd. (Udd.) G71 69 GG17
Old Mill Rd. (Camb.) G72 67 CC17
Old Mill Rd., Clyde. G81 5 L5
Old Mill Rd., Pais. PA2 45 H14
Old Renfrew Rd., Renf. PA4 32 P11
Old Rd. (Elder.), John. PA5 44 E14
Old Roundknowe Rd. 56 FF15
  (Udd.) G71
Old Rutherglen Rd. G5 52 W14
Old Shettleston Rd. G32 38 AA13
Old Sneddon St., Pais. PA3 30 K13
Old St., Clyde. G81 4 K5
Old Wd. Rd. (Bail.) G69 56 EE14
Old Wynd G1 36 W13
Oldhall Rd., Pais. PA1 47 M14
Olifard Av. (Both.) G71 69 HH18
Oliphant Cres., Pais. PA2 45 G16

Queen Elizabeth Sq. G5 52 W14
Queen Margaret Ct. G20 21 U10
Queen Margaret Cres. G12 21 U10
Hamilton Dr.
Queen Margaret Dr. G12 20 T10
Queen Margaret Dr. G20 21 U10
Queen Margaret Rd. G20 21 U10
Queen Mary Av. G42 51 V15
Queen Mary Av., Clyde. G81 5 M7
Queen Mary St. G40 52 X14
Queen Sq. G41 51 U15
Queen St. G1 36 W12
Queen St. (Ruther.) G73 53 Y16
Queen St., Pais. PA1 46 J14
Queen St., Renf. PA4 17 M10
Queen Victoria Dr. G13 19 Q10
Queen Victoria Dr. G14 19 Q10
Queen Victoria Gate G13 19 Q9
Queenbank Av. (Gart.) G69 27 GG8
Queens Av. (Camb.) G72 66 BB17
Queens Cres. G4 35 V11
Queens Cres. (Bail.) G69 41 GG13
Queens Cross G20 21 U10
Queens Dr. G42 51 U15
Queens Dr. (Cumb.) G68 70 NN1
Queens Dr. La. G42 51 V15
Queens Gdns. G12 20 T10
Victoria Cres. Rd.
Queens Pk. Av. G42 51 V15
Queens Pl. G12 20 T10
Queens Rd. (Elder.), John. 44 F15
PA5
Queensborough Gdns. 20 S10
G12
Queensby Av. (Bail.) G69 40 EE13
Queensby Rd.
Queensby Dr. (Bail.) G69 40 EE13
Queensby Rd.
Queensby Pl. (Bail.) G69 40 EE13
Queensby Rd.
Queensby Rd. (Bail.) G69 40 EE13
Rosebery St.
Queensferry St. G5 52 X15
Rosebery St.
Queenshill St. G21 22 X10
Queensland Ct. G52 33 Q13
Queensland Dr. G52 33 Q13
Queensland Gdns. G52 33 Q13
Queensland La. E. G52 32 P13
Kingsland Dr.
Queensland La. W. G52 33 Q13
Queensland Dr.
Queenslie Ind. Est. G33 39 CC12
Queenslie St. G33 37 Z11
Quendale Dr. G32 54 AA14
Quentin St. G41 51 U15
Quinton Gdns. (Bail.) G69 40 EE13

R

Raasay Dr., Pais. PA2 46 J16
Raasay Pl. G22 22 W8
Raasay St. G22 22 W8
Rachan St. G34 40 FF11
Radnor St. G3 35 U12
Argyle St.
Radnor St., Clyde. G81 5 L6
Raeberry St. G20 21 U10
Raeswood Dr. G53 48 N16
Raeswood Gdns. G53 48 N16
Raeswood Pl. G53 48 N16
Raeswood Rd. G53 48 N16
Raglan St. G4 35 V11
Raith Av. G44 64 W18
Raithburn Av. G45 64 W18
Raithburn Rd. G45 64 W18
Ralston Av. G52 48 N14
Ralston Av., Pais. PA1 48 N14
Ralston Ct. G52 48 N14
Ralston Dr. G52 48 N14
Ralston Path G52 48 N14
Ralston Dr.
Ralston Pl. G52 48 N14
Ralston Rd. (Bears.) G61 7 R5
Ralston Rd. (Barr.) G78 59 M19
Ralston St., Pais. PA1 47 L14
Seedhill Rd.
Ram St. G32 38 AA13
Rampart Av. G13 18 P8
Ramsay Av., John. PA5 43 D15

Ramsay Cres. (Mill.Pk.), 42 B15
John. PA10
Ramsay Pl., John. PA5 43 D15
Ramsay St., Clyde. G81 4 K6
Ranald Gdns. (Ruther.) G73 65 Z18
Randolph Av. (Clark.) G76 63 U19
Randolph Dr. (Clark.) G76 63 U19
Randolph Gdns. (Clark.) 63 U19
G76
Randolph Rd. G11 19 R10
Randolph Ter. (Camb.) G72 66 BB17
Hamilton Rd.
Ranfurley Rd. G52 32 N13
Rankine Pl., John. PA5 43 D14
Rankine St., John. PA5 43 D14
Rankines La., Renf. PA4 17 M10
Manse St.
Rannoch Av. (Bishop.) G64 11 Y7
Rannoch Dr. (Bears.) G61 8 S7
Rannoch Dr., Renf. PA4 17 M10
Rannoch Gdns. (Bishop.) 11 Y7
G64
Rannoch Pl., Pais. PA2 47 L14
Rannoch Rd. (Udd.) G71 57 GG15
Rannoch Rd., John. PA5 43 D15
Rannoch St. G44 63 V17
Raploch Av. G14 18 P10
Raploch La. G14 18 P10
Raploch Av.
Ratford St. G51 34 S12
Rathlin St. G51 34 S12
Ratho Dr. G21 22 X9
Rattray St. G32 54 AA14
Ravel Row G31 37 Z13
Ravel Wynd (Udd.) G71 57 HH16
Ravelston Rd. (Bears.) G61 7 R7
Ravelston St. G32 37 Z13
Ravens Ct. (Bishop.) G64 22 X8
Lennox Cres.
Ravenscliffe Dr. (Giff.) G46 62 S18
Ravenscraig Av., Pais. PA2 46 J15
Ravenscraig Dr. G53 60 P17
Ravenscraig Ter. G53 61 Q17
Ravenshall Rd. G41 50 T16
Ravenstone Rd. (Giff.) G46 62 T18
Ravenswood Av., Pais. PA2 45 G16
Ravenswood Dr. G41 50 T15
Ravenswood Rd. (Bail.) G69 40 FF13
Rayne Pl. G15 6 P6
Red Rd. G21 23 Y10
Red Rd. Ct. G21 23 Y10
Redan St. G40 36 X13
Redcastle Sq. G33 39 CC11
Redford St. G33 37 Z12
Redgate Pl. G14 18 P10
Redhill Rd. (Cumb.) G68 70 MM2
Redhurst Cres., Pais. PA2 45 H16
Redhurst La., Pais. PA2 45 H16
Redhurst Way, Pais. PA2 45 H16
Redlands La. G12 20 T10
Kirklee Rd.
Redlands Rd. G12 20 T10
Redlands Ter. G12 20 T10
Redlands Ter. La. G12 20 T10
Julian Av.
Redlawood Pl. (Camb.) G72 68 EE17
Redlawood Rd.
Redlawood Rd. (Camb.) G72 68 EE17
Redmoss St. G22 21 V9
Rednock St. G22 22 W10
Redpath Dr. G52 32 P13
Redwood Dr. G21 23 Y10
Foresthall Dr.
Redwood Pl. (Kirk.) G66 12 BB5
Redwood Rd. (Cumb.) G67 71 QQ3
Reelick Av. G13 18 N8
Reelick Quad. G13 18 N8
Reen Pl. (Both.) G71 69 HH18
Regent Moray St. G3 34 T11
Regent Pk. Sq. G41 51 U15
Regent Pk. Ter. G41 51 U15
Pollokshaws Rd.
Regent Pl., Clyde. G81 4 K6
Regent Sq. (Lenzie) G66 13 CC6
Regent St., Clyde. G81 4 K6
Regent St., Pais. PA1 31 L13
Regents Gate (Both.) G71 69 GG18
Regwood St. G41 50 T16
Reid Av. (Bears.) G61 8 S5

Reid Av. (Linw.), Pais. PA3 28 E13
Reid Pl. G40 52 X14
Muslin St.
Reid St. G40 52 X14
Reid St. (Ruther.) G73 53 Y16
Reidhouse St. G21 22 X10
Muir St.
Reidvale St. G31 36 X13
Renfield St. G2 35 V12
Renfield St., Renf. PA4 17 M10
Renfrew Ct. G2 35 V12
Renfrew St.
Renfrew La. G2 35 V12
Renfield St.
Renfrew Rd. G51 32 P11
Renfrew Rd., Pais. PA3 30 K13
Renfrew Rd., Renf. PA4 32 P11
Renfrew St. G2 35 V11
Renfrew St. G3 35 V11
Rennies Rd. (Inch.), Renf. 16 J8
PA4
Renshaw Dr. G52 32 P13
Renshaw Rd. (Elder.), 44 F15
John. PA5
Renton St. G4 36 W11
Renwick St. G41 35 U13
Scotland St.
Residdl Rd. (Stepps) G33 25 DD9
Reston Dr. G52 32 P13
Reuther Av. (Ruther.) G73 53 Y16
Revoch Dr. G13 18 P8
Rhannan Rd. G44 63 V17
Rhannan Ter. G44 63 V17
Rhindhouse Pl. (Bail.) G69 40 FF13
Rhindhouse Rd. (Bail.) G69 40 FF13
Swinton Av.
Rhindmuir Av. (Bail.) G69 40 FF13
Rhindmuir Cres. (Bail.) G69 40 FF13
Rhindmuir Dr. (Bail.) G69 40 FF13
Rhindmuir Gro. (Bail.) G69 40 FF13
Rhindmuir Rd. (Bail.) G69 40 FF13
Rhindmuir Vw. (Bail.) G69 40 FF13
Rhindmuir Wynd (Bail.) G69 40 FF13
Rhindmuir Cres.
Rhinds St., Coat. ML5 57 HH14
Rhinsdale Cres. (Bail.) G69 40 FF13
Rhumhor Gdns., John. PA10 42 B15
Rhymer St. G21 36 X11
Rhymie Rd. G32 55 CC14
Rhynie Dr. G51 34 S13
Riccarton St. G42 52 W15
Riccartsbar Av., Pais. PA2 46 J14
Richard St. G2 35 V12
Cadogan St.
Richard St., Renf. PA4 17 M10
Richmond Ct. (Ruther.) G73 53 Z16
Richmond Dr. (Bishop.) G64 11 Y6
Richmond Dr. (Camb.) G72 66 AA17
Richmond Dr. (Ruther.) G73 53 Z16
Richmond Dr. (Linw.), Pais. 28 E12
PA3
Richmond Gdns. (Chry.) 14 EE7
G69
Richmond Gro. (Ruther.) 53 Z16
G73
Richmond Pl. (Ruther.) G73 53 Z16
Richmond St. G1 36 W12
Richmond St., Clyde. G81 5 M7
Riddell St., Clyde. G81 5 M6
Riddon Av. G13 18 N8
Riddon Av., Clyde. G81 18 N8
Riddon Pl. G13 18 N8
Riddrie Cres. G33 38 AA12
Riddrie Knowes G33 38 AA12
Riddrie Ter. G33 23 Z10
Provanmill Rd.
Riddrievale Ct. G33 38 AA11
Riddrievale St. G33 38 AA11
Rigby St. G32 37 Z13
Rigg Pl. G33 39 DD12
Rigghead Av. (Cumb.) G67 71 PP1
Riggside Rd. G33 39 CC11
Riglands Way, Renf. PA4 17 M10
Riglaw Pl. G13 18 P8
Rigmuir Rd. G51 33 Q13
Rimsdale St. G40 37 Y13
Ringford St. G21 22 X10
Ripon Dr. G12 20 S9
Risk St. G40 36 X13

132

Street	Page	Grid
Rutland La. G51	35	U13
Govan Rd.		
Rutland Pl. G51	35	U13
Ryan Rd. (Bishop.) G64	11	Y7
Ryan Way (Ruther.) G73	65	Z18
Rye Cres. G21	23	Z9
Rye Rd. G21	23	Z9
Rye Way, Pais. PA2	45	G15
Ryebank Rd. G21	23	Z9
Ryecroft Dr. (Bail.) G69	40	EE13
Ryedale Pl. G15	6	P6
Ryefield Av., John. PA5	43	C15
Ryefield Pl., John. PA5	43	C15
Ryefield Rd. G21	23	Y9
Ryehill Pl. G21	23	Z9
Ryehill Rd. G21	23	Z9
Ryemount Rd. G21	23	Z9
Ryeside Rd. G21	23	Y9
Rylands Dr. G32	55	DD14
Rylands Gdns. G32	55	DD14
Rylees Cres. G52	32	N12
Rylees Pl. G52	32	N13
Rylees Rd. G52	32	N13
Ryvra Rd. G13	19	Q9

S

Street	Page	Grid
Sackville Av. G13	19	R9
Sackville La. G13	19	R9
Sackville Av.		
Saddell Rd. G15	6	P6
St. Abbs Dr., Pais. PA2	45	H15
St. Andrews Av. (Bishop.) G64	10	X7
St. Andrew's Av. (Both.) G71	69	HH19
St. Andrews Cres. G41	51	U14
St. Andrews Cres., Pais. PA3	30	J11
St. Andrews Cross G41	51	V14
St. Andrews Dr. G41	50	T15
St. Andrews Dr. (Abbots.), Pais. PA3	30	J12
St. Andrews Dr. W. (Abbots.), Pais. PA3	30	J11
St. Andrews La. G1	36	W13
Gallowgate		
St. Andrews Rd. G41	51	U14
St. Andrews Rd., Renf. PA4	31	M11
St. Andrews Sq. G1	36	W13
St. Andrews St. G1	36	W13
St. Anns Dr. (Giff.) G46	62	T19
St. Blanes Dr. (Ruther.) G73	64	X17
St. Boswell's Cres., Pais. PA2	45	H15
St. Brides Rd. G43	50	T16
St. Brides Way (Both.) G71	69	HH18
St. Catherines Rd. (Giff.) G46	62	T19
St. Clair Av. (Giff.) G46	62	T18
St. Clair St. G20	35	U11
Woodside Rd.		
St. Conval Pl. G43	50	S16
Shawbridge St.		
St. Cyrus Gdns. (Bishop.) G64	11	Z7
St. Cyrus Rd. (Bishop.) G64	11	Y7
St. Enoch Pl. G1	35	V13
Howard St.		
St. Enoch Sq. G1	35	V13
St. Enoch Wynd G2	35	V12
Argyle St.		
St. Fillans Rd. G33	25	CC9
St. Georges Cross G3	35	V11
St. Georges Pl. G20	35	V11
St. Georges Rd.		
St. Georges Rd. G3	35	V11
St. Germains (Bears.) G61	7	R6
St. Helena Cres., Clyde. G81	5	M5
St. Ives Rd. (Mood.) G69	15	GG6
St. James Av., Pais. PA3	29	H12
St. James Pl., Pais. PA3	30	K13
Love St.		
St. James Rd. G4	36	W12
St. James St., Pais. PA3	30	J13
St. Johns Ct. G41	51	U14
St. Johns Quad. G41	51	U14
St. Johns Rd. G41	51	U14
St. Johns Ter. G12	35	U11
Southpark Av.		
St. Joseph's Ct. G21	36	X11
St. Josephs Pl. G40	36	X13
Abercromby St.		
St. Joseph's Vw. G21	36	X11
St. Kenneth Dr. G51	33	R12
St. Kilda Dr. G14	19	R10
St. Leonards Dr. (Giff.) G46	62	T18
St. Margarets Pl. G1	36	W13
Bridgegate		
St. Mark Gdns. G32	38	AA13
St. Mark St.		
St. Mark St. G32	38	AA13
St. Marnock St. G40	37	Y13
St. Mary's Cres. (Barr.) G78	59	M19
St. Mary's Gdns. (Barr.) G78	59	M19
Heys St.		
St. Marys La. G2	35	V12
West Nile St.		
St. Marys Rd. (Bishop.) G64	10	X7
St. Michael's Ct. G31	37	Z13
St. Michael's La. G31	37	Z13
St. Mirren St., Pais. PA1	46	K14
St. Monance St. G21	22	X9
St. Mungo Av. G4	36	W12
St. Mungo Pl. G4	36	W12
St. Mungo St. (Bishop.) G64	22	X8
St. Mungo's Rd. (Cumb.) G67	70	NN3
St. Ninian St. G5	36	W13
St. Ninian Ter. G5	36	W13
Old Rutherglen Rd.		
St. Ninians Cres., Pais. PA2	46	K15
Rowan St.		
St. Ninians Rd., Pais. PA2	46	K15
St. Peters La. G2	35	V12
Blythswood St.		
St. Peters St. G4	35	V11
St. Rollox Brae G21	36	X11
St. Ronans Dr. G41	50	T15
St. Ronans Dr. (Ruther.) G73	65	Z17
St. Stephens Av. (Ruther.) G73	65	Z18
St. Stephens Cres. (Ruther.) G73	66	AA18
St. Valleyfield St. G21	22	X10
Ayr Rd.		
St. Vincent Cres. G3	34	T12
St. Vincent Cres. La. G3	35	U12
Corunna St.		
St. Vincent La. G2	35	V12
Hope St.		
St. Vincent Pl. G1	36	W12
St. Vincent St. G2	35	U12
St. Vincent St. G3	35	U12
St. Vincent Ter. G3	35	U12
Salamanca St. G31	37	Z13
Salen St. G52	33	R13
Salisbury Pl. G12	20	T10
Great Western Rd.		
Salisbury Pl., Clyde. G81	4	J5
Salisbury St. G5	51	V14
Salkeld St. G5	51	V14
Salmona St. G22	21	V10
Saltaire Av. (Udd.) G71	69	HH19
Salterland Rd. G53	60	N17
Salterland Rd. (Barr.) G78	60	N17
Saltmarket G1	36	W13
Saltmarket Pl. G1	36	W13
King St.		
Saltoun Gdns. G12	20	T10
Roxburgh St.		
Saltoun La. G12	20	T10
Ruthven St.		
Saltoun St. G12	20	T10
Salvia St. (Camb.) G72	66	AA17
Sanda St. G20	21	U10
Sandaig Rd. G33	39	DD13
Sandbank Av. G20	20	T9
Sandbank Dr. G20	20	T8
Sandbank St. G20	20	T9
Sandbank Ter. G20	20	T8
Sandend Rd. G53	48	P16
Sanderling Pl., John. PA5	43	C16
Sanderling Rd., Pais. PA3	30	J12
Sandfield St. G20	21	U9
Maryhill Rd.		
Sandford Gdns. (Bail.) G69	56	EE14
Scott St.		
Sandgate Av. G32	55	CC14
Sandhaven Rd. G53	48	P16
Sandholes, Pais. PA1	46	J14
Sandholm Pl. G14	18	N9
Sandholm Ter. G14	18	N9
Sandiefauld St. G5	52	W14
Sandielands Av., Ersk. PA8	16	J8
Sandilands St. G32	38	BB13
Sandmill St. G21	37	Y11
Sandra Rd. (Bishop.) G64	11	Z7
Sandringham Dr. (Elder.), John. PA5	44	E15
Glamis Av.		
Sandringham La. G12	20	T10
Kersland St.		
Sandwood Cres. G52	32	P13
Sandwood Rd.		
Sandwood Rd. G52	32	P13
Sandy La. G11	34	S11
Crawford St.		
Sandy Rd. G11	34	S11
Sandy Rd., Renf. PA4	31	M11
Sandyford Pl. G3	35	U12
Sandyford Pl. La. G3	35	U11
Elderslie St.		
Sandyford Rd., Pais. PA3	31	L12
Sandyford St. G3	34	T12
Sandyhills Cres. G32	54	BB14
Sandyhills Dr. G32	54	BB14
Sandyhills Gro. G32	55	CC15
Hamilton Rd.		
Sandyhills Pl. G32	54	BB14
Sandyhills Rd. G32	54	BB14
Sandyknowes Rd. (Cumb.) G67	71	PP4
Sanguhar Gdns. (Blan.) G72	68	EE19
Sannox Gdns. G31	37	Y12
Saracen Gdns. G22	22	W9
Saracen Head La. G1	36	W13
Gallowgate		
Saracen St. G22	22	W10
Sardinia La. G12	20	T10
Great George St.		
Sardinia Ter. G12	20	T10
Cecil St.		
Saucel, Pais. PA1	46	K14
Saucel St., Pais. PA1	46	K14
Saucelhill Ter., Pais. PA2	46	K14
Sauchenhall Rd. (Kirk.) G66	15	GG5
Sauchiehall La. G2	35	V12
Sauchiehall St.		
Sauchiehall St. G2	35	U12
Sauchiehall St. G3	35	U12
Saughs Av. G33	24	AA9
Saughs Dr. G33	24	AA9
Saughs Gate G33	24	AA9
Saughs Pl. G33	24	AA9
Saughs Av.		
Saughs Rd. G33	24	AA9
Saughton St. G32	38	AA12
Saunders Ct. (Barr.) G78	59	L18
John St.		
Savoy Arc. G40	52	X14
Main St.		
Savoy St. G40	52	X14
Sawfield Pl. G4	35	V11
Garscube Rd.		
Sawmill Rd. G11	33	R11
South St.		
Sawmillfield St. G4	35	V11
Saxon Rd. G13	19	Q8
Scadlock Rd., Pais. PA3	29	H13
Scalpay Pl. G22	22	W8
Scalpay St. G22	22	W8
Scapa St. G23	21	U8
Scapa St. G40	53	Y14
Springfield Rd.		
Scaraway Dr. G22	22	W8
Scaraway Pl. G22	22	W8
Scaraway St. G22	22	W8
Scaraway Ter. G22	22	W8
Scarba Dr. G43	62	S17
Scarrel Dr. G45	65	Y18
Scarrel Gdns. G45	65	Y18
Scarrel Rd. G45	65	Y18
Scarrel Ter. G45	65	Y18
Schaw Ct. (Bears.) G61	7	Q5

Schaw Dr. (Bears.) G61 7 R5
Schaw Rd., Pais. PA3 31 L13
Schipka Pas. G1 36 W13
Gallowgate
School Av. (Camb.) G72 66 BB17
School Rd. (Stepps) G33 25 DD9
School Rd., Pais. PA1 32 N13
School Wynd, Pais. PA1 30 K13
Scioncroft Av. (Ruther.) G73 53 Z16
Scone St. G21 22 W10
Sconser St. G23 9 U7
Scorton Gdns. (Bail.) G69 55 DD14
Scotland St. G5 35 U13
Scotland St. W. G41 34 T13
Scotsblair Av. (Kirk.) G66 13 CC5
Scotsburn Rd. G21 23 Z10
Scotstoun Mill Rd. G11 34 T11
Partick Bri. St.
Scotstoun Pl. G14 19 Q10
Scotstoun St.
Scotstoun St. G14 19 Q10
Scott Av., John. PA5 43 D16
Scott Dr. (Bears.) G61 7 Q5
Scott Rd. G52 32 N12
Scott St. G3 35 V11
Scott St. (Bail.) G69 56 EE14
Scott St., Clyde. G81 4 K6
Scotts Rd., Pais. PA2 47 M14
Seafar Rd. (Cumb.) G67 70 NN4
Seafield Dr. (Ruther.) G73 65 Z18
Seaforth Cres. (Barr.) G78 59 L18
Seaforth La. (Chry.) G69 15 HH7
Burnbrae Av.
Seaforth Rd. G52 32 P12
Seaforth Rd., Clyde. G81 5 L7
Seaforth Rd. N. G52 32 P12
Seaforth Rd. S. G52 32 P12
Seagrove St. G32 37 Z13
Seamill Path G53 60 N17
Seamill Pl. G53 60 N17
Seamill St. G53 60 N17
Seamore St. G20 35 U11
Seath Rd. (Ruther.) G73 53 Y15
Seath St. G42 52 W15
Seaward La. G41 35 U13
Seaward St.
Seaward St. G41 35 U13
Second Av. (Stepps) G33 24 BB9
Second Av. G44 63 V17
Second Av. (Bears.) G61 8 S6
Second Av. (Kirk.) G66 13 CC7
Second Av. (Udd.) G71 57 GG15
Second Av., Clyde. G81 5 L6
Second Av., Renf. PA4 31 M11
Second Gdns. G41 50 S14
Second St. (Udd.) G71 57 GG16
Seedhill, Pais. PA1 46 K14
Seedhill Rd., Pais. PA1 46 K14
Seggielea La. G13 19 Q9
Helensburgh Dr.
Seggielea Rd. G13 19 Q9
Seil Dr. G44 64 W18
Selborne Pl. G13 19 R9
Selborne Rd.
Selborne Pl. La. G13 19 R9
Selborne Rd.
Selborne Rd. G13 19 R9
Selby Gdns. G32 39 DD13
Selkirk Av. G52 49 Q14
Selkirk Av., Pais. PA2 45 H15
Selkirk Dr. (Ruther.) G73 53 Z16
Sella Rd. (Bishop.) G64 11 Z7
Selvieland Rd. G52 32 N13
Semple Pl. (Linw.), Pais. 28 E12
PA3
Seton Ter. G31 36 X12
Settle Gdns. (Bail.) G69 55 DD14
Seven Sisters (Kirk.) G66 13 DD5
Seventh Av. (Udd.) G71 57 GG16
Seyton Av. (Giff.) G46 62 T19
Shaftesbury St. G3 35 U12
Shaftesbury St., Clyde. G81 4 K7
Shafton Pl. G13 19 R8
Shafton Rd. G13 19 R8
Shakespeare Av., Clyde. 4 K6
G81
Shakespeare St. G20 21 U9
Shamrock Cotts. G13 19 R9
Crow Rd.

Shamrock St. G4 35 V11
Shandon St. G51 34 T12
Govan Rd.
Shandwick St. G34 40 EE12
Shanks Av. (Barr.) G78 59 M19
Shanks Cres., John. PA5 43 C15
Shanks St. G20 21 U9
Shannon St. G20 21 U9
Shapinsay St. G22 22 W8
Sharrocks St. G51 34 T13
Clifford St.
Shaw Pl. (Linw.), Pais. PA3 28 E13
Shaw St. G51 34 S12
Shawbridge St. G43 50 T16
Shawfield Dr. G5 52 X15
Shawfield Rd. G5 52 X15
Shawhill Rd. G41 50 T16
Shawhill Rd. G43 50 T16
Shawholm Cres. G43 50 S16
Shawlands Arc. G41 51 U16
Shawlands Sq. G41 51 U16
Shawmoss Rd. G41 50 T15
Shawpark St. G20 21 U9
Shearer La. G5 35 U13
Shearer Pl. G51 35 U13
Sheddons Pl. G32 38 AA13
Sheepburn Rd. (Udd.) G71 57 GG16
Sheila St. G33 24 AA10
Sheldrake Pl., John. PA5 43 C16
Shelley Ct. G12 20 S9
Shelley Rd.
Shelley Dr. (Both.) G71 69 HH18
Shelley Dr., Clyde. G81 5 L6
Shelley Rd. G12 19 R9
Sheppard St. G21 22 X10
Cowlairs Rd.
Sherbrooke Av. G41 50 T14
Sherbrooke Dr. G41 50 T14
Sherbrooke Gdns. G41 50 T14
Sherburn Gdns. (Bail.) G69 55 DD14
Sheriff Pk. Av. (Ruther.) G73 53 Y16
Sherwood Av. (Udd.) G71 69 HH17
Sherwood Av., Pais. PA1 31 L13
Sherwood Dr. (Thorn.) G46 62 S18
Sherwood Pl. G15 6 P6
Shetland Dr. G44 64 W18
Shettleston Rd. G31 37 Z13
Shettleston Rd. G32 38 AA13
Shettleston Sheddings G31 38 AA13
Shettleston Rd.
Shiel Ct. (Barr.) G78 59 L17
Shiel Rd. (Bishop.) G64 11 Y7
Shieldaig Dr. (Ruther.) G73 65 Y18
Shieldaig Rd. G22 21 V8
Shieldbridge Gdns. G23 9 U7
Shieldburn Rd. G51 33 Q12
Shieldhall Gdns. G51 33 Q12
Shieldhall Rd. G51 32 P12
Shields Rd. G41 35 U13
Shilford Av. G13 18 P8
Shillay St. G22 22 X8
Shilton Dr. G53 60 P17
Shinwell Av., Clyde. G81 5 M7
Shipbank La. G1 36 W13
Clyde St.
Shiskine Dr. G20 20 T8
Shiskine Pl. G20 20 T8
Shiskine St.
Shiskine St. G20 20 T8
Shore St. G40 52 X15
Shortbridge St. G20 21 U9
Shanks St.
Shortroods Av., Pais. PA3 30 J12
Shortroods Cres., Pais. PA3 30 J12
Shortroods Rd., Pais. PA3 30 J12
Shotts St. G33 39 CC12
Shuna Pl. G20 21 U9
Shuna St. G20 21 U9
Shuttle La. G1 36 W12
George St.
Shuttle St. G1 36 W12
Shuttle St. (Kilb.), John. 42 A14
PA10
Shuttle St., Pais. PA1 46 K14
Sidland Rd. G21 23 Z9
Sidlaw Av. (Barr.) G78 59 M19
Ochil Dr.
Sidlaw Rd. (Bears.) G61 6 P5
Sielga Pl. G34 40 EE12

Siemens Pl. G21 37 Y11
Siemens St. G21 37 Y11
Sievewright St. (Ruther.) 53 Z15
G73
Hunter Rd.
Silk St., Pais. PA1 30 K13
Silkin Av., Clyde. G81 5 M7
Silverburn St. G33 38 AA12
Silverdale St. G31 53 Z14
Silverfir St. G5 52 W14
Silvergrove St. G40 36 X13
Silverwells (Both.) G71 69 HH19
Silverwells Cres. (Both.) 69 HH19
G71
Simons Cres., Renf. PA4 17 M9
Simpson Ct. (Udd.) G71 69 GG17
Simpson Ct., Clyde. G81 5 L7
Simpson St. G20 21 U10
Simshill Rd. G44 63 V18
Sinclair Av. (Bears.) G61 7 R5
Sinclair Dr. G42 51 U16
Sinclair Gdns. (Bishop.) G64 23 Y8
Sinclair St., Clyde. G81 17 M8
Singer Rd., Clyde. G81 4 K6
Singer St., Clyde. G81 5 L6
Sir Michael Pl., Pais. PA1 46 J14
Sixth Av., Renf. PA4 31 M11
Sixth St. (Udd.) G71 57 GG15
Skaethorn Rd. G20 20 S8
Skaterig La. G13 19 R9
Skaterigg Dr. G13 19 R9
Skaterigg Gdns. G13 19 R9
Skaterigg Rd. G13 19 R9
Crow Rd.
Skelbo Path G34 40 FF11
Auchingill Rd.
Skelbo Pl. G34 40 FF11
Skene Rd. G51 34 S13
Skerray Quad. G22 22 W8
Skerray St. G22 22 W8
Skerryvore Pl. G33 38 BB12
Skerryvore Rd. G33 38 BB12
Skibo Dr. (Thorn.) G46 61 R18
Skibo La. (Thorn.) G46 61 R18
Skipness Dr. G51 33 R12
Skirsa Ct. G23 21 V8
Skirsa Pl. G23 21 U8
Skirsa Sq. G23 21 U8
Skirsa St. G23 21 U8
Skirving St. G41 51 U16
Skye Av., Renf. PA4 31 M11
Skye Ct. (Cumb.) G67 70 MM4
Skye Cres. (Old Kil.) G60 4 J5
Skye Cres., Pais. PA2 46 J16
Skye Dr. (Old Kil.) G60 4 J5
Skye Dr. (Cumb.) G67 70 MM4
Skye Gdns. (Bears.) G61 6 P5
Skye Pl. (Cumb.) G67 70 MM4
Skye Rd. (Cumb.) G67 70 MM4
Skye Rd. (Ruther.) G73 65 Z18
Skye St. G20 20 T8
Bantaskin St.
Slakiewood Av. (Gart.) G69 27 GG8
Slatefield St. G31 37 Y13
Sleads St. G41 35 U13
Sloy St. G22 22 W10
Smeaton St. G20 21 U9
Smith Cres., Clyde. G81 5 L5
Smith St. G14 33 R11
Smith Ter. (Ruther.) G73 53 Y15
Smithhills St., Pais. PA1 30 K13
Smiths La., Pais. PA3 30 K13
Smithy Ends (Cumb.) G67 71 PP1
Smithycroft Rd. G33 38 AA11
Snaefell Av. (Ruther.) G73 65 Z18
Snaefell Cres. (Ruther.) G73 65 Z17
Snuff Mill Rd. G44 63 V17
Society St. G31 37 Y13
Soho St. G40 37 Y13
Sollas Pl. G13 18 N8
Solway Pl. (Chry.) G69 26 FF8
Solway Rd. (Bishop.) G64 11 Z7
Solway St. G40 52 X15
Somerford Rd. (Bears.) G61 7 R7
Somerled Av., Pais. PA3 30 K11
Somerset Pl. G3 35 U11
Somerset Pl. Meuse G3 35 U11
Elderslie St.
Somervell St. (Camb.) G72 66 AA17

135

Stewart St. (Barr.) G78 59 M18
Stewart St., Clyde. G81 4 K6
Stewarton Dr. (Camb.) G72 66 AA17
Stewarton Rd. (Thorn.) G46 61 R19
Stewartville St. G11 34 S11
Stirling Av. (Bears.) G61 7 R7
Stirling Dr. (Bears.) G61 7 Q5
Stirling Dr. (Bishop.) G64 10 X6
Stirling Dr. (Ruther.) G73 65 Y17
Stirling Dr., John. PA5 43 C15
Stirling Fauld Pl. G5 35 V13
Stirling Gdns. (Bishop.) G64 10 X6
Stirling Rd. G4 36 W12
Stirling St. (Cumb.) G67 71 PP2
Stirling Way, Renf. PA4 31 M11
  York Way
Stirrat St. G20 20 T9
Stirrat St., Pais. PA3 29 H12
Stobcross Rd. G3 35 U12
Stobcross St. G3 35 U12
Stobhill Rd. G21 22 X8
Stobs Dr. (Barr.) G78 59 L17
Stobs Pl. G34 40 FF11
Stock Av., Pais. PA2 46 K14
Stock St., Pais. PA2 46 K15
Stockholm Cres., Pais. PA2 46 K14
Stockwell Pl. G1 36 W13
Stockwell St. G1 36 W13
Stoddard Sq. (Elder.), 44 F14
  John. PA5
  Glenpatrick Rd.
Stonedyke Gro. G15 6 P7
Stonefield Av. G12 20 T9
Stonefield Av., Pais. PA2 46 K15
Stonefield Cres., Pais. PA2 46 K15
Stonefield Dr., Pais. PA2 46 K15
Stonefield Gdns., Pais. PA2 46 K15
Stonefield Grn., Pais. PA2 46 K15
Stonelaw Dr. (Ruther.) G73 53 Y16
Stonelaw Rd. (Ruther.) G73 53 Y16
Stoneside Dr. G43 62 S17
Stoneside Sq. G43 62 S17
Stoney Brae, Pais. PA1 30 K13
Stoneyetts Cotts. (Chry.) 15 GG6
  G69
Stoneyetts Rd. (Chry.) G69 15 GG7
Stony Brae, Pais. PA2 46 K16
Stonyhurst St. G22 21 V10
Stonylee Rd. (Cumb.) G67 71 PP3
Storie St., Pais. PA1 46 K14
Stormyland Way (Barr.) G78 59 M19
Stornoway St. G22 22 W8
Stow Brae, Pais. PA1 46 K14
Stow St., Pais. PA1 46 K14
Strachur St. G22 21 V8
Straiton St. G32 38 AA12
Stranka Av., Pais. PA2 46 J14
Stranraer Dr. G15 7 Q7
  Moraine Av.
Stratford St. G20 21 U9
Strathallan La. G12 34 T11
  Highburgh Rd.
Strathallan Ter. G12 34 T11
  Caledon St.
Strathallon Pl. (Ruther.) G73 65 Z18
  Ranald Gdns.
Strathbran St. G31 53 Z14
Strathcarron Pl. G20 20 T9
  Glenfinnan Rd.
Strathcarron Rd., Pais. PA2 47 L16
Strathclyde Dr. (Ruther.) 53 Y16
  G73
Strathclyde Path (Udd.) G71 69 GG17
Strathclyde St. G40 53 Y15
Strathclyde Vw. (Both.) G71 69 HH19
Strathcona Dr. G13 19 R8
Strathcona Gdns. G13 20 S8
Strathcona Pl. (Ruther.) G73 65 Z18
Strathcona St. G13 19 R9
Strathdee Av., Clyde. G81 5 L5
Strathdee Rd. G44 63 U19
Strathdon Av. G44 63 U19
Strathdon Av., Pais. PA2 46 J15
Strathdon Dr. G44 63 U19
Strathendrick Dr. G44 63 U19
Strathkelvin Retail Pk. 11 Z6
  (Bishop.) G64
Strathmore Av. (Blan.) G72 68 FF19
Strathmore Av., Pais. PA1 47 M14

Strathmore Gdns. G12 35 U11
  Gibson St.
Strathmore Gdns. (Ruther.) 65 Z18
  G73
Strathmore Rd. G22 21 V8
Strathord Pl. (Chry.) G69 15 HH6
Strathord St. G32 54 BB14
Strathtay Av. G44 63 U19
Strathview Gdns. (Bears.) 7 Q6
  G61
Strathview Gro. G44 63 U19
Strathview Pk. G44 63 U19
Strathy Pl. G20 20 T9
  Glenfinnan Rd.
Strathyre Gdns. (Bears.) 8 S5
  G61
Strathyre Gdns. (Chry.) G69 15 HH7
  Heathfield Av.
Strathyre St. G41 51 U16
Stratton Dr. (Giff.) G46 62 S19
Strauss Av., Clyde. G81 6 N7
Stravaig Path, Pais. PA2 45 H16
Stravaig Wk., Pais. PA2 45 H16
Stravanan Av. G45 64 W19
Stravanan Ct. G45 64 X19
Stravanan Rd. G45 64 W19
Stravanan St. G45 64 W19
Stravanan Ter. G45 64 W19
Strenabey Av. (Ruther.) G73 65 Z18
Striven Gdns. G20 21 U10
Stroma St. G21 37 Y11
Stromness St. G5 51 V14
Strone Rd. G33 38 BB12
Stronend St. G22 21 V9
Stronsay Pl. (Bishop.) G64 11 Z7
Stronsay St. G21 37 Y11
Stronvar Dr. G14 18 P10
Stronvar La. G14 18 P10
  Larchfield Av.
Strowan Cres. G32 54 BB14
Strowan St. G32 54 BB14
Struan Av. (Giff.) G46 62 S18
Struan Gdns. G44 63 V17
Struan Rd. G44 63 V17
Struie St. G34 40 EE12
Stuart Av. (Ruther.) G73 65 Y17
Stuart Dr. (Bishop.) G64 22 X8
Succoth St. G13 19 R8
Suffolk St. G40 36 X13
  Kent St.
Sugworth Av. (Bail.) G69 40 EE13
Sumburgh St. G33 38 AA12
Summer St. G40 36 X13
Summerfield Cotts. G14 33 R11
  Smith St.
Summerfield Pl. G40 53 Y14
  Ardenlea St.
Summerfield St. G40 53 Y15
Summerhill Dr. G15 6 P6
Summerhill Gdns. G15 6 P6
Summerhill Pl. G15 6 P6
Summerhill Rd. G15 6 P6
Summerlee Rd. (Thorn.) 61 R18
  G46
Summerlee St. G33 39 CC12
Summertown Rd. G51 34 S12
Sunart Av., Renf. PA4 17 L10
Sunart Gdns. (Bishop.) G64 11 Y7
Sunart Rd. G52 33 R13
Sunart Rd. (Bishop.) G64 11 Y7
Sunningdale Rd. G23 20 T8
Sunningdale Wynd (Both.) 69 GG18
  G71
Sunnybank St. G40 53 Y14
Sunnylaw Dr., Pais. PA2 45 H15
Sunnylaw St. G22 21 V10
Sunnyside Av. (Udd.) G71 69 GG17
Sunnyside Dr. G15 6 P7
Sunnyside Dr. (Bail.) G69 41 GG13
Sunnyside Pl. G15 6 P7
Sunnyside Pl. (Barr.) G78 59 L19
Sunnyside Rd., Pais. PA2 46 J15
Surrey La. G5 51 V14
  Pollokshaws Rd.
Sussex St. G41 35 U13
Sutcliffe Ct. G13 19 R8
Sutcliffe Rd. G13 19 R8
Sutherland Av. G41 50 T14
Sutherland Dr. (Giff.) G46 62 T19

Sutherland La. G12 34 T11
  University Av.
Sutherland Rd., Clyde. G81 5 L7
Sutherland St., Pais. PA1 30 J13
Swallow Gdns. G13 18 N8
Swan La. G4 36 W11
Swan Pl., John. PA5 43 C16
Swan St. G4 36 W11
Swan St., Clyde. G81 4 K6
Swanston St. G40 53 Y15
Sween Dr. G44 63 V18
Sweethope Pl. (Both.) G71 69 HH18
Swift Cres. G13 18 N8
Swift Pl., John. PA5 43 C16
Swindon St., Clyde. G81 4 K6
Swinton Av. (Bail.) G69 40 FF13
Swinton Cres. (Bail.) G69 40 FF13
Swinton Cres., Coat. ML5 57 HH14
Swinton Dr. G52 32 P13
Swinton Gdns. (Bail.) G69 40 FF13
  Swinton Av.
Swinton Path (Bail.) G69 40 FF13
  Swinton Av.
Swinton Pl. G52 32 P13
Swinton Rd. (Bail.) G69 40 EE13
Swinton Vw. (Bail.) G69 40 FF13
  Swinton Av.
Switchback Rd. (Bears.) G61 7 R7
Sword St. G31 36 X13
Swordale Path G34 40 EE12
  Swordale Pl.
Swordale Pl. G34 40 EE12
Sycamore Av. (Lenzie) G66 13 CC5
Sycamore Av., John. PA5 44 E15
Sycamore Dr., Clyde. G81 5 L6
Sydenham La. G12 20 S10
  Crown Rd. S.
Sydenham Rd. G12 20 T10
Sydney Ct. G2 35 V12
  Argyle St.
Sydney St. G31 36 X13
Sydney St., Clyde. G81 4 J6
Sylvania Way, Clyde. G81 5 L7
Sylvania Way S., Clyde. G81 5 L7
Symington Dr., Clyde. G81 5 L7
Syriam Pl. G21 22 X10
  Syriam St.
Syriam St. G21 22 X10

T
Tabard Pl. G13 19 Q8
Tabard Pl. N. G13 19 Q8
  Tabard Rd.
Tabard Pl. S. G13 19 Q8
  Tabard Rd.
Tabard Rd. G13 19 Q8
Tabernacle La. (Camb.) G72 66 BB17
Tabernacle St. (Camb.) G72 66 BB17
Tain Pl. G34 40 FF12
Tait Av. (Barr.) G78 59 M18
Talbot Ct. G13 18 P9
Talbot Dr. G13 18 P9
Talbot Pl. G13 18 P9
Talbot Ter. G13 18 P9
Talbot Ter. (Udd.) G71 57 GG16
Talisman Rd. G13 19 Q9
Talisman Rd., Pais. PA2 45 G16
Talla Rd. G52 32 P13
Tallant Rd. G15 6 P6
Tallant Ter. G15 7 Q6
Tallisman, Clyde. G81 5 M7
  Onslow Rd.
Tambowie St. G13 19 R8
Tamshill St. G20 21 U9
Tamworth St. G40 37 Y13
  Rimsdale St.
Tanar Av., Renf. PA4 32 N11
Tanar Way, Renf. PA4 32 N11
Tandlehill Rd. (Mill.Pk.), 42 B18
  John. PA10
Tanera Av. G44 64 W18
Tanfield Av. G32 39 CC12
Tanfield Pl. G32 39 CC12
  Tanfield Av.
Tankerland Rd. G44 63 V17
Tanna Dr. G52 49 R14
Tannadice Av. G52 49 Q14
Tannahall Rd., Pais. PA3 29 H13

Tannahall Ter., Pais. PA3 29 H13
Tannahill Cres., John. PA5 43 D15
Tannahill Rd. G43 63 U17
Tannoch Dr. (Cumb.) G67 71 PP4
Tannoch Pl. (Cumb.) G67 71 PP4
Tannochside Dr. (Udd.) G71 57 HH15
Tannock St. G22 21 V10
Tantallon Dr., Pais. PA2 45 H15
Tantallon Rd. G41 51 U16
Tantallon Rd. (Bail.) G69 56 EE14
Tanzieknowe Av. (Camb.) 66 BB18
G72
Tanzieknowe Dr. (Camb.) 66 BB18
G72
Tanzieknowe Pl. (Camb.) 66 BB18
G72
Tanzieknowe Rd. (Camb.) 66 BB18
G72
Taransay St. G51 34 S12
Tarbert Av. (Blan.) G72 68 FF19
Tarbolton Dr., Clyde. G81 5 M6
Tarbolton Rd. G43 62 T17
Tarbolton Rd. (Cumb.) G67 71 PP3
Tarbolton Sq., Clyde. G81 5 M6
Tarbolton Dr.
Tarfside Av. G52 49 Q14
Tarfside Gdns. G52 49 Q14
Tarfside Oval G52 49 Q14
Tarland St. G51 33 R13
Tarras Dr., Renf. PA4 32 N11
Tarras Pl. (Camb.) G72 67 CC17
Tassie St. G41 50 T16
Tattershall Rd. G33 39 CC11
Tavistock Dr. G43 62 T17
Tay Av., Pais. PA2 45 G15
Tay Av., Renf. PA4 18 N10
Tay Cres. G33 38 AA11
Tay Cres. (Bishop.) G64 11 Y7
Tay Pl., John. PA5 43 C16
Tay Rd. (Bears.) G61 7 Q7
Tay Rd. (Bishop.) G64 11 Y7
Taylor Av. (Kilb.), John. 42 A14
PA10
Taylor Pl. G4 36 W12
Taylor St. G4 36 W12
Taylor St., Clyde. G81 17 M8
Taymouth St. G32 54 BB14
Taynish Dr. G44 64 W18
Teal Dr. G13 18 N8
Tealing Av. G52 49 Q14
Tealing Cres. G52 49 Q14
Teasel Av. G53 60 P18
Teith Av., Renf. PA4 32 N11
Teith Dr. (Bears.) G61 7 Q6
Teith Pl. (Camb.) G72 67 CC17
Teith St. G33 38 AA11
Telephone La. G12 34 T11
Highburgh Rd.
Telford Ct., Clyde. G81 5 L7
Telford Pl. (Cumb.) G67 71 PP4
Telford Rd. (Cumb.) G67 71 PP4
Templar Av. G13 7 Q7
Temple Gdns. G13 19 R8
Temple Pl. G13 19 R8
Temple Rd. G13 20 S8
Templeland Av. G53 49 Q15
Templeland Rd. G53 49 Q15
Templeton St. G40 36 X13
Tennant Rd., Pais. PA3 29 H13
Tennant St., Renf. PA4 17 M10
Tennyson Dr. G31 54 AA14
Tenters Way, Pais. PA2 45 H14
Tern Pl., John. PA5 43 C16
Terrace Pl. (Camb.) G72 67 DD17
Terregles Av. G41 50 T15
Terregles Cres. G41 50 T15
Terregles Dr. G41 50 T15
Teviot Av. (Bishop.) G64 11 Y6
Teviot Av., Pais. PA2 45 G16
Teviot Cres. (Bears.) G61 7 Q7
Teviot St. G3 34 T12
Teviot Ter. G20 21 U10
Sanda St.
Teviot Ter., John. PA5 43 C16
Thane Rd. G13 19 Q9
Thanes Gate (Udd.) G71 69 GG17
Castle Gate
Tharsis St. G21 36 X11
Third Av. (Millerston) G33 24 BB9

Third Av. G44 51 V16
Third Av. (Kirk.) G66 13 CC7
Third Av., Renf. PA4 31 M11
Third Gdns. G41 50 S14
Third St. (Udd.) G71 57 GG16
Thirdpart Cres. G13 18 N8
Thistle Bk. (Lenzie) G66 13 CC6
Thistle Cotts. G13 19 R9
Crow Rd.
Thistle St. G5 51 V14
Thistle St., Pais. PA2 46 J15
Thomas Muir Av. (Bishop.) 23 Y8
G64
Thomas St., Pais. PA1 45 H14
Thomson Av., John. PA5 43 D14
Thomson Dr. (Bears.) G61 7 R5
Thomson Gro. (Camb.) G72 54 BB16
Thomson Pl., Clyde. G81 5 M5
Thomson St. G31 37 Y13
Thomson St., John. PA5 43 D15
Thomson St., Renf. PA4 31 M11
Thorn Brae, John. PA5 44 E14
Thorn Dr. (Bears.) G61 7 Q5
Thorn Dr. (Ruther.) G73 65 Z18
Thorn Rd. (Bears.) G61 7 Q5
Thorn St. G11 34 S11
Dumbarton Rd.
Thornbank St. G3 34 T11
Yorkhill Par.
Thornbridge Av. G12 20 T9
Balcarres Av.
Thornbridge Av. (Bail.) G69 40 EE13
Bannercross Dr.
Thornbridge Gdns. (Bail.) 40 EE13
G69
Thornbridge Rd. (Bail.) G69 40 EE13
Thorncliffe Gdns. G41 51 U15
Thorncliffe La. G41 51 U14
Thorncroft Dr. G44 64 W18
Thornden Cotts. G14 18 N9
Dumbarton Rd.
Thornden La. G14 18 P10
Dumbarton Rd.
Thorndene (Elder.), John. 44 E14
PA5
Thornhill, John. PA5 44 E15
Thornhill Av. (Elder.), 44 E15
John. PA5
Thornhill Dr. (Elder.), John. 44 E15
PA5
Thornhill Gdns., John. PA5 44 E14
Armour St.
Thorniewood Gdns. (Udd.) 57 HH16
G71
Thorniewood Rd. (Udd.) 57 GG16
G71
Thornlea Dr. (Giff.) G46 62 T18
Thornley Av. G13 18 P9
Thornliebank Rd. G43 62 S17
Thornliebank Rd. 61 Q19
(Deaconsbank) G46
Thornliebank Rd. (Thorn.) 62 S18
G46
Thornly Pk. Av., Pais. PA2 46 K16
Thornly Pk. Dr., Pais. PA2 46 K16
Thornly Pk. Rd., Pais. PA2 46 K16
Thornside Rd., John. PA5 44 E14
Thornton La. G20 21 U8
Thornton St. G20 21 U8
Thorntree Way (Both.) G71 69 HH18
Thornwood Av. G11 34 S11
Thornwood Av. (Kirk.) G66 12 BB5
Thornwood Cres. G11 19 R10
Thornwood Dr.
Thornwood Dr. G11 33 R11
Thornwood Dr., Pais. PA2 45 H15
Thornwood Gdns. G11 34 S11
Thornwood Pl. G11 20 S10
Thornwood Quad. G11 19 R10
Thornwood Dr.
Thornwood Rd. G11 33 R11
Thornwood Ter. G11 33 R11
Thornyburn Dr. (Bail.) G69 56 FF14
Thornyburn Pl. (Bail.) G69 56 FF14
Three Ell Rd. G51 34 T12
Govan Rd.
Threestonehill Av. G32 38 BB13
Thrums Av. (Bishop.) G64 11 Z7
Thrums Gdns. (Bishop.) G64 11 Z7

Thrush Pl., John. PA5 43 C16
Thrushcraig Cres., Pais. PA2 46 K15
Thurso St. G11 34 T11
Dumbarton Rd.
Thurston Rd. G52 32 P13
Tibbermore Rd. G11 20 S10
Tillet Oval, Pais. PA3 30 J12
Tillie St. G20 21 U10
Tillycairn Av. G33 39 CC11
Tillycairn Dr. G33 39 CC11
Tillycairn Pl. G33 25 DD10
Tillycairn Rd. G33 39 DD11
Tillycairn St. G33 39 DD11
Tilt St. G33 38 AA11
Tintagel Gdns. (Chry.) G69 15 GG6
Tinto Dr. (Barr.) G78 59 L19
Tinto Rd. G43 62 T17
Tinto Rd. (Bears.) G61 6 P5
Tinto Rd. (Bishop.) G64 11 Z7
Fintry Cres.
Tinto Sq., Renf. PA4 31 L11
Ochil Rd.
Tinwald Av. G52 32 N13
Tinwald Path G52 32 P13
Tiree Av., Pais. PA2 46 J16
Tiree Av., Renf. PA4 31 M11
Tiree Ct. (Cumb.) G67 70 MM4
Tiree Dr. (Cumb.) G67 70 MM4
Tiree Gdns. (Bears.) G61 6 P5
Tiree Rd. (Cumb.) G67 70 MM4
Tiree St. G21 37 Z11
Tirry Way, Renf. PA4 32 N11
Morriston Cres.
Titwood Rd. G41 50 T15
Tiverton Av. G32 55 CC14
Tobago Pl. G40 36 X13
Tobago St. G40 36 X13
Tobermory Rd. (Ruther.) 65 Z18
G73
Todburn Dr., Pais. PA2 46 K16
Todd St. G31 37 Z12
Todholm Rd., Pais. PA2 47 L15
Todholm Ter., Pais. PA2 47 L15
Tofthill Av. (Bishop.) G64 10 X7
Tofthill Gdns. (Bishop.) G64 10 X7
Toll La. G51 34 T13
Paisley Rd. W.
Tollcross Rd. G31 37 Z13
Tollcross Rd. G32 37 Z13
Tolsta St. G23 9 U7
Tontine La. G1 36 W13
Bell St.
Tontine Pl. (Ruther.) G73 66 AA18
Toppersfield (Mill.Pk.), 43 C15
John. PA10
Torbreck St. G52 33 R13
Torbrex Rd. (Cumb.) G67 71 PP3
Torburn Av. (Giff.) G46 62 S18
Tordene Path (Cumb.) G68 70 MM2
Torgyle St. G23 8 T7
Tormore St. G51 33 Q13
Tormusk Dr. G45 65 Y18
Tormusk Gdns. G45 65 Y18
Tormusk Gro. G45 65 Y18
Tormusk Rd. G45 65 Y18
Torness St. G11 34 T11
Torogay Pl. G22 22 X8
Torogay St. G22 22 W8
Torogay Ter. G22 22 W8
Toronto Wk. G32 55 CC16
Torphin Cres. G32 38 BB13
Torphin Wk. G32 38 BB13
Torr Rd. (Bishop.) G64 11 Z7
Torr St. G22 22 W10
Torran Rd. G33 39 DD12
Torrance Rd. (Torrance) G64 11 Z5
Torrance St. G21 22 X10
Springburn Way
Torridon Av. G41 50 S14
Torrin Rd. G23 8 T7
Torrington Av. (Giff.) G46 62 S19
Torrington Cres. G32 55 CC14
Torrisdale St. G42 51 U15
Torryburn Rd. G21 23 Z10
Torwood La. (Chry.) G69 15 HH7
Burnbrae Av.
Toryglen Rd. (Ruther.) G73 52 X16
Toryglen St. G5 52 W15
Toward Ct. (Blan.) G72 69 GG19

Toward Rd. G33	39	CC12	Tweedvale Av. G14	18	N9	Verona Av. G14	19	Q10
Tower Av. (Barr.) G78	59	M18	Tweedvale Pl. G14	18	N9	Verona La. G14	19	Q10
Tower Cres., Renf. PA4	31	L11	Twinlaw St. G34	40	FF11	*Verona Av.*		
Tower Dr., Renf. PA4	31	L11	Tylnley Rd., Pais. PA1	31	M13	Vesalius St. G32	38	BB13
Tower Pl. G20	20	T9	Tyndrum Rd. (Bears.) G61	8	S5	Vicarfield Pl. G51	34	S12
Glenfinnan Dr.			Tyndrum St. G4	36	W11	*Vicarfield St.*		
Tower Pl., John. PA5	43	D15	Tyne St. G14	33	Q11	Vicarfield St. G51	34	S12
Tower Rd., John. PA5	43	D15	Tynecastle Cres. G32	38	BB12	Vicarland Pl. (Camb.) G72	66	BB18
Tower St. G41	35	U13	Tynecastle Pl. G32	38	BB12	Vicarland Rd. (Camb.) G72	66	BB17
Tower Ter., Pais. PA1	46	J14	Tynecastle St. G32	38	BB12	Vicars Wk. (Camb.) G72	66	BB17
Towerhill Rd. G13	7	Q7	Tynwald Av. (Ruther.) G73	65	Z18	Victoria Bri. G1	36	W13
Towerhill Ter. G21	23	Y10				Victoria Bri. G5	36	W13
Broomfield Rd.						Victoria Circ. G12	20	T10
Towerside Cres. G53	48	P15	**U**			Victoria Cres. G12	20	T10
Towerside Rd. G53	48	P15	Uddingston Rd. (Both.) G71	69	HH18	*Dowanside Rd.*		
Towie Pl. (Udd.) G71	69	GG17	Uig Pl. G33	39	DD13	Victoria Cres. La. G12	20	T10
Townhead Pl. (Udd.) G71	57	HH16	Uist Cres. (Stepps) G33	25	DD10	*Victoria Cres. Rd.*		
Townhead Rd. (Gart.) G69	41	HH11	Uist St. G51	33	R12	Victoria Cres. Pl. G12	20	T10
Townhead Ter., Pais. PA1	46	J14	Ulundi Rd., John. PA5	43	C15	*Bowmont Ter.*		
Townmill Rd. G31	36	X12	Ulva St. G52	33	R13	Victoria Cres. Rd. G12	20	T10
Townsend St. G4	36	W11	Unden Pl. G13	19	R8	Victoria Cross G42	51	V15
Tradeston St. G5	35	V13	Underwood La., Pais. PA1	30	J13	*Victoria Rd.*		
Trafalgar St. G40	52	X14	Underwood Rd. (Ruther.)	65	Z17	Victoria Dr., Renf. PA4	17	L10
Trafalgar St., Clyde. G81	4	K6	G73			Victoria Dr. E., Renf. PA4	31	M11
Trainard Av. G32	54	AA14	Underwood Rd., Pais. PA3	30	J13	Victoria Gdns. (Barr.) G78	59	L18
Tranent Pl. G33	38	AA12	Underwood St. G41	51	U16	Victoria Pk. Cor. G14	19	Q10
Traquair Av., Pais. PA2	45	G16	*Tantallon Rd.*			Victoria Pk. Dr. N. G14	19	R10
Traquair Dr. G52	48	P14	Union Pl. G1	35	V12	Victoria Pk. Dr. S. G14	19	Q10
Treeburn Av. (Giff.) G46	62	S18	*Gordon St.*			Victoria Pk. Gdns. N. G11	19	R10
Trees Pk. Av. (Barr.) G78	59	L18	Union St. G1	35	V12	Victoria Pk. Gdns. S. G11	19	R10
Trefoil Av. G41	50	T16	Union St., Clyde. G81	17	M8	Victoria Pk. La. N. G14	19	Q10
Tresta Rd. G23	21	V8	Union St., Pais. PA2	46	K15	Victoria Pk. La. S. G14	19	Q10
Trident Way, Renf. PA4	31	M11	Unity Pl. G4	35	V11	*Westland Dr.*		
Newmains Rd.			*St. Peters St.*			Victoria Pk. St. G14	19	Q10
Trinity Av. G52	49	Q14	University Av. G12	34	T11	Victoria Pl. (Ruther.) G73	53	Y16
Trinity Dr. (Camb.) G72	67	CC18	University Gdns. G12	34	T11	*Greenbank St.*		
Trinley Brae G13	7	Q7	University of Glasgow G12	34	T11	Victoria Rd. (Stepps) G33	25	CC9
Trinley Rd. G13	7	Q7	University Pl. G12	34	T11	Victoria Rd. G42	51	V15
Trondra Path G34	39	DD12	*University Av.*			Victoria Rd. (Lenzie) G66	13	CC6
Trondra Pl. G34	39	DD12	Unsted Pl., Pais. PA1	46	K14	Victoria Rd. (Ruther.) G73	65	Y17
Trondra Rd. G34	39	DD12	Uphall Pl. G33	38	AA12	Victoria Rd. (Barr.) G78	59	L18
Trongate G1	36	W13	Upland Rd. G14	19	Q10	Victoria Rd., Pais. PA2	46	J15
Troon Gdns. (Cumb.) G68	71	PP1	Upper Bourtree Ct.	65	Z18	Victoria St. (Ruther.) G73	53	Y16
Troon St. G40	53	Y14	(Ruther.) G73			Victory Dr. (Kilb.), John.	42	B14
Trossachs Ct. G20	21	V10	*Upper Bourtree Dr.*			PA10		
Trossachs St.			Upper Bourtree Dr.	65	Y18	*Glentyan Av.*		
Trossachs Rd. (Ruther.) G73	65	Z19	(Ruther.) G73			Viewbank (Thorn.) G46	62	S18
Trossachs St. G20	21	V10	Upper Glenburn Rd.	7	Q5	Viewfield Av. (Bishop.) G64	22	X8
Troubridge Av. (Mill.Pk.),	42	B15	(Bears.) G61			Viewfield Av. (Lenzie) G66	13	CC5
John. PA10			Ure Pl. G4	36	W12	Viewfield Av. (Bail.) G69	39	DD13
Troubridge Cres. (Mill.Pk.),	42	B15	*Montrose St.*			Viewfield Av. (Blan.) G72	69	GG19
John. PA10			Urquhart Cres., Renf. PA4	31	M11	Viewfield Dr. (Bishop.) G64	22	X8
Truce Rd. G13	18	P8	Urrdale Rd. G41	34	S13	Viewfield Dr. (Bail.) G69	39	DD13
Truro Rd. (Chry.) G69	15	GG6	Usmore Pl. G33	39	DD13	Viewfield La. G12	35	U11
Tryst Rd. (Cumb.) G67	70	NN3				*Gibson St.*		
Tudor La. S. G14	19	Q10				Viewfield Rd. (Bishop.) G64	22	X8
Orleans Av.			**V**			Viewfield Rd., Coat. ML5	57	HH14
Tudor Rd. G14	19	R10	Vaila Pl. G23	21	U8	Viewfield Ter. G12	35	U11
Tudor St. (Bail.) G69	55	DD14	*Vaila St.*			*Southpark Av.*		
Tullis Ct. G40	52	X14	Vaila St. G23	21	U8	Viewglen Ct. G45	64	W19
Tullis St. G40	52	X14	Vale Wk. (Bishop.) G64	23	Z8	Viewmount Dr. G20	20	T8
Tulloch St. G44	63	V17	Valetta Pl., Clyde. G81	4	J6	Viewpark Av. G31	37	Y12
Tullochard Pl. (Ruther.) G73	65	Z18	Valeview Ter. G42	51	V16	Viewpark Dr. (Ruther.) G73	65	Y17
Tummel St. G33	38	AA11	Vallantine Cres. (Udd.) G71	57	HH16	Viewpoint Pl. G21	22	X9
Tummell Way, Pais. PA2	45	G15	Vallay St. G22	22	W8	Viewpoint Rd. G21	22	X9
Tunnel St. G3	35	U12	Valley Vw. (Camb.) G72	67	CC17	Viking Rd. (Thorn.) G46	61	R18
Finnieston St.			*Caledonian Circuit*			Viking Way, Renf. PA4	31	M11
Turnberry Av. G11	20	S10	Valleyfield St. G21	22	X10	*Vanguard Way*		
Turnberry Dr. (Ruther.) G73	64	X17	*Ayr St.*			Villafield Av. (Bishop.) G64	11	Y6
Turnberry Gdns. (Cumb.)	70	NN1	Van St. G31	37	Z13	Villafield Dr. (Bishop.) G64	11	Y6
G68			Vancouver La. G14	19	Q10	Villafield Ln. (Bishop.) G64	11	Y6
Turnberry Pl. (Ruther.) G73	64	X17	*Vancouver Rd.*			Village Gdns. (Blan.) G72	69	GG19
Turnberry Rd. G11	20	S10	Vancouver Pl., Clyde. G81	4	J6	Village Rd. (Camb.) G72	67	DD17
Turnberry Wynd (Both.) G71	69	GG18	Vancouver Rd. G14	19	Q10	Villiers Ct. G31	36	X13
Turnbull St. G1	36	W13	Vanguard St., Clyde. G81	5	M7	*Sword St.*		
Turner Rd. G21	36	X11	Vanguard Way, Renf. PA4	31	M11	Vine St. G11	34	S11
Turner Rd., Pais. PA3	30	K12	Varna La. G14	19	R10	Vinicombe La. G12	20	T10
Turnlaw Rd. (Camb.) G72	66	BB19	Varna Rd. G14	19	R10	*Vinicombe St.*		
Turnlaw St. G5	52	W14	Vasart Pl. G20	21	U10	Vinicombe St. G12	20	T10
Turret Cres. G13	19	Q8	*Caithness St.*			Vintner St. G4	36	W11
Turret Rd. G13	19	Q8	Veitchs Ct., Clyde. G81	4	K5	Violet St., Pais. PA1	47	L14
Turriff St. G5	51	V14	*Dumbarton Rd.*			Virginia Bldgs. G1	36	W12
Tweed Av., Pais. PA2	45	G15	Vennacher Rd., Renf. PA4	17	L10	*Virginia St.*		
Tweed Cres. G33	38	AA11	Vennard Gdns. G41	51	U15	Virginia Ct. G1	36	W12
Tweed Cres., Renf. PA4	18	N10	Vere St. G22	22	W10	*Virginia St.*		
Tweed Dr. (Bears.) G61	7	Q6	Vermont Av. (Ruther.) G73	65	Y16	Virginia Pl. G1	36	W12
Tweed Pl., John. PA5	43	C16	Vermont St. G41	35	U13	Virginia St. G1	36	W12
Tweedsmuir (Bishop.) G64	11	Z7	Vernon Dr. (Linw.), Pais.	28	E13	Viscount Av., Renf. PA4	31	M11
Tweedsmuir Rd. G52	48	P14	PA3			Viscount Gate (Both.) G71	69	GG17

Voil Dr. G44 63 V18
Vorlich Ct. (Barr.) G78 59 M19
Vulcan St. G21 22 X10
  Ayr St.

W

Waddell Ct. G5 36 W13
Waddell St. G5 52 W14
Waldemar Rd. G13 19 Q8
Waldo St. G13 19 R8
Walker Ct. G11 34 S11
  Walker St.
Walker Dr. (Elder.), John. 44 E15
PA5
Walker Path (Udd.) G71 57 HH16
Walker Sq. G20 20 T8
  Bantaskin St.
Walker St. G11 34 S11
Walker St., Pais. PA1 46 J14
Walkerburn Rd. G52 48 P14
Walkinshaw Cres., Pais. 29 H13
PA3
  Ferguslie Pk. Av.
Walkinshaw Rd., Renf. PA4 16 J10
Walkinshaw St. G40 53 Y14
Walkinshaw St., John. PA5 43 D14
Walkinshaw Way, Pais. PA3 30 J12
  Broomdyke Way
Wallace Av. (Elder.), John. 44 F14
PA5
Wallace Pl. (Blan.) G72 69 GG19
Wallace Rd., Renf. PA4 31 L11
Wallace St. G5 35 V13
Wallace St. (Ruther.) G73 53 Y16
Wallace St., Clyde. G81 17 L8
Wallace St., Pais. PA3 30 K13
Wallacewell Cres. G21 23 Y9
Wallacewell Pl. G21 23 Y9
Wallacewell Quad. G21 23 Z9
Wallacewell Rd. G21 23 Y9
Wallbrae Rd. (Cumb.) G67 71 PP4
Wallneuk, Pais. PA1 30 K13
  Incle St.
Wallneuk Rd., Pais. PA3 30 K13
Walls St. G1 36 W12
Walmer Cres. G51 34 T13
Walmer Ter. G51 34 T13
  Paisley Rd. W.
Walnut Cres. G22 22 W9
Walnut Cres., John. PA5 44 E15
Walnut Dr. (Kirk.) G66 12 BB5
Walnut Pl. G22 22 W9
Walnut Rd. G22 22 W9
Walter St. G31 37 Z12
Walton St. G41 51 U16
Walton St. (Barr.) G78 59 M18
Wamba Av. G13 19 R8
Wamba Pl. G13 19 R8
  Wamba Av.
Wandilla Av., Clyde. G81 5 M7
Wanlock St. G51 34 S12
Warden Rd. G13 19 Q8
Wardhill Rd. G21 23 Y9
Wardhouse Rd., Pais. PA2 46 J16
Wardie Path G33 39 DD12
Wardie Pl. G33 40 EE12
Wardie Rd. G33 40 EE12
Wardie Rd. G34 40 EE12
Wardlaw Av. (Ruther.) G73 53 Y16
Wardlaw Dr. (Ruther.) G73 53 Y16
Wardlaw Rd. (Bears.) G61 7 R7
Wardpark Rd. (Cumb.) G67 71 QQ1
Wardrop St. G51 34 S12
Wardrop St., Pais. PA1 46 K14
Ware Path G34 40 EE12
Ware Rd. G34 39 DD12
Warilda Av., Clyde. G81 5 M7
Warnock St. G31 36 X12
  Wishart St.
Warp La. G3 35 U12
  Argyle St.
Warren St. G42 51 V15
Warriston Cres. G33 37 Z12
Warriston Pl. G32 38 BB12
Warriston St. G33 37 Z12
Warroch St. G3 35 U12
Washington Rd., Pais. PA3 30 K12
Washington St. G3 35 V13

Water Brae, Pais. PA1 46 K14
  Forbes Pl.
Water Rd. (Barr.) G78 59 M18
Water Row G51 34 S12
Waterfoot Av. G53 49 Q16
Waterford Rd. (Giff.) G46 62 S18
Waterloo La. G2 35 V12
  Waterloo St.
Waterloo St. G2 35 V12
Watermill Av. (Lenzie) G66 13 CC6
Waterside La. (Mill.Pk.), 43 C15
John. PA10
Waterside St. G5 52 W14
Waterside Ter. (Mill.Pk.), 43 C15
John. PA10
  Kilbarchan Rd.
Watling St. (Udd.) G71 57 GG16
Watson Av. (Ruther.) G73 52 X16
Watson Av. (Linw.), Pais. 28 E13
PA3
Watson St. G1 36 W13
Watson St. (Udd.) G71 69 GG17
Watt Low Av. (Ruther.) G73 64 X17
Watt Rd. G52 32 N12
Watt St. G5 35 U13
Waukglen Av. G53 60 P19
Waukglen Cres. G53 61 Q18
Waukglen Dr. G53 60 P18
Waukglen Gdns. G53 60 P19
Waukglen Path G53 60 P18
  Waukglen Dr.
Waukglen Rd. G53 60 P18
Waulkmill Av. (Barr.) G78 59 M18
Waulkmill St. (Thorn.) G46 61 R18
Waverley, Clyde. G81 5 M7
  Onslow Rd.
Waverley Ct. (Both.) G71 69 HH19
Waverley Cres. (Cumb.) 70 MM4
G67
Waverley Dr. (Ruther.) G73 53 Z16
Waverley Gdns. G41 51 U15
Waverley Gdns. (Elder.), 44 F15
John. PA5
Waverley Rd., Pais. PA2 45 G16
Waverley St. G41 51 U15
Waverley Ter. G31 37 Y13
  Whitevale St.
Waverley Way, Pais. PA2 45 G16
  Waverley Rd.
Weardale La. G33 39 CC12
Weardale St. G33 39 CC12
Weaver La. (Kilb.), John. 42 B14
PA10
  Glentyan Av.
Weaver St. G4 36 W12
Weaver Ter., Pais. PA2 47 L14
Weavers Av., Pais. PA2 45 H14
Weavers Gate, Pais. PA1 45 H14
Weavers Rd., Pais. PA2 45 H14
Webster St. G40 53 Y14
Webster St., Clyde. G81 18 N8
Wedderlea Dr. G52 32 P13
Weensmoor Pl. G53 60 P18
Weensmoor Rd. G53 60 P17
Weeple Dr. (Linw.), Pais. 28 E13
PA3
Weighhouse Clo., Pais. PA1 46 K14
Weir Av. (Barr.) G78 59 M19
Weir St., Pais. PA3 30 K13
Weirwood Av. (Bail.) G69 55 DD14
Weirwood Gdns. (Bail.) G69 55 DD14
Welbeck Rd. G53 60 P17
Welfare Av. (Camb.) G72 67 CC18
Well Grn. G43 50 T16
Well Rd. (Kilb.), John. PA10 42 B14
Well St. G40 36 X13
Well St., Pais. PA1 30 J13
Wellbank Pl. (Udd.) G71 69 GG17
  Church St.
Wellbrae Ter. (Chry.) G69 15 GG7
Wellcroft Pl. G5 51 V14
Wellfield Av. (Giff.) G46 62 S18
Wellfield St. G21 22 X10
Wellhouse Cres. G33 39 DD12
Wellhouse Path G34 39 DD12
Wellhouse Rd. G33 39 DD12
Wellington La. G2 35 V12
  West Campbell St.
Wellington Pl., Clyde. G81 4 J6

Wellington Rd. (Bishop.) 11 Z6
G64
Wellington St. G2 35 V12
Wellington St., Pais. PA3 30 J13
  Caledonia St.
Wellington Way, Renf. PA4 31 M11
  Tiree Av.
Wellmeadow Rd. G43 62 S17
Wellmeadow St., Pais. PA1 46 J14
Wellpark St. G31 36 X12
Wells St., Clyde. G81 4 K6
Wellshot Dr. (Camb.) G72 66 AA17
Wellshot Rd. G32 54 AA14
Wellside Dr. (Camb.) G72 67 CC18
Wemyss Gdns. (Bail.) G69 56 EE14
Wendur Way, Pais. PA3 30 J12
  Abbotsburn Way
Wenlock Rd., Pais. PA2 46 K15
Wentworth Dr. G23 9 U7
West Av. (Stepps) G33 25 CC9
West Av. (Udd.) G71 69 HH17
West Av., Renf. PA4 17 M10
West Brae, Pais. PA1 46 J14
West Campbell St. G2 35 V12
West Campbell St., Pais. 45 H14
PA1
West Chapelton Av. 7 R6
  (Bears.) G61
West Chapelton Cres. 7 R6
  (Bears.) G61
West Chapelton Dr. 7 R6
  (Bears.) G61
West Chapelton La. 7 R6
  (Bears.) G61
  West Chapelton Av.
West Coats Rd. (Camb.) G72 66 AA18
West Cotts. (Gart.) G69 26 EE10
West Ct., Clyde. G81 4 K6
  Little Holm
West George La. G2 35 V12
  West Campbell St.
West George St. G2 35 V12
West Graham St. G4 35 V11
West Greenhill Pl. G3 35 U12
West La., Pais. PA1 45 H14
West Lo. Rd., Renf. PA4 17 L10
West Nile St. G1 35 V12
West Princes St. G4 35 U11
West Regent La. G2 35 V12
  Renfield St.
West Regent St. G2 35 V12
West Rd. (Kilb.), John. PA10 42 B14
West St. G5 51 V14
West St., Clyde. G81 18 N8
West St., Pais. PA1 46 J14
West Thomson St., Clyde. 5 L6
G81
West Whitby St. G31 53 Z14
Westbank Ct. G12 35 U11
  Gibson St.
Westbank La. G12 35 U11
  Gibson St.
Westbank Quad. G12 35 U11
  Gibson St.
Westbank Ter. G12 35 U11
  Gibson St.
Westbourne Cres. (Bears.) 7 Q5
G61
Westbourne Dr. (Bears.) 7 Q5
G61
Westbourne Gdns. La. G12 20 T10
  Lorraine Rd.
Westbourne Gdns. N. G12 20 T10
Westbourne Gdns. S. G12 20 T10
Westbourne Gdns. W. G12 20 T10
Westbourne Rd. G12 20 S10
Westbourne Ter. La. G12 20 S10
  Westbourne Rd.
Westbrae Dr. G14 19 R10
Westburn Av. (Camb.) G72 67 CC17
Westburn Av., Pais. PA3 29 H13
Westburn Cres. (Ruther.) 52 X16
G73
Westburn Dr. (Camb.) G72 66 BB17
Westburn Fm. Rd. (Camb.) 66 BB17
G72
Westburn Rd. (Camb.) G72 68 EE17
Westburn Way, Pais. PA3 29 H13
  Westburn Av.

Westclyffe St. G41   51   U15
Westend (Bears.) G61   8   S7
Maryhill Rd.
Westend Pk. St. G3   35   U11
Wester Cleddens Rd.   11   Y7
  (Bishop.) G64
Wester Common Dr. G22   21   V10
Wester Common Rd. G22   21   V10
Wester Common Ter. G22   21   V10
Wester Rd. G32   55   CC14
Westerburn St. G32   38   AA12
Westercraigs G31   36   X12
Westergreens Av. (Kirk.)   13   CC5
  G66
Parkburn Av.
Westerhill Rd. (Bishop.) G64   11   Y6
Westerhill St. G22
Westerhouse Rd. G34   40   EE11
Westerkirk Dr. G23   9   U7
Western Av. (Ruther.) G73   52   X16
Western Isles Rd. (Old Kil.)   4   J5
  G60
Western Rd. (Camb.) G72   66   AA18
Westerton Av. (Bears.) G61   19   R8
Westfield Av. (Ruther.) G73   52   X16
Westfield Cres. (Bears.) G61   7   R7
Westfield Dr. G52   32   P13
Westfield Dr. (Bears.) G61   7   R7
Westfield Rd. (Thorn.) G46   61   R19
Westfield Vills. (Ruther.)   52   X16
  G73
Westfields (Bishop.) G64   10   X6
Westhouse Av. (Ruther.)   52   X16
  G73
Westhouse Gdns. (Ruther.)   52   X16
  G73
Westknowe Gdns.   65   Y17
  (Ruther.) G73
Westland Dr. G14   19   Q10
Westland Dr. La. G14   19   Q10
Westland Dr.
Westlands (Bishop.) G64   10   X6
Westlands Gdns., Pais. PA2   46   J15
Westminster Gdns. G12   20   T10
Kersland St.
Westminster Ter. G3   35   U12
North Claremont St.
Westmoreland St. G42   51   V15
Westmuir Pl. (Ruther.) G73   52   X16
Westmuir St. G31   37   Z13
Westpark Dr., Pais. PA3   29   H13
Westray Circ. G22   22   W9
Westray Ct. (Cumb.) G67   70   NN4
Westray Pl. G22   22   W8
Westray Pl. (Bishop.) G64   11   Z7
Ronaldsay Dr.
Westray Rd. (Cumb.) G67   70   MM4
Westray Sq. G22   22   W8
Westray St. G22   22   W8
Westside Gdns. G11   34   S11
Particklhill Rd.
Westwood Av. (Giff.) G46   62   S18
Westwood Gdns., Pais. PA3   29   H13
Westwood Quad., Clyde.   5   M7
  G81
Westwood Rd. G43   62   S17
Weymouth Dr. G12   20   S9
Whamflet Av. (Bail.) G69   40   FF12
Wheatfield Rd. (Bears.) G61   7   Q7
Wheatlands Dr. (Kilb.),   42   B14
  John. PA10
Wheatlands Fm. Rd.   42   B14
  (Kilb.), John. PA10
Whin Dr. (Barr.) G78   59   L18
Whin St., Clyde. G81   5   L6
Whinfield Av. (Camb.) G72   54   AA16
Whinfield Path G53   60   P18
Whinfield Rd. G53   60   P18
Whinhill Rd. G53   48   P14
Whinhill Rd., Pais. PA2   47   L15
Whins Rd. G41   50   T15
Whirlow Gdns. (Bail.) G69   40   EE13
Whirlow Rd. (Bail.) G69   40   EE13
Whistlefield (Bears.) G61   7   R6
Whitacres Path G53   60   P18
Whitacres Pl. G53   60   P18
Whitacres Rd. G53   60   P18
Whitburn St. G32   38   AA12
White St. G11   34   S11

White St., Clyde. G81   17   M8
Whitecraigs Pl. G23   21   U8
Whitefield Av. (Camb.) G72   66   BB18
Whitefield Rd. G51   34   T13
Whiteford Rd., Pais. PA2   47   L15
Whitehall Ct. G3   35   U12
Whitehall St. G3   35   U12
Whitehaugh Av., Pais. PA1   31   L13
Whitehaugh Cres. G53   60   P18
Whitehaugh Dr., Pais. PA1   31   L13
Whitehaugh Path G53   60   P18
Whitehaugh Rd. G53   60   P18
Whitehill Av. (Stepps) G33   25   CC9
Whitehill Av. (Cumb.) G68   70   MM3
Whitehill Fm. Rd. (Stepps)   25   CC9
  G33
Whitehill Gdns. G31   37   Y12
Garthland Dr.
Whitehill La. (Bears.) G61   7   Q6
Whitehill Rd.
Whitehill Rd. (Stepps) G33   25   CC8
Whitehill Rd. (Bears.) G61   7   Q5
Whitehill Rd. (Kirk.) G66   25   CC8
Whitehill St. G31   37   Y12
Whitehurst (Bears.) G61   7   Q5
Whitehurst Pk. (Bears.) G61   7   Q5
Whitekirk Pl. G15   6   P7
Whitelaw St. G20   20   T8
Whitelawburn Av.   66   AA18
  (Camb.) G72
Whitelawburn Rd.   66   AA18
  (Camb.) G72
Whitelawburn Ter.   66   AA18
  (Camb.) G72
Whiteloans (Both.) G71   69   HH18
Wordsworth Way
Whitemoss Av. G44   63   U18
Whitesbridge Av., Pais. PA3   45   G14
Whitesbridge Clo., Pais. PA3   45   G14
Whitestone Av. (Cumb.) G68   70   MM2
Dungoil Av.
Whitevale St. G31   37   Y13
Whithope Rd. G53   60   N18
Whithope Ter. G53   60   N18
Whithorn Cres. (Mood.) G69   15   GG6
Whitriggs Rd. G53   60   N18
Whitslade St. G34   40   EE11
Whittingehame Dr. G12   19   R9
Whittingehame Dr. G13   19   R9
Whittingehame Gdns. G12   20   S9
Whittingehame La. G13   19   R9
Whittingehame Dr.
Whittliemuir Av. G44   63   U18
Whitton Dr. (Giff.) G46   62   T18
Whitton St. G20   20   T8
Whitworth Dr., Clyde. G81   5   L7
Whitworth St. G20   21   V9
Whyte Av. (Camb.) G72   66   AA17
Wickets, The, Pais. PA1   47   L14
Wigton St. G4   21   V10
Wigtoun Pl. (Cumb.) G67   71   PP2
Wilderness Brae (Cumb.)   71   PP2
  G67
Wilfred Av. G13   19   Q8
Wilkie Rd. (Udd.) G71   69   HH18
William St. G2   35   V12
William St. G3   35   U12
William St., Clyde. G81   5   L5
William St., John. PA5   43   D14
William St., Pais. PA1   46   J14
William Ure Pl. (Bishop.)   11   Y5
  G64
Williamson Pl., John. PA5   44   E15
Williamson St. G31   53   Z14
Williamson St., Clyde. G81   5   L6
Williamwood Dr. G44   63   U19
Williamwood Pk. G44   63   U19
Williamwood Pk. W. G44   63   U19
Willock Pl. G20   21   U8
Willoughby Dr. G13   19   R9
Willoughby La. G13   19   R9
Willoughby Dr.
Willow Av. (Bishop.) G64   23   Y8
Willow Av. (Lenzie) G66   13   CC5
Willow Av. (Elder.), John.   44   F15
  PA5
Hillview Rd.
Willow Dr., John. PA5   43   D15
Willow La. G32   54   BB15

Willow Pl., John. PA5   44   E15
Willow St. G13   19   R8
Willowbank Cres. G3   35   U11
Willowbank St. G3   35   U11
Willowdale Cres. (Bail.) G69   56   EE14
Willowdale Gdns. (Bail.)   56   EE14
  G69
Willowford Rd. G53   60   N18
Wilmot Rd. G13   19   Q9
Wilson Av. (Linw.), Pais.   28   E13
  PA3
Wilson St. G1   36   W12
Wilson St., Pais. PA1   46   J14
William St.
Wilson St., Renf. PA4   17   M10
Wilsons Pl., Pais. PA1   46   K14
Seedhill
Wilton Cres. G20   21   U10
Wilton Cres. La. G20   21   U10
Wilton Cres.
Wilton Dr. G20   21   U10
Wilton Gdns. G20   21   U10
Wilton Mans. G20   21   U10
Wilton St.
Wilton St. G20   21   U10
Wiltonburn Path G53   60   P18
Wiltonburn Rd. G53   60   P18
Wilverton Rd. G13   19   R8
Winchester Dr. G12   20   S9
Windhill Pl. G43   62   T17
Windhill Rd.
Windhill Rd. G43   62   S17
Windlaw Ct. G45   64   W19
Windlaw Gdns. G44   63   U18
Windlaw Pk. Gdns. G44   63   U18
Windlaw Rd. G45   64   W19
Windlaw Rd. (Clark.) G76   64   W19
Windmill Cres. G43   62   S17
Windmill Rd.
Windmill Pl. G43   62   T17
Windmill Rd.
Windmillcroft Quay G5   35   V13
Windsor Cres., Clyde. G81   5   L6
Windsor Cres. (Elder.),   44   E15
  John. PA5
Windsor Cres., Pais. PA1   31   L13
Windsor Path (Bail.) G69   41   GG13
Park Rd.
Windsor Rd., Renf. PA4   31   M11
Windsor St. G20   35   V11
Windsor St. G32   39   CC13
Windsor Ter. G20   35   V11
Windsor Wk. (Udd.) G71   57   HH16
Windyedge Cres. G13   19   Q9
Windyedge Pl. G13   19   Q9
Wingfield Gdns. (Both.) G71   69   HH19
Blairston Av.
Winifred St. G33   23   Z10
Winning Ct. (Blan.) G72   69   GG19
Ness Dr.
Winning Row G31   38   AA13
Winton Av. (Giff.) G46   62   T19
Winton Dr. G12   20   T9
Winton Gdns. (Udd.) G71   57   GG16
Winton La. G12   20   T9
Wirran Pl. G13   18   N8
Wishart St. G31   36   X12
Wisner Ct. (Thorn.) G46   61   R18
Wiston St. (Camb.) G72   67   DD17
Woddrop St. G40   53   Y15
Wolseley St. G5   52   W14
Wood Fm. Rd. (Thorn.) G46   62   S19
Wood La. (Bishop.) G64   23   Y8
Wood Quad., Clyde. G81   18   N8
Wood St. G31   37   Y12
Wood St., Pais. PA2   47   L14
Woodbank Cres.,   43   D15
  John. PA5
Woodburn Rd. G43   62   T17
Woodburn Way (Cumb.)   70   MM3
  G68
Woodcroft Av. G11   19   R10
Woodcroft Ter. G11   19   R10
Crow Rd.
Woodend (Giff.) G46   62   S19
Milverton Rd.
Woodend Ct. G32   55   DD15
Woodend Dr. G13   19   R9
Woodend Dr., Pais. PA1   47   M14

Woodend Gdns. G32   55 DD15
Woodend La. G13   19 R9
Woodend Dr.
Woodend Pl. (Elder.), John. 44 E15
PA5
Malloch Cres.
Woodend Rd. G32   55 CC15
Woodgreen Av. G44   64 W17
Woodhall St. G40   53 Y15
Woodhead Av. (Both.) G71 69 HH19
Old Bothwell Rd.
Woodhead Cres. (Udd.) G71 57 GG16
Woodhead Path G53   60 P17
Woodhead Rd. G53   60 N17
Woodhead Rd. (Chry.) G69 26 EE9
Woodhead Ter. (Chry.) G69 26 EE8
Woodhill Gro. (Bishop.) G64 23 Z8
Woodhill Rd.
Woodhill Rd. G21   23 Y9
Woodhill Rd. (Bishop.) G64 11 Y7
Woodholm Av. G44   64 W17
Woodhouse St. G13   19 R8
Woodilee Cotts. (Kirk.) G66 13 DD5
Woodilee Rd. (Kirk.) G66 13 DD5
Woodland Av. (Gart.) G69 27 GG8
Woodland Av., Pais. PA2 46 K16
Woodland Cres. (Camb.) 66 BB18
G72
Woodland Vw. (Cumb.) G67 71 PP2
Braehead Rd.
Woodland Way (Cumb.) 71 PP2
G67
Woodlands Av. (Both.) G71 69 HH18
Woodlands Ct. (Thorn.) G46 61 R19
Woodlands Rd.
Woodlands Cres. (Thorn.) 61 R18
G46
Woodlands Cres. (Both.) 69 HH18
G71
Woodlands Dr. G4   35 U11
Woodlands Gdns. (Both.) 69 GG18
G71
Woodlands Gate G3   35 U11
Woodlands Gate (Thorn.) 61 R18
G46

Woodlands Pk. (Thorn.) G46 61 R19
Woodlands Rd. G3   35 U11
Woodlands Rd. (Thorn.) G46 61 R19
Woodlands Ter. G3   35 U11
Woodlands Ter. (Both.) G71 69 HH18
Woodlea Dr. (Giff.) G46 62 T18
Woodlinn Av. G44   63 V17
Woodneuk Rd. G53   60 P17
Woodneuk Rd. (Gart.) G69 27 GG9
Woodneuk Ter. (Gart.) G69 27 GG9
Woodrow Circ. G41   50 T14
Woodrow Pl. G41   50 T14
Maxwell Dr.
Woodrow Rd. G41   50 T14
Woods La., Renf. PA4   17 M10
Woodside Av. (Thorn.) G46 62 S18
Woodside Av. (Lenzie) G66 13 CC5
Woodside Av. (Ruther.) G73 53 Z16
Woodside Cres. G3   35 U11
Woodside Cres. (Barr.) G78 59 M19
Woodside Cres., Pais. PA1 46 J14
William St.
Woodside Pl. G3   35 U11
Woodside Pl. La. G3   35 U11
Elderslie St.
Woodside Rd. G20   21 U10
Woodside Ter. G3   35 U11
Woodside Ter. (Bishop.) 10 W6
G64
Woodside Ter. La. G3   35 U11
Woodlands Rd.
Woodstock Av. G41   50 T15
Woodstock Av., Pais. PA2 45 G16
Woodvale Av. (Bears.) G61 8 S7
Woodvale Dr., Pais. PA3 29 H13
Woodville Pk. G51   34 S13
Woodville St.
Woodville St. G51   34 S13
Wordsworth Way (Both.) 69 HH18
G71
Works Av. (Camb.) G72 67 DD17
Wraes Av. (Barr.) G78   59 M18
Wraes Vw. (Barr.) G78   58 K19
Wren Pl., John. PA5   43 C16
Wright Av. (Barr.) G78   59 L19
Wright St., Renf. PA4   31 L11
Wrightlands Cres., Ersk. 16 K8
PA8
Wykeham Pl. G13   19 Q9
Wykeham Rd. G13   19 Q9
Wynd, The (Cumb.) G67 71 PP1
Wyndford Dr. G20   20 T9
Wyndford Pl. G20   20 T9
Wyndford Rd.

Wyndford Rd. G20   20 T9
Wyndham Ct. G12   20 T10
Wyndham St.
Wyndham St. G12   20 T10
Wynford Ter. (Udd.) G71 57 HH16
Myrtle Rd.
Wyper Pl. G40   37 Y13
Gallowgate
Wyvil Av. G13   7 R7
Wyvis Av. G13   18 N8
Wyvis Pl. G13   18 N8
Wyvis Quad. G13   18 N8

Y

Yair Dr. G52   32 P13
Yarrow Ct. (Camb.) G72 67 DD17
Yarrow Gdns. G20   21 U10
Yarrow Gdns. La. G20   21 U10
Yarrow Gdns.
Yarrow Rd. (Bishop.) G64 11 Y6
Yate St. G31   37 Y13
Yetholm St. G14   18 N9
Yew Dr. G21   23 Y10
Foresthall Dr.
Yew Pl., John. PA5   44 E15
Yoker Ferry Rd. G14   18 N9
Yoker Mill Gdns. G13   18 N8
Yoker Mill Rd. G13   18 N8
Yokerburn Pl. G13   18 N8
Yoker Mill Rd.
Yokerburn Ter., Clyde. G81 17 M8
York Dr. (Ruther.) G73 65 Z17
York La. G2   35 V12
York St.
York St. G2   35 V13
York St., Clyde. G81   5 M7
York Way, Renf. PA4   31 M11
Yorkhill La. G3   34 T12
Yorkhill St.
Yorkhill Par. G3   34 T11
Yorkhill Quay G3   34 S12
Yorkhill St. G3   34 T12
Young Pl. (Udd.) G71   57 HH16
Young St., Clyde. G81   5 L6
Young Ter. G21   23 Y10

Z

Zambesi Dr. (Blan.) G72 68 FF19
Zena Cres. G33   23 Z10
Zena Pl. G33   23 Z10
Zena St. G33   23 Z10
Zetland Rd. G52   32 N12